The War
of the
Antichrist
with the Church
and Christian Civilization

The War
of the
Antichrist
with the Church
and Christian Civilization

Monsignor George F. Dillon, DD
Edited by Joshua Charles

TAN Books
Gastonia, North Carolina

Nihil Obstat: W. Fortune, D.D., *Censor Theologus Deputatus*
                    Die 3 Mensis Maii, 1885

Imprimatur: Gulielmus J. Canon. Walsh, *Vic. Cap. Dublin*
                    Die 4 Mensis Maii, 1885

Originally published in 1885 as *The War of Antichrist with the Church and Christian Civilization* by M.H. Gill & Son (London and New York) from a series of lectures delivered by Monsignor Dillon in 1884.

Cover design by Andrew Schmalen

Cover image: Satan presiding at the Infernal Council by John Martin (1824) via Wikimedia Commons, Public domain.

ISBN: 978-1-5051-2847-5
Kindle ISBN: 978-1-5051-2848-2
ePUB ISBN: 978-1-5051-2849-9

Published in the United States by
TAN Books
PO Box 269
Gastonia, NC 28053
www.TANBooks.com

Printed in the United States of America

Dedicated to Our Lady of Fatima, Our Lady of
Victory, Queen of the Rosary, Seat of Wisdom,
Holy Theotokos, Ark of the New Covenant.
Pray for us, for the defeat of Freemasonry, and for the
conversion of Freemasons around the world!

-Joshua Charles

Contents

Chapter 1: Introduction   **1**

Reasons for selecting the Subject—"Catholic Institute" a Society such as those commended by Leo XIII, in the Bull *Humanum Genus*—Necessity of keeping Youth from bad Associations—Necessity of unmasking Secret Societies—Words of Leo XIII—Freemasonry and Secret Societies with us—On the Continent—All Secret Associations Atheistic, and intensely hostile to the Church, Christianity, and Social order—Union of all Secret Societies—All knowingly, or otherwise, under a central direction and control—Fraud and Force—Review of Atheistic Organization since the first French Revolution—Features of its Progress.

Chapter 2: The Rise of Atheism in Europe   **7**

The Spirit of Private Judgment advocated by Protestants ends in doubt—Disbelief in the Divinity of Christ—Bayle, Spinosa—Deism, Pantheism, Atheism—Atheism Absolute—Infidelity in England and Germany—Supreme in France though.

Chapter 3: Voltaire   **11**

His efforts to advance Atheism—His Parentage, Education and Early Life—Corruption of the Age—European Courts,

Chapter 17: Lord Palmerston 161

Incredulity natural regarding the role attributed to Palmerston by Father Deschamps—Proofs from Henry Misley and Louis Blanc—History of Palmerston—Change from Conservative to Ultra-Liberal—His policy against the Pope and Europe, Masonic—Not in the interests of England—Unites Italy and Germany—Palmerston, Mazzini, and Louis Napoleon—Palmerston defies the Queen, Cabinet, and Country for Masonic ends—Inutility of his Dismissal for acting without authority, and interpolating Dispatches—Isolation of England made inevitable by his policy.

NOTES: Testimony of Eckert—Jewish Illuminated Lodges in London—Testimony of Mr. F. Fugh O'Donnell, MP.

Chapter 18: War of the Intellectual Party 175

Diffusion of Atheism and Immorality during the reign of Palmerston—Attacks on the Christian Marriage Laws—On the Sabbath—On the Christian Customs of Social and Public Life—On Primary Education—On Religious Instruction—Queen's Colleges in Ireland—Attacks commenced on Religious Education in England, successful by the aid of Masonry—Education of Females in purely Secular and Master Schools—University Education—Contempt for Religion made fashionable.

NOTE: Monsignor Dupanloup on the Freemason War against Christian Education.

Chapter 19: The War Party under Palmerston 189

Mazzini prepares Europe for the Revolutions of 1848—Napoleon III obtains influence with the Chief—War for the weakening of Russia, for the severance of Austria from Russia, and for the unification of Italy—War on the Temporalities of

Editor's Introduction

IT SEEMS STRANGE to republish a book that was first published in 1885. But the times call for it.

In 1884, Pope Leo XIII promulgated his iconic encyclical on Freemasonry, *Humanum Genus*. In that document, he asked the Catholic clergy that it "be your first rule of all to tear away the mask from Freemasonry, and let it be seen as it really is."

Later that year, an Irish priest, Monsignor George F. Dillon, answered this call by delivering a series of lectures on Freemasonry which were made into a book, originally published in 1885, entitled *War of Antichrist with the Church and Christian Civilization*. Leo XIII thanked him for his efforts in a letter included in this book. He even paid for the Italian translation and the printing of several thousand copies.

It is this book which is now republished in its entirety,[1] with footnotes and explanations, and, to our knowledge, for the first time since its original publication.

Why are we republishing this work now? Put simply, because its "prophecies" about Freemasonry and its designs on the world have come true. Many of them had already been articulated by numerous sovereign pontiffs of the Catholic Church throughout the eighteenth and nineteenth centuries.

---

[1] There was a previous version published in 1965 under the title *Grand Orient Freemasonry Unmasked*. But this version did not include everything Monsignor Dillon wrote, nor the various explanatory footnotes we have provided.

But Monsignor Dillon's work shows how they were being brought to pass—the dark harvest of which seems to be near completion in our own times. As such, this work sheds invaluable light on the nature of the times in which we live.

At the same time, by republishing this work, we are not thereby claiming every assertion made by Monsignor Dillon is true. Many, if not all of them, likely are. Our interest in this text, and thus our desire to republish it for the consideration of Catholics in the twenty-first century, was twofold: the endorsement of Pope Leo XIII, who more than any other pontiff raised his apostolic voice against the wolves of Freemasonry; and the by now obvious and undeniable extent to which the Masonic program as described by Pope Leo and Monsignor Dillon has been realized across the world, and especially the post-Christian West. Is this by design? Many popes, and Monsignor Dillon, believed such a design was afoot. We are content to leave readers to their own conclusions.

So, what is the Masonic program? According to Pope Leo XIII, it is nothing less than the destruction of Christian civilization, and the resurrection of pre-Christian civilization on its ruins according to the principles of naturalism, in which man's unaided reason and will are supreme, and divine grace plays no role. Freemasonry believes itself to be the custodian of the "original" primeval revelation to mankind—a "revelation" that can unite all mankind regardless of their particular religions. This "revelation" is the religion of nature and the unfolding of its secrets, the knowledge of which can be attained by reason alone and "redeem" mankind from its delusions, among which are the idea that any particular religion is true or salvific.

The Catholic Church, on the contrary, has always taught that mankind lives under the weight of original sin inherited from our first parents. Those parents deliberately chose to disobey God, and thereby fell from a state in which divine grace inhabited their souls, and empowered their reason, appetites, and wills to conform to their final end, namely, eternal life with God, which the Church calls the "beatific vision," and teaches is the reward for obedience. With their fall, their reason, appetites, and wills became weakened, and thereby rendered them incapable of attaining the end for which God created them. Not only that, but they were also rendered incapable of even fully obeying the natural law, which even in their damaged state, they could still know by reason. We have inherited that fallen human nature. But God, in His mercy, reconciled human nature to Himself through the passion and resurrection of Jesus Christ, making it possible for divine grace to inhabit human souls once again, empowering them to obey God and attain their final end in heaven by being united to Christ in the sacraments.

Thus, the Church teaches that human nature, on its own, is incapable of saving itself, of growing in perfection, and thus attaining its final end. It must receive God's assistance—His grace—to do so.

Freemasonry is based on the exact opposite principle. Nature is capable of saving itself. It is capable of its own perfection. Divine power need not be received from the outside, for it is already within everyone and everything, waiting to be uncovered through the *gnosis* (secret knowledge) of Freemasonry. As such, and as Pope Leo XIII warned, it invariably ends in nature worship and pantheism.

It is for this reason we describe what Pope Leo XIII called "naturalism" as *sola natura*, or "nature alone." Upon this basis, Freemasonry not only denies the reality of original sin but also declares that man's reason is all-powerful and nature is capable of its own perfection apart from divine grace. Whereas the Church has always declared that the salvation of mankind is achieved within Christ, the second Adam, Freemasonry contends that the first Adam, without divine grace, is sufficient. Man does not require something from God in order to be united with his fellows. They are their own source of salvation. This is the "fraternity" so often proposed by Freemasonry—a "fraternity" of nature bereft of divine grace, united in the first Adam that shall be confined to the flames of hell, and ignoring entirely, if not outright hostile to, the second Adam, in whom alone man may find eternal life.

It is upon the basis of the first Adam that Freemasonry seeks to build not only individuals but also societies, and ultimately a global civilization—a civilization built on the power of human reason alone, indifferent at best, and hostile at worst, to the very divine grace that has been gifted to it in Christ, the second Adam, in whose name alone it can be saved.

The Two Swords

What we will call the "Masonic program" detailed by Pope Leo XIII and Monsignor Dillon cannot be adequately understood apart from the Church's doctrine of the Two

Swords. While the doctrine of the "Two Swords" reached the height of its development in the Middle Ages, its origins are ancient, and most famously articulated by Pope Saint Gelasius I in a letter to Emperor Anastasius I in AD 494, in which he writes as follows:

> For there are, Your Imperial Majesty, two principles by which this world is principally governed: the sacred authority of the pontiffs and the royal power; between the two, the burden of priests is all the heavier, as they are obliged to give an accounting before the divine justice even for those very kings of men.
>
> For you are, most merciful son, aware that through your dignity, you indeed preside over mankind, but nevertheless, you bow devoutly to those who are the leaders in divine matters, and from them you seek the source of your salvation; and you understand that, in receiving the sacraments of heaven and in administering them (as appropriate), you must be a follower, according to the rule of religion, rather than the leader. And so you realize that in these matters you are dependent upon their judgment and must not want them to be subject to your will.
>
> If, then, religious leaders themselves recognize, in what concerns the order of public discipline, that authority has been bestowed upon you by a dispensation from above, and therefore obey your laws, so that in worldly things they may not even appear to oppose . . . an impossible decision, with what feelings, I ask you, is it fitting and proper for you to obey those

who have been assigned to the administration of the venerable mysteries?

Hence, just as no small risk impends for pontiffs if they remained silent about what pertains to the worship of the Deity, so there is no trivial danger for persons who—perish the thought!—show disrespect when they ought to show obedience. And if it is appropriate for the hearts of the faithful to be submissive to all priests in general when they are properly attending to godly concerns, how much the more is compliance to be accorded the leader of that See which the most high Godhead has wished to give preeminence over all priests and which the subsequent devotion of the universal Church also has continually exalted?

In this regard Your Charity has obviously noticed that no one has ever been able to lift himself up by any merely human devising to the privilege or the acknowledged position of the person whom the voice of Christ has put before all the rest, whom the venerable Church has always acknowledged and devoutly regards as primate. That which has been decided by God's judgment can be attacked by human presumptuousness, but it cannot be vanquished by any power whatsoever.[2]

---

[2] Pope Gelasius I, "Letter to Emperor Anastasius I" (AD 494), in Heinrich Denzinger, *Enchiridion symbolorum definitionum et declarationum de rebus fidei et morum: Compendium of Creeds, Definitions and Declarations on Matters of Faith and Morals*, eds. Peter Hünermann, Robert Fastiggi, and Anne Englund Nash, 43rd ed. (San Francisco: Ignatius Press, 2012), 347.

The root of the doctrine of the Two Swords is Christ's words delivered just prior to His ascension: "All authority in heaven and on earth has been given to me" (Mt 28:18). Christ explicitly delegated authority to His Church, and Scripture is clear that the authority of states also comes from God. As such, all humanity—including civil government—has a duty to submit to the second Adam, Christ the King. The Church can never impose such submission on non-believers by violence. But the duty remains, nonetheless.

Under the doctrine of the Two Swords, the Church has consistently taught that God established two authorities by which man is enabled to meet his end, both natural and supernatural: the Temporal Sword for his natural end and the Spiritual Sword for his supernatural end; the one for earthly matters, the other for heavenly matters; the one for the common good of all, the other for the supernatural good of all; the one constituted by nature, the other by grace.

Under this doctrine, the purpose of the Temporal Sword is to uphold the common good, and the purpose of the Spiritual Sword is to enable man to reach his supernatural end—namely, eternal salvation. The ultimate "common good," that good shared by men in virtue of their being bearers of God's image, is to see God face to face forever—the beatific vision. The Temporal Sword cannot achieve this. But it can, in its role as provider of the common temporal good, help create a society in which all are genuinely free to "work out your own salvation with fear and trembling" (Phil 2:12), rightly worship God, obey His commandments, and thus achieve the beatific vision. As such, the Temporal Sword submitted to Christ the King recognizes it can never effect eternal salvation (hence the Church's consistent teaching against obtaining converts by violence), and as such must submit to the Spiritual Sword on matters of faith and morals. In its merely natural capacity, it must encourage and protect a society in which human law accords with natural law, the pursuit of eternal salvation is unobstructed, and where, ideally, the Church herself is provided various aids by which to carry out her mission. The state saves no one. But as an authority established by God, it must never interfere with, and, to the extent possible, should positively assist men in their pursuit of eternal salvation.

The Temporal Sword has its own proper jurisdiction, derived from nature, which the Church cannot infringe upon. But it does not have jurisdiction over matters of religion and morals, of which the Church is the authoritative and infallible teacher. As such, the state, regardless of its form, cannot be auto-defining. As an authority derived from the same nature which has been damaged by original sin, the Temporal Sword requires grace to properly discern the moral law established by God. The moral law can be known by reason. But since reason itself has been damaged by original sin, the aid of grace is required for it to be known with certainty. Therefore, the Temporal requires the aid of the Spiritual Sword, whose infallible teaching of the moral law is absolutely binding. No autocrat dictating from on high or vote bubbling up from the people below can presume to contradict it, for its source is God, who is the source of all authority.

Likewise, as the supernatural society created by God in order to dispense the divine grace required for salvation to the world, the Church has an absolute right from God Himself to engage in its mission—at the very minimum—unhindered by any earthly power, which is itself established by God. Therefore, the Temporal Sword must not interfere with or obstruct the Spiritual Sword in the execution of its mission.

The reason the Temporal Power must ultimately be submitted in matters of faith and morals to the Spiritual Power is because human nature is incapable of keeping the natural law, given the damage done to it by original sin. Thus, only the grace provided by the supernatural society of the Church can enable human beings to keep the natural law, and the Temporal Power to uphold it. This is why the naturalism of Freemasonry is so pernicious, for it claims that nature can reach its end without the assistance of divine grace, and that the Temporal Power can effect the common good without the Spiritual Power. Our nature, such as it is, may be compared to a swimmer in an ocean who cannot keep his head above water because his limbs are paralyzed, or otherwise incapacitated. He must have a flotation device to help him do so. That "flotation" device, that thing which enables human nature to keep even the natural law (keeping one's head above water, in our analogy) is divine grace.

Therefore, because of original sin, the Temporal Power that has formally separated itself from the Spiritual Power will thereby render itself incapable of even legislating in accord with the natural law. One need only observe the current status of post-Christian societies to see that this is true. The masonic principle of *sola natura*, as such, implicitly rejects the reign of Christ the King, and any religion that would claim divine authority to teach on matters of faith and morals. Hence the essential incompatibility of Freemasonry and Catholicism.

With this understanding in place, the Masonic program laid out by Pope Leo XIII and Monsignor Dillon begins to make sense in light of the doctrine of the Two Swords. In short, the fullness of Christendom (imperfect and subject to corruption prior to Our Lord's return) existed wherever both swords were submitted to Christ the King. As such, they acted in concert. They remained separate entities—one constituted by nature, the other by grace; one for the purpose of man's temporal good, the other for his supernatural good. But in Christendom, the Temporal Sword, though constituted by nature, nonetheless recognized the voice of Christ its King, and His presence among His people by virtue of their baptism, and therefore recognized the authority of the Spiritual Sword in all religious and moral matters.

Therefore, the destruction of Christendom envisioned by Freemasonry necessarily involves not only a direct attack on the Church herself but an apostasy of the Temporal Sword from the Spiritual Sword, and therefore from Christ the King. Christendom is destroyed when its temporal powers believe the lie that they may reach their end without divine grace—that their nature may become godlike without God. In so doing, it is falling for the lie of the serpent in the Garden: "You will not die. For God knows that when you eat of it your eyes will be opened, and you will be like God, knowing good and evil" (Gn 3:4–5). But this is precisely the point—that our damaged human nature *cannot* perfectly know what is good and evil, let alone will the good without divine grace.

Thus, the Masonic program seeks to destroy Christendom, and in its place inaugurate a "world republic" inspired by what Pope Leo XIII called "naturalism," and we describe as *sola natura*, "nature alone." These are not the ravings of a "conspiracy theorist" but the consistent warnings of many supreme pontiffs throughout the eighteenth and nineteenth centuries—preeminently Pope Leo XIII. That program primarily consists of the following pillars, each of which was intended to sever the state from the Church, to secularize the Temporal Sword and society, to undermine the Church from within, and thereby destroy both powers established by God to rightly govern the world:

1. the complete separation of the state from the Church;
2. the idea of "popular sovereignty" as the only basis for any government authority;
3. religious indifferentism;
4. placing marriage under the jurisdiction of the state, making it "civil," and encouraging easy divorce laws that reduce marriage to nothing more than a civil contract like any other;
5. the secularizing of education;
6. the encouragement of moral decay among the populace as a means to secure their obedience to the Masonic program once it reaches its global climax; and finally,
7. the destruction of the temporal and spiritual authority of the pope.

Of portentous significance in light of the revelations of Our Lady of Fatima three decades later concerning the "errors of Russia," Pope Leo XIII and Monsignor Dillon both contend that Freemasonry was the prime mover behind the cause of worldwide Socialism and Communism, with which it intended to establish its envisioned world republic on the basis of the ideals of *Liberté, égalité, fraternité*. They declared this decades before the birth of the Soviet Union and other socialist and communist states.

Given that this book was written by Monsignor Dillon, a brief survey of the warnings of Pope Leo XIII himself which inspired Monsignor Dillon's lectures are in order. The italicized words are those we wish to emphasize.

Freemasonry's Ultimate Goal: The Destruction of Christendom

First, the pontiff made clear that Freemasonry intended nothing less than the destruction of Christian civilization.

For example, in *Humanum Genus*, he observes as follows:

> No longer making any secret of their purposes, they [the Freemasons] are now *boldly rising up against God Himself.* They are *planning the destruction of holy Church publicly and openly*, and this with the set purpose of *utterly despoiling the nations of Christendom*, if it were possible, of the blessings obtained for us through Jesus Christ our Savior. . . .
>
> . . . From what We have above most clearly shown, that which is *their ultimate purpose forces itself into view—namely, the utter overthrow of that whole religious and political order of the world which the Christian teaching has produced, and the substitution of a new state of things in accordance with their ideas, of which the foundations and laws shall be drawn from mere naturalism.* . . .

... To wish to destroy the religion and the Church which God Himself has established, and whose perpetuity He insures by His protection, and *to bring back after a lapse of eighteen centuries the manners and customs of the pagans*, is signal folly and audacious impiety. . . . In this insane and wicked endeavor we may almost see *the implacable hatred and spirit of revenge with which Satan himself is inflamed against Jesus Christ.*[3]

In an 1890 encyclical on Freemasonry in Italy, *Dall'alto dell'Apostolico Seggio*, Pope Leo XIII repeated the same assertion: "It is the plan of the sects [all secret societies, preeminently Freemasons] that is now unfolding itself in Italy, especially in what relates to the Catholic religion and the Church, *with the final and avowed purpose, if it were possible, of reducing it to nothing.*"[4] The goal of the "Masonic sect," Leo stated, was "to destroy the religion of Christ."[5]

Likewise, in 1892, in another encyclical on Freemasonry delivered to the Italian people, *Custodi di Quella Fede*, Leo declared, "This war [against Catholicism] is directed at the same time against the heavenly and the earthly kingdoms, against the faith of our ancestors, and the culture which they handed on to us." The "chief source" of this war, he declared, is the "masonic sect."[6] The pope decried the fact that "a people redeemed by divine blood have thus returned to . . . the shames of paganism."[7] He continued: "After nineteen

---

[3] Pope Leo XIII, *Humanum Genus* (1884), nos. 2, 10, 24.
[4] Pope Leo XIII, *Dall'alto dell'Apostolico Seggio* (1890), no. 2.
[5] Pope Leo XIII, *Dall'alto* (1890), no. 11.
[6] Pope Leo XIII, *Custodi di Quella Fede* (1892), no. 2.
[7] Pope Leo XIII, *Custodi* (1892), no. 8.

centuries of Christian civilization, this sect [Freemasonry] tries to *overthrow the Catholic Church and to cut off its divine sources.* It absolutely denies the supernatural, repudiating every revelation and all the means of salvation which revelation shows us."[8] He declared Freemasonry to be "an enemy of God, Church, and country."[9]

That same year, in another encyclical on Freemasonry, this time addressed to the Italian bishops, *Inimica Vis,* in a manner similar to Pope Saint Pius X's declaration that modernism was the synthesis of all heresies, Pope Leo declared that Freemasonry was the embodiment of *every* enemy that had ever sought the destruction of the Catholic Church:

> The spirit of all previous groups hostile to Catholic institutions has come to life again in that group called the Masonic sect, which, strong in manpower and resources, *is the leader in a war against anything sacred.* . . . We have deliberately endeavored to reveal the secrets of this pernicious sect and the means by which *it labors for the destruction of the Catholic enterprise.*[10]

He repeats elsewhere that it is "the impious aspiration of the sects to overthrow the Catholic religion and the papacy."[11] In Italy, they sought "to establish the new settlement of the Italian Peninsula upon the ruins of the Catholic Religion"[12]—a project they ultimately intended to be global in scope.

---

8   Pope Leo XIII, *Custodi* (1892), no. 9.
9   Pope Leo XIII, *Custodi* (1892), no. 10.
10 Pope Leo XIII, *Inimica Vis* (1892), nos. 1, 2.
11 Pope Leo XIII, *Dall'alto* (1890), no. 16.
12 Pope Leo XIII, *Dall'alto* (1890), no. 18.

The first and most fundamental pillar of the Masonic program is the absolute and total separation of Church and state. This would be achieved not only by positive legislation but by the inculcation of the idea of popular sovereignty, or the idea that all sovereignty is inherent in the people, who may choose their governors as they will, which implicitly rejects the authority of God. Finally, both ideas would result from, and further encourage, the great scourge of the modern epoch—namely, religious indifferentism.

Separation of Church and State, Popular Sovereignty, and Religious Indifferentism

Based on its naturalistic principles, Freemasonry necessarily denies the existence of any supernaturally constituted society—namely, the Catholic Church. As such, it denies that the Church is the infallible teacher of faith and morals, and thus endeavors to entirely separate it from the state, which it insists can and should exist on an entirely "natural" foundation.

Pope Leo XIII made this clear in *Humanum Genus*: "By a long and persevering labor, they [the Freemasons] endeavor to bring about this result—namely, *that the teaching office and authority of the Church may become of no account in the civil State*; and for this same reason *they declare to the people and contend that Church and State ought to be altogether disunited.* By this means *they reject from the laws and from the commonwealth the wholesome influence of the Catholic religion*; and they consequently imagine that *States ought to be constituted without any regard for the laws and precepts of the Church.*"[13]

---

[13] Pope Leo XIII, *Humanum Genus* (1884), no. 13.

From such premises it necessarily follows that all religions are fundamentally the same, and thus equally irrelevant, to the state. As the pope explained, this is the religious indifferentism that is the unique scourge of the modern epoch: "They thereby teach *the great error of this age—that a regard for religion should be held as an indifferent matter, and that all religions are alike.* This manner of reasoning is calculated to bring about the ruin of all forms of religion, and *especially of the Catholic religion,* which, as it is the only one that is true, cannot, without great injustice, be regarded as merely equal to other religions."[14]

For this reason, he urged the following elsewhere: "Every familiarity should be avoided, not only with those impious libertines who openly promote the character of the sect, but also with *those who hide under the mask of universal tolerance, respect for all religions,* and the craving to *reconcile the maxims of the Gospel with those of the revolution.* These men seek *to reconcile Christ and Belial, the Church of God and the state without God.*"[15]

But the total separation of Church and state was also intrinsically linked with the broader idea of popular sovereignty, in which, according to a popular phrase of the eighteenth century (including in early America), *vox populi, vox Dei,* "the voice of the people is the voice of God":

> Then come their doctrines of politics, in which the naturalists lay down that *all men have the same right, and are in every respect of equal and like condition*; that

---

[14] Pope Leo XIII, *Humanum Genus* (1884), no. 16.
[15] Pope Leo XIII, *Custodi* (1892), no. 15.

each one is *naturally free*; that *no one has the right to command another*; that it is *an act of violence to require men to obey any authority other than that which is obtained from themselves*. According to this, therefore, all things belong to the free people; power is held by the command or permission of the people, so that, *when the popular will changes, rulers may lawfully be deposed and the source of all rights and civil duties is either in the multitude or in the governing authority when this is constituted according to the latest doctrines*. It is held also that *the State should be without God*; that in the various forms of religion there is *no reason why one should have precedence of another*; and that they are *all to occupy the same place*.[16]

In short, the idea of popular sovereignty, understood this way, made permanent revolution into a principle of politics. Nothing could be conserved so long as "the people" thought otherwise. Their will, no doubt often inflamed by their passions, became law. Swept away is the Christian idea articulated by Saint Paul that every person should "be subject to the governing authorities. For there is no authority except from God, and those that exist have been instituted by God. Therefore he who resists the authorities resist what God has appointed, and those who resist will incur judgment" (Rom 13:1–2). The Catholic Church has long recognized "exceptions" to this general principle. That genuinely tyrannical rulers can, in some instances, be lawfully resisted, is affirmed throughout the ages. After all, the first supreme

---

[16] Pope Leo XIII, *Humanum Genus* (1884), no. 22.

pontiff himself testified that "we must obey God rather than men" (Acts 5:29). However, Freemasonry not only asserts an exception to this general principle but overturns it entirely. The origin of authority is no longer divine but earthly. It no longer commands obedience but must itself obey. As such, the state has been detached from any transcendent source of reason and morality, and is instead found merely on the supposed will of "the people," who themselves have been absolved of any duty to obey Christ's Church and the natural law. They act accordingly, and take the place of God, having appointed themselves the fount of all legitimate authority.

In its total separation of Church and state, Pope Leo warned that the Masonic agenda for secularizing the state went even further than paganism: "To have in public matters no care for religion, and in the arrangement and administration of civil affairs to have no more regard for God than if He did not exist, is *a rashness unknown to the very pagans*; for in their heart and soul the notion of a divinity and the need of public religion were so firmly fixed that they would have thought it easier to have [a] city without foundation than a city without God."[17]

This spiritual revolution would necessarily lead to a temporal revolution, for, "in this," the pontiff observed, "they prepare the way for not a few bolder men who are hurrying on even to worse things, in their endeavor to obtain equality and community of all goods by the destruction of every distinction of rank and property."[18] He was referring to Socialists and Communists, who the pope everywhere identified

---

[17] Pope Leo XIII, *Humanum Genus* (1884), no. 24.
[18] Pope Leo XIII, *Humanum Genus* (1884), no. 23.

with the Masonic program and its false, egalitarian idea of "equality." "In the commonwealth," he notes, "there is an almost infinite dissimilarity of men, as parts of the whole. If they are to be all equal, and each is to follow his own will, the State will appear most deformed."[19] The pope warned where such political principles would lead: "*A change and overthrow of all things will necessarily follow.* Yea, this change and overthrow is *deliberately planned and put forward by many associations of communists and socialists*; and to their undertaking, the sect of Freemasons is not hostile, but *greatly favors their designs*, and *holds in common with them their chief opinions.*"[20]

"Would that all men would judge of the tree by its fruit, and would acknowledge the seed and origin of the evils which press upon us, and of the dangers that are impending!" he warned.[21]

Civil Marriage, Easy Divorce, and Secular Education

With the total separation of Church and state, the will of the people established as absolutely sovereign, and religious indifferentism, the Masonic program then entailed the establishment of civil marriage, wrenching it out of the jurisdiction of the Church and legislating divorce laws that make breaking the marriage contract as easy—if not easier—than breaking other merely civil contracts. In this, Masonry completes the work begun by Protestantism, which denied the sacramental nature of marriage and frequently redefined it as under the jurisdiction

---

[19] Pope Leo XIII, *Humanum Genus* (1884), no. 26.
[20] Pope Leo XIII, *Humanum Genus* (1884), no. 27.
[21] Pope Leo XIII, *Humanum Genus* (1884), no. 28.

of the state. This phalanx directed at the heart of the family would be supported by the secularizing of all education in order to ensure the rising generation would be devoid of religious and moral principles in accord with divine and even natural law.

With the establishment of state-sanctioned religious indifferentism, Pope Leo warned even those truths which may be known by reason—namely, the existence of God, the immaterial nature of the soul, and the soul's immortality— would be overthrown,[22] resulting in a catastrophic collapse in morals in the name of a false "freedom":

> When these truths are done away with, which are as the principles of nature and important for knowledge and for practical use, it is easy to see what will become of both public and private morality. . . . If these be taken away, as the naturalists and Freemasons desire, *there will immediately be no knowledge as to what constitutes justice and injustice, or upon what principle morality is founded.* And, in truth, the teaching of morality which alone finds favor with the sect of Freemasons, and in which they contend that youth should be instructed, is that which they call "civil," and "independent," and "free," namely, that which does not contain any religious belief. But how insufficient such teaching is, how wanting in soundness, and how easily moved by every impulse of passion, is sufficiently proved by its sad fruits, which have already begun to appear. For, *wherever, by removing Christian education, this teaching has begun more completely to rule, there goodness and*

---

[22] Pope Leo XIII, *Humanum Genus* (1884), no. 17.

integrity of morals have begun quickly to perish, mon-
strous and shameful opinions have grown up, and the
audacity of evil deeds has risen to a high degree.[23]

The target would then be the family—both the marriage of the
parents and the education of the children, both of which would
fall under the jurisdiction of the state. The agenda outlined by
Pope Leo XIII appears to be a *fait accompli* in our own day:

> What refers to domestic life in the teaching of the nat-
> uralists is almost all contained in the following decla-
> rations: that *marriage belongs to the genus of commercial*
> *contracts, which can rightly be revoked by the will of those*
> *who made them, and that the civil rulers of the State have*
> *power over the matrimonial bond*; that *in the education*
> *of youth nothing is to be taught in the matter of religion as*
> *of certain and fixed opinion*; and each one must be left
> at liberty to follow, when he comes of age, *whatever he*
> *may prefer*. To these things the Freemasons fully assent;
> and not only assent, but have long endeavored to *make*
> *them into a law and institution*. For in many countries,
> and those nominally Catholic, it is enacted that no
> marriages shall be considered lawful except those con-
> tracted by the civil rite; in other places *the law permits*
> *divorce*; and in others every effort is used to *make it*
> *lawful as soon as may be*. Thus, *the time is quickly com-*
> *ing when marriages will be turned into another kind of*
> *contract—that is into changeable and uncertain unions*
> *which fancy may join together, and which the same when*
> *changed may disunite.* . . .

---

[23] Pope Leo XIII, *Humanum Genus* (1884), no. 19.

> . . . If they [marriages] are deprived of their sacred
> character, and made dissoluble, *trouble and confusion
> in the family will be the result*, the *wife being deprived of
> her dignity* and the *children left without protection as to
> their interests and wellbeing.*[24]

With the rupture between husband and wife instantiated
in law, the secularization of education could proceed apace.
The pope once again describes a plan whose realization we
cannot but acknowledge in our own day:

> With the greatest unanimity the sect of the Freema-
> sons also *endeavors to take to itself the education of
> youth. They think that they can easily mold to their opin-
> ions that soft and pliant age, and bend it whither they
> will; and that nothing can be more fitted than this to
> enable them to bring up the youth of the State after their
> own plan.* Therefore, in the education and instruction
> of children they allow no share, either of teaching or
> of discipline, to the ministers of the Church; and in
> many places they have procured that *the education of
> youth shall be exclusively in the hands of laymen*, and
> that *nothing which treats of the most important and most
> holy duties of men to God shall be introduced into the
> instructions on morals.*[25]

Pope Leo repeated the same warning elsewhere in even more
strident language:

---

[24] Pope Leo XIII, *Humanum Genus* (1884), nos. 21, 24.
[25] Pope Leo XIII, *Humanum Genus* (1884), no. 21.

By the entirely lay education which is now demanded, from the first elements to the higher teaching of the universities, *so that the rising generations, as far as this can be effected by the State, have to grow up without any idea of religion, and without the first essential notions of their duties towards God. This is to put the axe to the root.* No more universal and efficacious means could be imagined of *withdrawing society, and families, and individuals, from the influence of the Church and of the faith.* To lay Clericalism (or Catholicism) waste in its foundations and in its very sources of life, namely, *in the school and in the family*: such is the authentic declaration of Masonic writers.[26]

As this agenda began to be implemented, the result was an education system that had become not merely neutral but actively hostile and competitive with parents: *"Masonry has taken control of the public schools*, leaving private schools, paternal schools, and those directed by zealous ecclesiastics and religious of both sexes *to compete in the education of Christian youth.* Christian parents especially *should not entrust the education of their children to uncertain schools."*[27]

Moral Decay

Pope Leo also warned that the moral decay that was being inculcated by secularized education was in fact an intentional encouragement of the passions of the population in

---

[26] Pope Leo XIII, *Dall'alto* (1890), no. 4.
[27] Pope Leo XIII, *Custodi* (1892), no. 18.

order to make them more pliant and controllable. He writes as follows:

> Wherefore we see that *men are publicly tempted by the many allurements of pleasure*; that there are journals and pamphlets with *neither moderation nor shame*; that stage-plays are *remarkable for license*; that designs for works of art are shamelessly sought in the laws of a so called verism; that *the contrivances of a soft and delicate life are most carefully devised*; and that all *the blandishments of pleasure* are diligently sought out *by which virtue may be lulled to sleep*. Wickedly, also, but at the same time quite consistently, do those act *who do away with the expectation of the joys of heaven*, and bring down all happiness to the level of mortality, and, as it were, sink it in the earth. Of what We have said the following fact, astonishing not so much in itself as in its open expression, may serve as a confirmation. For, since generally *no one is accustomed to obey crafty and clever men so submissively as those whose soul is weakened and broken down by the domination of the passions*, there have been in the sect of the Freemasons some who have *plainly determined and proposed that, artfully and of set purpose, the multitude should be satiated with a boundless license of vice*, as, when this had been done, it *would easily come under their power and authority for any acts of daring*.[28]

Monsignor Dillon further supports this case with the examples of the letters of the Alta Vendita (see chapter 14) and

---

[28] Pope Leo XIII, *Humanum Genus* (1884), no. 20.

Piccolo Tigre (see chapter 15), both of which were discovered by the popes while they still controlled the Papal States and published by them.

The Destruction of the Papacy

Finally, perhaps the most important goal of the Masonic program was the destruction of both the temporal and spiritual authority of the papacy, the first of which was achieved *de facto* with the destruction of the Papal States in 1870, and all but achieved *de jure* with the 1929 Lateran Treaty. As Catholics, we believe the spiritual authority of the papacy will remain until the return of Our Lord. But as Church history shows, whether through moral corruption or such scandalous events as the Avignon papacy and the western schism, it can be undermined from within to a certain degree as well. We leave the reader to their own conclusions in light of Pope Leo's warnings.

Beginning in *Humanum Genus*, Leo made the Masonic program's goals with respect to the papacy clear:

> *But against the apostolic see and the Roman Pontiff the contention of these enemies has been for a long time directed.* The Pontiff was first, for specious reasons, thrust out from the bulwark of his liberty and of his right, *the civil princedom*; soon, he was unjustly driven into a condition which was unbearable because of the difficulties raised on all sides; and *now the time has come when the partisans of the sects openly declare, what in secret among themselves they have for a long time plotted, that the sacred power of the Pontiffs must be abolished,*

*and that the papacy itself, founded by divine right, must
be utterly destroyed. . . .* They especially desire to assail
the Church with irreconcilable hostility, and that they
will never rest *until they have destroyed whatever the
supreme Pontiffs have established for the sake of religion.*[29]

In his encyclical *Dall'alto*, to the bishops of Italy in 1890,
Pope Leo declared the same warning: "*Possessed by the spirit
of Satan*, whose instrument they are, they burn like him with
a deadly and implacable hatred of Jesus Christ and of His
work; and they endeavor by every means *to overthrow and
fetter it.* This war is at present waged more than elsewhere in
Italy, in which the Catholic religion has taken deeper root;
and *above all in Rome, the center of Catholic unity, and the
See of the Universal Pastor and Teacher of the Church.*"[30] He
continued:

The war began by *the overthrow of the civil power of
the Popes*, the downfall of which, according to the
secret intentions of the real leaders, afterwards openly
avowed, was, under a political pretext, to be the means
of enslaving at least, if not of *destroying the supreme
Spiritual Power of the Roman Pontiffs. . . .*

. . . Instead, the Masonic influence is to make itself
*felt in all the circumstances of social life, and to become
master and controller of everything.* Hereby the way will
be smoothed *towards the abolition of the Papacy*; Italy
will thus be free from its implacable and deadly enemy;
and *Rome, which in the past was the center of universal*

---

[29] Pope Leo XIII, *Humanum Genus* (1884), no. 15.
[30] Pope Leo XIII, *Dall'alto* (1890), no. 2.

Theocracy will in the future be the center of universal secularization, whence the Magna Charta of human liberty is to be proclaimed in the face of the whole world. Such are the authentic declarations, aspirations, and resolutions, of Freemasons or of their assemblies. . . .

. . . It suffices to take note of the kind of future, in the social and political order, which is being prepared for Italy *by men whose object is—and they make no secret of it—to wage an unrelenting war against Catholicism and the Papacy.*[31]

In such warnings, we hear the words of Christ to Saint Peter that "Satan demanded to have you, that he might sift you like wheat" (Lk 22:31). But as Catholics, we also trust Our Lord when He says in the very next verse, "but I have prayed for you that your faith may not fail; and when you have turned again, strengthen your brethren" (v. 32).

The Theology and Philosophy of Freemasonry

In addition to summarizing the various goals of the Masonic program, Pope Leo XIII also summarized Freemasonry's "theology" and philosophy, which he described with the word "naturalism":

Now, the fundamental doctrine of the naturalists, which they sufficiently make known by their very name, is that *human nature and human reason ought in all things to be mistress and guide.* Laying this down, they care little for duties to God, or pervert them by

---

[31] Pope Leo XIII, *Dall'alto* (1890), nos. 4, 6, 10.

erroneous and vague opinions. For *they deny that any-thing has been taught by God*; they allow no dogma of religion or truth which cannot be understood by the human intelligence, *nor any teacher who ought to be believed by reason of his authority*. And since it is the special and exclusive duty of the Catholic Church fully to set forth in words truths divinely received, to teach, besides other divine helps to salvation, the authority of its office, and to defend the same with perfect purity, *it is against the Church that the rage and attack of the enemies are principally directed.*[32]

This "naturalism," which we have described as *sola natura*, is the belief that human nature is not damaged by original sin and is capable of perfecting itself and arriving at truth on its own, apart from divine revelation, and any religious authority whatsoever. In a well-known work on Freemasonry published a few decades before *Humanum Genus*, Félix Dupanloup, the bishop of Orleans, and considered a "liberal" by the standards of the time, confirmed Pope Leo's warnings with testimony from Freemasons themselves. "What, in fact, is the principle [of Freemasonry]? Free-thinking," he says. He goes on to quote multiple contemporary Masonic sources who describe Freemasonry as follows:

> "Free-thinking is the fundamental principle of Free-masonry." "Not restrained, but complete and univer-sal liberty." "A liberty which shall be absolute, without limit, *in its fullest extent*." "Absolute liberty of conscience is the only basis of Freemasonry." "Freemasonry is, in

---

[32] Pope Leo XIII, *Humanum Genus* (1884), no. 12.

fact, above all dogmas." "Above all religions." "Liberty of conscience is superior to all forms of religious belief." "Freemasonry is an institution withdrawn from all the hypotheses of the mystics." "Freemasons ought, in consequence, to place themselves not only above different religions, but entirely above all belief in any God whatsoever." "We will be our *own priests* and our own gods." "This unlimited, complete, and universal liberty is a right."

It is this "liberty," untethered to any objective and absolute truth, that the Masonic program intends to spread to every part of the world, amounting to nothing but this, that "every man did what was right in his own eyes" (Jud. 21:25).[33]

Dupanloup elsewhere described the Masonic program as follows:

The doctrines which prevail in the lodges are impiety—that is, *the radical negation of Christianity*; and the negation, implicit but real, not only of Jesus Christ, but of *all* religion, all kinds and forms of Divine worship. *This is the 'progress' of which she dreams for humanity*. And the political form which she pursues to realize these designs, and upon which to build *this new society—without belief, without worship, without Christ, and without God*—is *the Republic which everywhere is to be substituted for monarchies*; but a *democratic and socialist Republic*.

---

[33] Monsignor Dupanloup, *A Study of Freemasonry* (Newark, NJ: J.J. O'Connor & Co., 1876), 44–45.

> *Now we see what is at the bottom of all this Masonic*
> *work,* whatever may be the illusions of or the incon-
> sequence of such-or-such a Freemason, a good and
> honest man perhaps, too easily deceived. This is the
> meaning of all her mighty symbols.[34]

It is upon such a basis, Dupanloup asserts, that Masonry
seeks to erect its own "temple of unity and fraternity"—a
unity, as we said, that is rooted in the first Adam, not the
second:

> Ah! this *temple of unity and fraternity* that you wish to
> build, my poor deceived brethren, it exists; but *it is a*
> *building raised by the hand of God, and not by the hand*
> *of men.* Its foundations are not laid on ruinous nega-
> tions, but rest on a faith which is as firm as it is fertile.
> *It is the great Catholic Church.* Enter into it, you also,
> and you will find your place marked there. This temple
> of God invites all men to take shelter within its walls.
> Jesus Christ died for you as well as for us. He is the
> Savior, the Illuminator of all the human race. Come
> then to Him.[35]

Likewise, in *Inimica vis,* Pope Leo XIII affirmed that this new
"temple of unity and fraternity" of which Dupanloup spoke
was animated by the principles of naturalism—that is, nature,
apart from grace: "*They wish to see the religion founded by God*
repudiated and all affairs, private as well as public, regulated by

---

[34] Dupanloup, 140.
[35] Dupanloup, 154.

the principles of naturalism alone; this is what, in their impiety and stupidity, *they call the restoration of civil society*."[36]

Albert Pike, a thirty-third degree Freemason (the highest rank) and a widely recognized masonic authority, wrote in *Morals and Dogma*—a book intended just for masons— words that support this contention: "Masonry, when properly expounded, is at once *the interpretation of the great book of nature*, the recital of physical and astronomical phenomena, the purest philosophy, and the place of deposit, where, as in a Treasury, are *kept in safety all the great truths of the primitive revelation, that form the basis of all religions*."[37]

Indeed, Pike calls this knowledge of nature "magic": "Magic is that which it is; it is by itself, like the mathematics; for it is *the exact and absolute science of Nature and its laws*."[38] This "magic," which he defines as an exact knowledge of nature, Pike contends is the means by which a Freemason may know and understand "truth" with absolute certainty. "It supplies the human mind with an instrument of philosophical and religious certainty," he says of magic. This is Freemasonry's faux replacement of infallible apostolic authority with the supposedly "incontestable verity" of "magic." By knowledge of and use of such "magic," Freemasons may thereby become immensely powerful: "Thus there is an Absolute, in the matters of the Intelligence and of Faith. The *Supreme Reason* has not left the gleams of the human understanding to vacillate at hazard. There is *an incontestable verity*, there is *an infallible*

---

[36] Pope Leo XIII, *Inimica vis* (1892), no. 8.
[37] Albert Pike, *Morals and Dogma of the Ancient and Accepted Scottish Rite of Freemasonry* (Charleston, SC: Supreme Council of the Thirty-Third Degree for the Southern Jurisdiction of the United States, 1871), 625.
[38] Pike, 841.

method of knowing this verity, and by the knowledge of it, those who accept it as a rule may *give their will a sovereign power that will make them the masters of all inferior things and of all errant spirits;* that is to say, will *make them the Arbiters and Kings of the World."*[39]

Note Pike's assertion that such power can be exercised on "errant spirits" as well as on matter. The implications of this are certainly disturbing. "The Secret of the Occult Sciences," he says, "is that of Nature itself, the Secret of the generation of the Angels and Worlds, that of the Omnipotence of God."[40] Such "errant spirits" are apparently "angels"—or what the Church would more likely call demons (fallen angels).

It is here that the truly diabolical nature of the Masonic project becomes clear. By Pike's own admission, Masonry's goal is to transform the Tree of Knowledge into the Tree of Life:

> *"Ye shall be like the Elohim, knowing good and evil,"* had the Serpent of Genesis said, and the Tree of Knowledge became the Tree of Death.
>
> For six thousand years the Martyrs of Knowledge toil and die at the foot of this tree, *that it may again become the Tree of Life.*[41]

Incidentally, Masonry's own system of dating, "in the year of Masonry," putatively begins in 4000 BC. Thus, the six thousand years referred to by Pike would take the world to the year 2000.

---

[39] Pike, 842.
[40] Pike, 844.
[41] Pike, 844.

Thus, while Masonry claims "nature" is the path to absolute truth, it denies the existence of divinely revealed truth, as this would necessarily transcend man's reason, requiring him to believe something that nature could not disclose to him. With respect to the claims of divine revelation, Freemasonry contends one can only have opinions, but not certainty. As such, there is no authority competent to judge disputes about it, as Pike confirms: "No man can say that he hath as sure possession of the truth as of a chattel. When men entertain opinions diametrically opposed to each other, and each is honest, *who shall decide which hath the Truth*; and how can either say with certainty that *he* hath it? We know not what *is* the truth. . . . No man is responsible for the rightness of his faith; but only for the *up*rightness of it."[42]

Upon this denial of revealed religion, Pike asserts that we are incapable of adjudicating competing religious tenets with the same level of divine authority that are claimed for them. In this, Freemasonry fundamentally agrees with Protestantism, which likewise denies that there is any living apostolic voice deputized by God (i.e. the Catholic Church) to adjudicate religious controversies. In place of the Catholic Church, Pike contends that Freemasonry is the true "Holy Empire" in which men of all religions devoted to being "good" may unite and live in peace. Once again, this unity is based upon the first Adam, rather than the second. It is a unity built upon damaged nature, bereft of and denying the necessity of grace. It is a unity in which Christ not only is not King, but can never be King.

With no authority competent to umpire in religious matters, Masonry contends that all men have a "right" to

---

[42] Pike, 166.

believe whatever they wish, and all such beliefs are, in some sense, equally true. As such, private opinion on matters of supposedly "revealed" religion can never bind anyone, let alone serve as the basis of universal human fraternity. "No man truly obeys the Masonic law who *merely* tolerates those whose religious opinions are opposed to his own," Pike contends. "Every man's opinions are his own private property, and the rights of all men to maintain each his own are perfectly equal." He continues:

> The Mason's creed goes farther than that. No man, it holds, has any right in any way to interfere with the religious belief of another. It holds that each man is *absolutely sovereign as to his own belief*, and that belief is a matter *absolutely foreign* to all who do not entertain the same belief; and that, if there were any right of persecution at all, it would in all cases be a mutual right; because one party has the same right as the other to sit as judge in his own case; and *God is the only magistrate that can rightfully decide between them.* To that great Judge, Masonry refers the matter; and opening wide its portals, *it invites to enter there and live in peace and harmony the Protestant, the Catholic, the Jew, the Moslem*; every man who will lead a truly virtuous and moral life, love his brethren, minister to the sick and distressed, and believe in the One, *All-Powerful, All-Wise, everywhere-Present God, Architect, Creator, and Preserver of all things.*[43]

---

[43] Pike, 167.

One thus sees in Freemasonry the seeds of that religious indifferentism the popes so often warned about—the belief that
each religion is as good as the others because God has not
really spoken to man through His Son Jesus Christ, through
whom He has provided the grace necessary to heal human
nature; nor does He govern His people through the Catholic
Church. Freemasonry speaks of universal toleration. And yet,
this is merely a prelude to the acceptance of the "universal
religion" of Masonry described in Pike's own words as follows:
"Masonry is the universal morality which is suitable to the
inhabitants of every clime, to the man of every creed."[44]

As such, Masonry's chief enemy must be he who claims
to resolve the very disputes which the Mason pseudo-piously
contends can only be resolved by God, who could not really
have meant it when he said to Saint Peter, "I will give you the
keys of the kingdom of heaven, and whatever you bind on
earth shall be bound in heaven, and whatever you loose on
earth shall be loosed in heaven," (Mt 16:19) or to all the other
apostles, "Truly, I say to you, whatever you bind on earth shall
be bound in heaven, and whatever you loose on earth shall be
loosed in heaven" (Mt 18:18). The same apostles to whom
He said, "He who hears you hears me, and he who rejects you
rejects me, and he who rejects me rejects him who sent me"
(Lk 10:16). The same apostles, along with those men they
had already begun appointing to succeed them, who rendered
decisions for the whole Church with the justification "it has
seemed good to the Holy Spirit and to us" (Acts 15:28). Nor
could the apostle be right when he calls this Church "the pillar and bulwark of the truth" (1 Tm 3:15).

---

[44] Pike, 161.

Thus, it comes as no surprise that the Catholic Church—which claims to possess this same apostolic authority from God, and to be the supreme teacher of articles of faith and morality—would be the archenemy of Freemasonry, which claims *for itself* a similar catholicity of religious principles and morals. As the Catholic Church calls all humanity to union in Christ, Masonry calls all into a unity where Christ is no longer essential but only one among many. His claims are revered, but only insofar as they are respected alongside every other religious leader's claims. In short, Christ is made nothing, along with His Church.

"It is not possible to create a true and genuine Brotherhood upon any theory of the baseness of human nature,"[45] says Pike, in an explicit disavowal of original sin. In its place, he asserts that nature is sufficient as it is. Thus, the Freemasonic idea that true "fraternity" may be found in Adam (man's ungraced nature). Under this Masonic regime of "fraternity," the competing claims of different religions simply don't matter. What matters is the common nature we share with one another—a nature which Masonry claims is not damaged by original sin and capable of its own perfection without grace. It is no wonder, then, that Pike declared Freemasonry "incessantly tends toward spiritual perfection, and the fusion of the creeds and Nationalities of Mankind."[46] Masonry's purpose is thus the abolition of all meaningful distinctions between religions and nations on a worldwide scale. Masonry shall be the one true religion, the one true society to which all men may belong, the one true *universal temple*.

---

[45] Pike, 856.
[46] Pike, 625.

By its project to unite humanity in "fraternity" on the basis of the first Adam, rather than the second Adam, Masonry shows itself to be a diabolical *pseudo-temple*. As such, it is, in the truest sense of the word, the anti-Church—a counter-temple built on *sola natura* rather than the grace merited by the passion and resurrection of Jesus Christ.

The "Mysteries" of the Masonic Anti-Church

As a pseudo-temple, an anti-church, Freemasonry claims to be the custodian of its own set of "mysteries," or "sacraments." In their own words, these "mysteries" are those of the pagan religions which preceded the rise of the Catholic Church, which "suppressed" them. But now, in modern days, these "mysteries" are rising once again, with the avowed goal of destroying the very Church that so long suppressed them.

Pike, in *Morals and Dogma*, explicitly says that Masonry *is* the ancient mystery system derived from ancient Egypt, and from there adapted throughout the pagan world that dominated the globe prior to Christianity:

> Masonry, successor of the Mysteries, *still follows the ancient manner of teaching. . . .* Though *Masonry is identical with the ancient Mysteries*, it is so only in this qualified sense: that it presents but an imperfect image of their brilliancy, the ruins only of their grandeur, and a system that has experienced progressive alterations, the fruits of social events, political circumstances, and the ambitious imbecility of its improvers. After leaving Egypt, the Mysteries were modified by the habits of the different nations among whom they were introduced,

and especially by the religious systems of the countries into which they were transplanted. To maintain the established government, laws, and religion, was the *obligation of the Initiate everywhere*; and everywhere they were *the heritage of the priests*, who were *nowhere willing to make the common people co-proprietors with themselves* of philosophical truth.[47]

This apparent unwillingness on the part of the ancient "elites" to share their "knowledge" has been maintained in Freemasonry, in which those who are outside are referred to as the "profane" and must never be allowed to know its "secrets." Later in the same work, Pike is even more explicit: "The *Occult Science of the Ancient Magi* was concealed under *the shadows of the Ancient Mysteries*: it was imperfectly revealed or rather disfigured by the Gnostics; it is guessed at under the obscurities that cover *the pretended crimes of the Templars*; and it is found enveloped in enigmas that seem impenetrable, in *the Rites of the Highest Masonry*."[48]

Pope Leo XIII makes similar assertions as the Masons themselves—that such occult mysteries conceal their ideas and plans not only from outsiders but also from lower-level Masons: "There are many things *like mysteries* which it is the fixed rule to *hide with extreme care*, not only from strangers, *but from very many members*, also; such as their *secret and final designs, the names of the chief leaders*, and certain *secret and inner meetings*, as well as their decisions, and the ways and means of carrying them out."[49]

---

[47] Pike, 22, 23.
[48] Pike, 839.
[49] Pope Leo XIII, *Humanum Genus* (1884), no. 9.

These masonic "mysteries," he says, are enforced by a series of oaths—a fact which is now common knowledge: "The sect of the Freemasons shows itself insolent and proud of its success, and seems as if it would put no bounds to its pertinacity. Its followers, *joined together by a wicked compact and by secret counsels*, give help one to another, and excite one another to an audacity for evil things."[50]

These mysteries, said another thirty-third degree Freemason, J. D. Buck, who played a leading role in the 1893 Parliament of Religions (the beginning of the "ecumenical" movement), are rising once again after centuries of suppression by the Catholic Church: "These ancient institutions, derided, anathematized, misrepresented, persecuted, and *suppressed*, as they have been *for the last fifteen hundred years*, will, *in the age that is now dawning*, demonstrate their beneficence and their power; and the marvel will be, that the ignorance and brutality of man could have so long succeeded *in suppressing them*."[51]

Buck, quoting another Freemason, claims there have been two forces that have existed in perpetual conflict with one another since the dawn of man. One is the side of "light," "liberty," and "reason," while the other stands for "darkness," "oppression," and "superstition." The former is Freemasonry, the latter is the Catholic Church: "*From the dawn of civilization to the present moment two active and opposing forces have been engaged in deadly conflict over the destiny of human intelligence*. . . . At the very *cradle of humanity* these two forces arrayed themselves in an *irrepressible conflict*. At that point

---

[50] Pope Leo XIII, *Humanum Genus* (1884), no. 37.
[51] J. D. Buck, *Mystic Masonry* (Chicago: Indo-American Book Company, 1911), 215.

the struggle began. From that point forward throughout all the subsequent ages, even to the present time, it has continued unabated. *At no time within the limits of authentic history has the conflict reached a more critical stage than in this, the dawning of the twentieth Christian century.*"[52]

Freemasons such as Manly P. Hall speak in very similar terms as Pike and Buck in books such as *The Secret Teachings of All Ages*, *The Secret Destiny of America*, and *The Lost Keys of Freemasonry.*

This is why Pope Leo declared that in Freemasonry "is revived the contumacious spirit of the demon, together with his unsubdued perfidy and deceit."[53] Whether its claims about itself are true or not, Freemasonry conceives of itself as the custodian of the ancient pagan mysteries which were suppressed by the Catholic Church, and are now rising once again to exact their revenge, which it expresses through its own allegories of avenging the death of Masonic heroes such as Hiram Abiff and Jacques de Molay, the last Grand Master of the Knights Templar.

Papal and Canonical Condemnations of Freemasonry

Since 1738, at least eight supreme pontiffs have condemned Freemasonry in one form or another:

- Pope Clement XII, *In eminenti apostolatus* (1738)
- Pope Benedict XIV, *Providas Romanorum* (1751)

---

[52] J. D. Buck, *The Genius of Freemasonry and the Twentieth-Century Crusade* (Chicago: Indo-American Book Company, 1914), 178–79, 180–81.

[53] Pope Leo XIII, *Humanum Genus* (1884), mo. 37.

- Pope Pius VII, *Ecclesiam a Jesu Christo* (1821)
- Pope Leo XII, *Quo Graviora: On Secret Societies* (1826)
- Pope Pius VIII, *Traditi Humilitati: On His Program for His Pontificate* (1829)
- Pope Pius VIII, *Litteris altero* (1830)
- Pope Gregory XVI, *Mirari vos: On Liberalism and Religious Indifferentism* (1832)
- Pope Pius IX, *Qui pluribus: On Faith and Religion* (1846)
- Pope Pius IX, *Quibus quantisque malis* (1849)
- Pope Pius IX, *Quanta cura: Condemning Current Errors* (1864)
- Pope Pius IX, *Multiplices inter: Pleading for Unity of Spirit* (1853)
- Pope Pius IX, *Apostolicae Sedis moderationi* (1869)
- Pope Pius IX, *Etsi multa: On the Church in Italy, Germany, and Switzerland* (1873)
- Pope Leo XIII, *Etsi Nos: On Conditions in Italy* (1882)
- Pope Leo XIII, *Humanum Genus* (1884)
- Pope Leo XIII, *Officia sanctissimo: On the Church in Bavaria* (1887)
- Pope Leo XIII, *Dall'alto dell'Apostolico Seggio: Freemasonry in Italy* (1890)
- Pope Leo XIII, *Custodi di Quella Fede: On Freemasonry* (1892)
- Pope Leo XIII, *Inimica vis: On Freemasonry* (1892)
- Pope Leo XIII, *Praeclara gratulationis publicae: The Reunion of Christendom* (1894)
- Pope Leo XIII, *Annum ingressi* (1902)

Membership in Masonic sects has also been condemned in Canon Law since Pope Saint Pius X promulgated the 1917 Code. Canon 2334 of the 1917 *Code of Canon Law*, for example, explicitly named Freemasonry and imposes an automatic excommunication for membership in Masonic sects that can only be lifted by Rome: "Those giving their name to masonic sects or other associations of this sort that machinate against the Church or legitimate civil powers *contract by that fact excommunication simply reserved to the Apostolic See.*"[54]

After Vatican II, and prior to the promulgation of the 1983 code, Cardinal Seper, prefect of the Congregation for the Doctrine of the Faith, issued a formal declaration clarifying that the prohibitions against masonic membership remained in full force.[55] While Freemasonry is not explicitly mentioned in the 1983 *Code of Canon Law*, Canon 1374 nonetheless serves the same function as Canon 2334 under the 1917 Code: "A person who joins an association which plots against the Church is to be *punished with a just penalty*; however, a person who promotes or directs an association of this kind is to be punished with an interdict."[56]

Canon 1448 of the *Code of Canons of Oriental Churches*— the eastern Catholic rites—has a similar prohibition: "One who joins *an organization which plots against the Church*, is to be punished with an appropriate penalty."[57]

---

[54] Edward N. Peters, curator, *The 1917 Pio-Benedictine Code of Canon Law* (San Francisco: Ignatius Press, 2001), 740.

[55] Franjo Cardinal Seper, *Declaration Concerning Status of Catholics Becoming Freemasons* (February 17, 1981).

[56] Vatican, *Code of Canon Law, Can. 1374* (1983).

[57] *Code of Canons of Oriental Churches* (1990).

The new Code's lack of any explicit mention of Freemasonry led to a request for clarification from then prefect of the Congregation for the Doctrine of the Faith, Cardinal Ratzinger, who later became Pope Benedict XVI. Soon after the release of the 1983 Code, he left no room for doubt that the Church's teaching and prohibition remained unchanged: *"Therefore the Church's negative judgment in regard to Masonic association remains unchanged* since their principles have always been considered *irreconcilable with the doctrine of the Church* and therefore membership in them remains forbidden. The faithful who enroll in Masonic associations are in a state of *grave sin* and may not receive Holy Communion."[58]

Leo XIII and the Significance of *The War of the Antichrist with the Church and Christian Civilization*

As we have already stated, we do not presume to declare with certainty that Monsignor Dillon's case is without any error, or accurate in every respect. However, it is indeed of great value in light of two facts: the remarkable and eerie extent to which its description of the Masonic program aligns with the state of the world nearly 140 years later; and its endorsement by Pope Leo XIII, whose encyclicals also corroborate its most important claims. Shortly after its publication, a Catholic magazine, *The Month*, reported on the pontiff's endorsement in its September 1885 issue:

> Mgr. [sic] Dillon's work has already been honored
> by the Holy Father himself with so marked and so

---

[58] Vatican, Joseph Cardinal Ratzinger, *Declaration on Masonic Associations* (November 26, 1983).

unusual an approbation that there is no need for us to accord it any further praise than merely to take note of the fact. The book was presented to His Holiness, accompanied by an Italian version of its table of contents, and of long extracts from its principal sections, and *Leo the Thirteenth was pleased to order that the Italian version should be completed, and the book printed and published at Rome at his own expense.* We offer Mgr. Dillon our congratulations on this high mark of approval of the Sovereign Pontiff, and proceed to give such of our readers as have not yet seen the book an outline of its general plan and contents.[59]

For Leo XIII, Freemasonry was no idle threat. Its goal was nothing less than the destruction of Christian civilization—a goal which, according to his 1894 encyclical *Praeclara gratulationis publicae*, involved a direct attack on the papacy itself:

There is likewise *a great danger threatening unity* on the part of that association which goes by the name of Freemasons, whose fatal influence for a long time past oppresses Catholic nations in particular. Favored by the agitations of the times, and waxing insolent in its power and resources and success, it strains every nerve to *consolidate its sway and enlarge its sphere.* It has already sallied forth from its hiding-places, where it hatched its plots, into the throng of cities, and as if to

[59] *The Month: A Catholic Magazine and Review, No. 256, Twenty-Second Year, October 1885* (London: Office of the Month, 48 South St. Grosvenor Sq., 1885), 141.

defy the Almighty, *has set up its throne in this very city of Rome, the Capital of the Catholic world.*

What is the meaning of this particularly ominous phrase: that Freemasonry has "set up its throne in this very city of Rome"? It's unclear. But it is perhaps not mere coincidence that the prayer to Saint Michael the Archangel authored and promulgated by Pope Leo XIII to the whole Church uses strikingly similar language in one of its lesser-known sections:

> Most cunning enemies have filled with bitterness and drenched with gall the Church, the Spouse of the Lamb without spot, and have lifted impious hands against all that is most sacred in it. *Even in the holy place where the See of Blessed Peter and the chair of truth was set up to enlighten the world, they have raised the abominable throne of their impiety with the iniquitous hope that the Shepherd may be stricken and the flock scattered abroad.* Arise, then, unconquerable Prince, defend the people of God against the assaults of the reprobate spirits, and give them the victory.[60]

Thus, in the prayer to Saint Michael the Archangel, Pope Leo XIII speaks of the setting up of a diabolical throne in Rome for the purpose of striking at the papacy itself so that the unity of the Church may be disrupted—which is exactly how he described the goals of the Masonic program throughout his entire pontificate. Not only that, but his prayer also

---

[60] *The New Raccolta, or, Collection of Prayers and Good Works to which the Sovereign Pontiffs have Attached Holy Indulgences; Published in 1898 by Order of His Holiness, Pope Leo XIII* (Philadelphia: Peter F. Cunningham & Son, 1903), 364–65.

alludes to the words of Zechariah 13:7, which were quoted by Our Lord Himself (Matt. 26:31; Mark 14:27) as a prophecy of His passion: "*Strike the shepherd, that the sheep may be scattered*; I will turn my hand against the little ones."

It is thus perhaps no coincidence that the *Catechism of the Catholic Church* compares the final persecution of the Church by Antichrist with the passion of Our Lord. This apparent connection is strengthened by Pope Leo XIII's allusion to the Old Testament prophecy of Christ's passion and the fact that the prayer is addressed to Saint Michael the Archangel, who is often associated with the end times, given his appearance in both the prophet Daniel, and the Apocalypse:

> Before Christ's second coming the Church must *pass through a final trial that will shake the faith of many believers*. The persecution that accompanies her pilgrimage on earth will *unveil the "mystery of iniquity" in the form of a religious deception* offering men an apparent solution to their problems at the price of *apostasy from the truth*. . . .
>
> The Church will enter the glory of the kingdom *only through this final Passover, when she will follow her Lord in his death and Resurrection*. The kingdom will be fulfilled, then, *not by a historic triumph of the Church through a progressive ascendancy, but only by God's victory over the final unleashing of evil*, which will cause his Bride to come down from heaven. God's triumph over *the revolt of evil* will take the form of the Last Judgment after the final cosmic upheaval of this passing world.[61]

---

[61] *CCC* 675, 677.

Like Pope Leo XIII, Monsignor Dillon lays out the details of this plot against the papacy throughout his book. But the significance of Pope Leo XIII's endorsement goes even further, for, as Monsignor Dillon details, the supreme pontiff long warned that the Masonic program ultimately sought the handing of the Temporal Sword from Christ to Satan across the globe. As such, its goal was to gain control of governments throughout the world. We repeat: these are not the claims of a wild-eyed "conspiracy theorist" on the internet but of the Vicar of Christ on earth, following in a long line of predecessors who warned of essentially the same thing:

> But what is most disastrous is, that wherever it has set its foot *it penetrates into all ranks and departments of the commonwealth, in the hope of obtaining at last supreme control.* This is, indeed, a great calamity: for its depraved principles and iniquitous designs are well known. Under the pretense of *vindicating the rights of man and of reconstituting society*, it attacks Christianity; it rejects revealed Doctrine, denounces practices of Piety, the Divine Sacraments, and every Sacred thing as superstition; it strives to *eliminate the Christian Character from Marriage and the family and the education of youth*, and from *every form of instruction*, whether public or private, and to *root out from the minds of men all respect for Authority, whether human or Divine*. On its own part, it preaches the *worship of nature*, and maintains that by the principles of nature are truth and probity and justice to be measured and regulated. In this way, as is quite evident, *man is being driven to adopt customs and habits of life akin to those*

of the heathen, only more corrupt in proportion as the incentives to sin are more numerous.[62]

The pope warned that indeed the power of Freemasonry had increased to such a degree that it exercised immense control in numerous states, and only sought more: "In consequence, the sect of Freemasons grew with a rapidity beyond conception in the course of a century and a half, until it came to be able, by means of fraud or of audacity, *to gain such entrance into every rank of the State as to seem to be almost its ruling power.*"[63]

"The Freemasons," he declared, "have endeavored to make them [states] their allies and powerful helpers for the destruction of the Christian name." He continued: "Having, by these artifices, insured their own safety and audacity, they have begun *to exercise great weight in the government of States*; but nevertheless they are prepared to *shake the foundations of empires*, to *harass the rulers of the State*, to accuse, and to cast them out, *as often as they appear to govern otherwise than they themselves could have wished.*"[64]

He issued similar warnings in *Dall'alto*:

> This system is adopted and carried out wherever Freemasonry uses its impious and wicked action; and, as its action is widespread, so is *this anti-Christian system* widely applied. But the application becomes more speedy and general, and is pushed more to extremes, *in countries where the government is more under the control of*

---

[62] Pope Leo XIII, *Praeclara gratulationis publicae* (1894).
[63] Pope Leo XIII, *Humanum Genus* (1884), no. 7.
[64] Pope Leo XIII, *Humanum Genus* (1884), no. 28.

the sect and better promotes its interest. . . . Here the direction of public affairs, in what concerns religion, is wholly in conformity with the aspirations of the sects; and for accomplishing their aspirations, they find avowed supporters and ready instruments in those who hold the public power.[65]

The pontiff is not saying that Freemasons are behind every wound inflicted on the Church nor that there is a Mason under every rock. In fact, both Leo XIII and Monsignor Dillon repeatedly emphasize that there can be Masons who are in outward appearance good men, and that many of its lower grades know absolutely nothing about the intentions of the higher ones. Nonetheless, it remains the case that Freemasonry is the "implacable enemy" of the Church and plans to use civil governments as the primary means of attacking Her:

> *We do not wish to exaggerate the masonic power* by attributing to its direct and immediate action all the evils which presently preoccupy Us. However, you can clearly see its spirit in the facts which We have just recorded and in many others which We could recall. That spirit, which is *the implacable enemy of Christ and of the Church*, tries all ways, uses all arts, and prevails upon all means. It seizes from the Church its first-born daughter [France] and seizes from Christ His favored nation [Italy], the seat of His Vicar on earth and the center of Catholic unity. . . . Proud of its successes, the sect herself has spoken out and told us all its past accomplishments and future goals. *It regards the public powers as its instruments. . . .*

---

[65] Pope Leo XIII, *Dall'alto* (1890), no. 5.

> . . . The facts say that masonic patriotism is no less
> than *sectarian egotism which yearns to dominate every-*
> *thing, particularly the modern states which unite and con-*
> *centrate everything in their hands.* The facts say that in
> the plans of masonry, the names of political indepen-
> dence, equality, civilization, and progress *aimed to facil-*
> *itate the independence of man from God* in our country.[66]

In his apostolic letter *Annum ingressi*, Pope Leo XIII provided a revealing summary of his condemnations of Freemasonry, and its goals for the world:

> Abiding personification of the revolution, *it constitutes*
> *a sort of retrogressive society whose object is to exercise an*
> *occult suzerainty over the established order and whose*
> *whole purpose is to make war against God and against*
> *His Church.* There is no need of naming it, for all will
> recognize in these traits the society of Freemasons. . .
> While denouncing its destructive tendency, its errone-
> ous teachings and *its wicked purpose of embracing in its*
> *far-reaching grasp almost all nations,* and *uniting itself*
> *to other sects which its secret influences puts in motion,*
> directing first and afterwards retaining its members by
> the advantages which it procures for them, *bending gov-*
> *ernments to its will,* sometimes by promises and some-
> times by threats, it has succeeded in entering all classes
> of society, and forms *an invisible and irresponsible state*
> *existing within the legitimate state.* Full of the *spirit of*
> *Satan* who, according to the words of the Apostle,
> knows how to transform himself at need into an angel
> of light, it gives prominence to *its humanitarian object,*

---

[66] Pope Leo XIII, *Custodi* (1892), nos. 6, 8.

but it sacrifices everything to its sectarian purpose and protests that it has no political aim, while in reality *it exercises the most profound action on the legislative and administrative life of the nations,* and while loudly professing its respect for authority and even for religion, has for *its ultimate purpose, as its own statutes declare, the destruction of all authority as well as of the priesthood,* both of which it holds up as the enemies of liberty.[67]

The pope specifically observes that this masonic conspiracy is centrally directed, as evidenced by the fact that it adopts the same means throughout the world:

It becomes more evident day by day that *it is to the inspiration and the assistance of this sect that we must attribute in great measure the continual troubles with which the Church is harassed,* as well as the recrudescence of the attacks to which it has recently been subjected. For the simultaneousness of the assaults in the persecutions which have so suddenly burst upon us in these later times, like a storm from a clear sky, that is to say without any cause proportionate to the effect; the uniformity of means employed to inaugurate this persecution, namely, *the press, public assemblies, theatrical productions*; the *employment in every country of the same arms,* to wit, calumny and public uprisings, *all this betrays clearly the identity of purpose and a program drawn up by one and the same central direction.* All this is only *a simple episode of a prearranged plan carried out on a constantly widening field to multiply the ruins of which we speak.*

---

[67] Pope Leo XIII, *Annum ingressi* (1902).

He continues, "Thus they are endeavoring by every means in their power first to *restrict and then to completely exclude religious instruction from the schools so as to make the rising generation unbelievers or indifferent to all religion*; as they are endeavoring by the daily press to *combat the morality of the Church*, to ridicule its practices and its solemnities. It is only natural, consequently, that *the Catholic priesthood*, whose mission is to preach religion and to administer the sacraments, should be *assailed with a special fierceness*." Leo again asserts that the ultimate object of the conspiracy is the papacy:

> We must not be astonished that the most beloved children are struck when *the father himself, that is to say, the head of Catholicity, the Roman Pontiff, is no better treated*. The facts are known to all. *Stripped of the temporal sovereignty* and consequently of *that independence which is necessary to accomplish his universal and divine mission*; forced in Rome itself to shut himself up in his own dwelling because the enemy has laid siege to him on every side, he has been compelled in spite of the derisive assurances of respect and of the precarious promises of liberty to *an abnormal condition of existence which is unjust and unworthy of his exalted ministry*. We know only too well the difficulties that are each instant created to thwart his intentions and to outrage his dignity. It only goes to prove what is every day more and more evident that *it is the Spiritual Power of the head of the Church which little by little they aim at destroying when they attack the Temporal Power*

of the Papacy. Those who are the real authors of this spoliation have not hesitated to confess it.

Likewise, Pope Leo asserted that the facts of this conspiracy are "so connected together as in their series to reveal with fullest evidence a system of which they [the Masons] are the actual operation and development. The system is not new; but the audacity, the fury, the rapidity with which it is now carried out, is new."[68]

It bears mentioning a fascinating anecdote provided by Catholic scholar, Vatican expert, and journalist Dr. Robert Moynihan, which he shared in April 2020. He recounted a discussion he had with Cardinal Ratzinger several years before he became pope, in which the eminent churchman made a stunning remark:

> I recall a conversation that I had with then Cardinal Ratzinger a few years before he became pope. We were in his apartment, not far from St. Anne's Gate. We were discussing his conflict with Cardinal Walter Casper over the question of Universal Church and Particular Church which was much in the media at that time. I asked the Cardinal where the greatest danger to the authentic Catholic faith lies. "Is it in our own selves, our own sins and weaknesses. Is this what is the greatest danger to the Church or is it something else, some external enemy?"
>
> *He looked at me directly in the eyes and then after a moment's pause, as if he were reflecting, he said:* "It is Freemasonry."

---

[68] Pope Leo XIII, *Dall'alto* (1890), no. 2.

I never forgot that conversation as it was [a] fixed point that brought to a conclusion a long series of questions that had concerned me up until that meeting and have concerned me since.[69]

This naturally raises the question: How should Catholics respond not only to Freemasonry but also to the world system which, if not directly established by it, is nonetheless consonant with its ideology and is everywhere taken for granted across most of the formerly Christian world in the twenty-first century? Pope Leo XIII addresses this question as best as anyone:

> Let Us then show you masonry as an enemy of God, Church, and country. Recognize it as such once and for all, and with all the weapons which reason, conscience, and faith put in your hands, defend yourselves from such a proud foe. Let no one be taken in by its attractive appearance or allured by its promises; do not be seduced by its enticements or frightened by its threats. *Remember that Christianity and masonry are essentially irreconcilable, such that to join one is to divorce the other. You can no longer ignore such incompatibility between Catholic and mason, beloved children: you have been warned openly by Our predecessors, and We have loudly repeated the warning.* . . .
>
> . . . Does the sect try to enslave the Church and to put it at the feet of the state as a humble servant? You

---

[69] Robert Moynihan, "*Letter #8: The Long Hand,*" *Inside the Vatican*, April 23, 2020, https://insidethevatican.com/news/newsflash/letter-8-the-long-hand/.

must then demand and claim for it the freedom and independence due it before the law. Does masonry seek to tear apart Catholic unity, sowing discord even in the clergy itself, arousing quarrels, fomenting strife, and inciting insubordination, revolt, and schism? By tightening the sacred bond of charity and obedience, you can thwart its plans, bring to naught its efforts, and disappoint its hopes. . . .

Redouble your prayers so that God might be with you in a greater abundance of grace, fighting and triumphing with you. Accompany your prayers with the practice of the Christian virtues, especially charity toward the needy. Seek God's mercies with humility and perseverance, renewing every day the promises of your baptism.[70]

Catholics, as with all trials, must ultimately respond with prayer, penance, and spiritual and corporal acts of mercy.

When it comes to Freemasonry, however, there is a great danger that any one of us can be drawn into an endless rabbit hole of "conspiracy theories." Has there been a conspiracy to overturn Christian civilization? Yes, there has. The vicars of Christ have repeatedly said so. This is not a "conspiracy theory." However, no Catholic should cultivate an unhealthy obsession with determining the precise nature of the inner sanctum of Masonry and other secret societies. It is sufficient to know that its ideology of naturalism and *sola natura* is the arch-enemy of the grace of God, and as such the Catholic Church. It is sufficient to know that the agenda it pursues—that of the total separation of Church and state; the replacement of the

---

[70] Pope Leo XIII, *Custodi* (1892), nos. 10, 19, 21.

authority of God with the authority of the people; religious indifferentism; transforming marriage into a purely "civil" matter; easy divorce laws; secular education; moral decay; the destruction of both the temporal and spiritual authority of the papacy; and all of it aligned with Socialist, Communist, and ultimately Pantheistic movements—is diabolical, and must be resisted. It is sufficient to know it has been condemned by the Church in the most scathing terms possible—perhaps more than any other "heresy" of the last three centuries. The exact nature and content of its symbols, oaths, and methods is, for the vast majority of Catholics, a distraction more likely to disturb their peace and waste the time and effort they owe to God than to achieve any comparable good.

This book's purpose is to help Catholics see that there does in fact exist a diabolical enemy, Freemasonry. It has, in fact, conspired to overturn Christian civilization, the fruit of which we see everywhere around us, including the lives of many Catholics who have adopted the very religious indifference Freemasonry so insidiously promoted. This cannot be dismissed as a mere "conspiracy theory." The salvation of souls is at stake.

As such, the Catholic's duty is first and foremost to work out his own salvation with fear and trembling, and do all he can for the salvation of others—to love God with all his heart, soul, mind, and strength, and his neighbor as himself.

Let all our efforts be subservient to these ends, never allowing an unhealthy curiosity with the forces of darkness to distract us from the true light of Jesus Christ, in whom alone is found salvation and eternal life.

Editor's Note

THROUGHOUT THIS REPUBLISHED version of *The War of the Antichrist with the Church and Christian Civilization*, we substituted modern American spelling where appropriate. The footnotes consist of four categories: (1) original footnote; (2) original citation; (3) editor's footnote; and (4) editor's citation.

The first is a footnote originally included in the same place by Monsignor Dillon. Some of these footnotes are quite extensive, and in such cases, we made them into appendices at the end of their respective chapters to improve the flow of the text.

The second is a citation originally included by Monsignor Dillon within the text of the book that we have made into a footnote to improve the flow of the text.

The third is a footnote created by us to explain or provide more detail about what Monsignor Dillon has written. Most often, these are short biographical summaries of the various historical figures he mentions.

The fourth is a footnote created by us which includes a citation not originally provided by Monsignor Dillon.

Monsignor Dillon makes several statements about Jewish involvement in some of the conspiracies he outlines. In the interest of historical integrity, and the fact that Monsignor Dillon mentions many other nationalities that played a prominent role in the plots he unfolds, we have retained these statements. We do not believe his intentions were animated by racial, religious, or any other anti-Semitic hatred of Jews. Likewise, we reject any and all forms of anti-Semitism.

Finally, while the original work published by Monsignor Dillon simply referred to "Antichrist" in the title, we saw fit to change this to "the Antichrist," as this seems to better accord with modern usage.

Letter from His Holiness Pope Leo XIII

Leo XIII, Pope.

Beloved Son, health and Apostolic Benediction.

The presentation which you have recently made to Us of your work in English on the war of anti-Christ against the Church and against that true civilization brought by her into the world, is a new proof of your fidelity. To this work is added and bound up in the same volume a smaller one on the wrong done to the patrimony which the Apostolic See had dedicated for the propagation of the Christian name.

The reason which led you to compose the greater work is abundantly made known to Us from what you have condensed in the very beginning of the volume. You desired, as is evident by your writings, to describe chiefly those things which, in the last century and in our own, have been done by those perverse combinations of men whom a common hatred of virtue and truth binds together in an impious league against God and against His Christ. On which account the very gravity itself of your subject tacitly exhorts Us that whenever any time should be given to Us from Our cares, that time We should willingly devote to the reading of your volume.

For the noble zeal which aroused you to write of the atrocious war by which the religion of Christ is assailed gives Us reason to hope that in the discharge of the ministry of the word you will assiduously labor to cause the faithful deeply to abhor those criminal societies condemned by Us and by Our predecessors, and understanding their most mischievous evil nature, not permit themselves to be ensnared by their fraudulent arts.

Meanwhile returning you thanks due for the gift you have made to Us, and praying an ample abundance of Divine blessing upon you, We most lovingly in the Lord impart to you as a pledge of our paternal affection the Apostolic Benediction.

Given at St. Peter's, Rome, this 5th day of September, in the year 1885, being the eighth of Our Pontificate.

Leo XIII, Pope.

Original Latin

Leo XIII, Pope

Dilecte Fili, Salutem et Apostolicam Benedictionera.

Novum obsequii tui testimonium praebuit Nobis oblatum a Te munus libri anglico sermone conscripti, de bello Antichristi contra Ecclesiam varaeque bumanitatis cultum ab Ipsa illatum. Huic adjectus est eodemque volumine comprehensus libellus de violato patrimonio, quod Apostolica Sedes Christiano nomine propagando addixerat. Quae mens tua fuerit in majore opere concinando, satis nobis elucet ex lis quae in ipsa fronte libri es complexus. Persequi scilicet voluisti pottissimum scriptione tua, quae superiore saeculo et Nostro gesta sunt ad Ecclesiae reique publicae perniciem a pravis coetibus hominum, quos commune virtutis et veritatis odium impio foedere consociavit adversus Dominum et adversus Christum ejus. Quare ipsa argumenti gravitas Nos tacite hortatur ut si quid temporis vacuum a curis Nobis suppetat illud lectioni voluminis tui impertiamus libenter. Nobis autem zelus qui te excitavit ut de atroci bello scriberes quo Christi religio impetitur Nobis spem facit te in ministerio verbi obeundo impigre daturum operam, ut fideles a noxiis illis societatibus vehementer abhorreant, perspectaque earum indole pessima non sinant sese fraudolosis illarum artibus illaquear. Debitas interim pro oblato numere tibi gratias agentes, et amplam coelestium donorum copiamadprecantes, Apostolicam Benedictionem paternae caritatis testem peramanter in Domino impertimus.

Datum Romae apud S. Petrum Die V, Septembris Anno MDCCCLXXXV, Pontificatus Nostri Octavo.

LEO P.P. XIII.

Letter from the Congregation of Propaganda

Rome, August 25, 1885

I RETAIN WITH great pleasure the copy which you have presented to me of the book you recently published, containing your lectures upon Freemasonry, and upon the Congregation of the Propaganda. Although I have not as yet been able to read the whole of it on account of the grave occupations of my position, yet even from that little which I have read, and much more from the knowledge which I possess of your ability, I am quite certain that your work will prove of great advantage. Moreover the sentiments which you have expressed in favor of this sacred Congregation of Propaganda will cause the merits of that evangelizing work to be better understood, and conciliate more and more towards it the esteem not only of Catholics but even of non-Catholics. Thanking you then for the offering you have made me and wishing you every blessing.

I am,
Yours most affectionately,
JOHN CARDINAL SIMEONI, Prefect.
+ D. Archbishop of Tyre,
Secretary.

Original Italian

Ho molto gradito la copia che V. S. mi ha presentato del libro da Lei teste posto a stampa, in cui ha raccolto le sue dissertazioni sulla Framassoneria e sulla Congregazione di Propaganda. Quantunque io non l'abbia ancora letto interamente, attese le gravi occupazioni della mia carica, pur tuttavia, e da quel poco che ho percorso, e molto più dalla conoscenza che ho della sua abilità, mi rendo certo che la sua opera sarà per riuscire di molto vantaggio. I sentimenti poi che Ella ha espresso in favore di questa S. C. di Propaganda, faranno sempre meglio conoscere la benemerenza di quest' opera evangelizzatrice, e concilierà alla medesima sempre più la stima, non solo dei cattolici, ma altresì degli eterodossi.

Mgr. Giogio Dillon
Ringraziandola quindi dell' offerta
che mi fa fatto, le auguro ogni bene.
Di V.S.

Affmo
GIOVANNI CARD. SIMEONI, Prefetto.
+ D. Arcivescovo di Tiro,
Segretario.

Preface

"Upon great social movements, upon discontented populations, upon corruption, distraction, and contention, they rely to bring their one redoubted enemy, the Catholic Church, to what they call the tomb. . . . Now, if the following pages prove anything, it is that over the whole world there exists a formidable conspiracy—the War of Antichrist—carried on by a secret directory ruling every form of secret society on earth, and losing no chance of seducing men from God by first bringing them, under some pretense or other, within its ranks."

—Monsignor Dillon

THE FOLLOWING PAGES contain the substance of two Lectures given a few months ago in Edinburgh. The selection of the subjects upon which they treat, and, indeed, the fact of their being delivered at all, were, it may be said, accidental. The author, a missionary priest, was, after over twenty years' labor in Australia, compelled for health reasons to visit Europe: and during the past season took advantage of an opportunity to make a tour through Scotland. His object in visiting that historic land was first to gratify his Scotch friends and converts in Australia by a sojourn, however brief, in a country, and in several special localities of it, which he knew to be very dear to them; and next to satisfy his own desire of seeing the progress of religion in that as well as in other portions of the British Isles which he had already visited. The condition of the Church in Ireland, and her advance amidst the adverse influences with which she was to contend in England and Scotland, are of intense interest to Australian Catholics; and an Australian missionary who visits these countries is supposed to bring back much information regarding the state of religion in each one of them. Scotland besides is so full of historic reminiscences, and so favored by nature with splendid scenery, that a visit to Europe is incomplete without a look upon its rugged hills, its romantic lakes and lovely valleys, now made so interesting by the works of Sir Walter Scott and other writers. The land once evangelized by Columba and his bands of missionary saints, has besides an indescribable charm for a Catholic missionary. He went, therefore, with great pleasure to Scotland, and he cannot speak too highly or too thankfully of the kindness which the Venerable Archbishop of Glasgow, the Bishops and the Clergy he happened to meet with showed him.

But, with the exception of a Sunday sermon to oblige the good pastor of whatever locality he happened to pass through, it was his fixed intention not to speak publicly during his rather rapid progress through the country. It happened, however, that on coming to Edinburgh he found an old and very dear friend and College companion in charge of the most populous Catholic district of the metropolis, and in deference to the earnest solicitations of that friend, he departed from his resolution and gave during the few days his stay lasted, first, a lecture on Secret Societies for the benefit of a large and flourishing Catholic Association for men;

and secondly, as a sequel to that, a lecture on the Spoliation of the Propaganda.

Both lectures were delivered extemporaneously; that is to say, so far as the language which conveyed their substance was concerned. The matter, however, had been made familiar to the speaker by many years of observation and reading. Very flattering, and, in some cases, very full reports of them appeared in Catholic newspapers. The report of the principal Protestant organ of public opinion in Edinburgh (the *Scotsman*) was very fair, but another paper bitterly resented what it chose to consider an attack on "Freemasonry and Freedom." It was not, however, so much in the hope of diverting Protestants from Freemasonry as in the desire to show to Catholics that all kinds of secret societies were as bad as, if not worse than, Freemasonry—were, in fact, united with, and under the rule of the worst form of Freemasonry—that the lecturer essayed [attempted] to speak at all upon the subject. If what he said could influence anyone outside the Church from joining the worse than folly of British Masonry, he would rejoice as a result; but his principal aim was to save his own co-religionists from an evil far more pernicious to them than British Masonry has ever been to Protestants. In this latter design, he was glad to learn that he had considerable success; and amongst those who heard or read his utterances, very many expressed a desire to see what he happened to have said in a permanent form. Notwithstanding the difficulties of doing this with any effect during a vacation tour, he determined, at whatever cost to himself, to gratify their wishes, and therefore took advantage of a few weeks' rest, while spending Christmas in his *Alma*

Mater—All Hallows' College, Dublin—to put both lectures into the shape in which he now presents them to such as may desire to read them.

It must, however, be remembered that these lectures are nothing more than what they were originally; that is, casual discourses, and not formal and exhaustive treatises on the subjects upon which they touch. For convenience he has divided each one into separate headings; and where necessary to illustrate the text, he has added notes. These are necessary in order to form a clear idea of the whole matter treated. Notes, however, are not always proofs; and proofs however difficult to be obtained against opponents' intent on concealment, must, nevertheless, be forthcoming in order to convince. He has, therefore, embodied in the text several documents which were only referred to, or but partially quoted in the spoken lectures. Those now occupy many pages of the lecture upon Secret Societies, and will, he believes, be read with considerable interest by such as have not previously been acquainted with them. "The Permanent Instruction" and the letters of Vindex and Piccolo Tigre, originally published by M. Cretineau-Joly from the archives of the Alta Vendita, after they were fortunately discovered by the Roman police, are of this class. Certain extracts are also given of equal value. Most of these documents have been translated into English from French translations of the original Italian and German; and the one passage, that of Mr. Robison on Freemasonry as the cause of the first French Revolution, is taken from a translation from the English into French, re-done into English, as it was impossible to find the original English work of Mr. Robison, which, though extremely valuable, is, he believes, long out of print. The documents regarding the Spoliation of the Propaganda have been translated from the Latin and Italian originals. He has endeavored to translate all such documents as literally as possible, so as to preserve their value as evidence.

The first lecture, which he has entitled the war of Antichrist with the Church and Christian Civilization, is intended to treat, in as brief space as possible, the whole question of Secret, Atheistic Organization, its origin, its nature, its history in the last century and in this, and its unity of satanic purpose in a wonderful diversity of forms. To do this with effect, it was necessary to go over a large area of ground, and to touch upon a great variety of topics. The writer was conscious that much of this ground and many of these topics would be very much better known to a large number of his readers than to himself. Nearly every matter he had to speak about had been already very frequently handled ably and exhaustively in our Catholic reviews, magazines, and newspapers. But notwithstanding this fact, very few, if any, attempts have been made in our language to treat the subject as a whole. Many articles which he has seen, proposed to treat some one feature only of the Atheistic conspiracy—for example, Freemasonry; or the Infidel war upon Christian education and Christian institutions; or the Revolution in Italy; or the efforts of sectaries against the Temporal Power of the Pope, and against the welfare of Christian States generally. Several writers appeared to assume as known that which was really unknown to very many; and few touched at all upon the fact—a fact, no doubt, difficult to prove from the strict and ably guarded secrecy which protects it—of the supreme direction given to the universality of secret societies from a guiding, governing, and—even to the rank and file of the members of the secret societies themselves—unknown and invisible junta ceaselessly sitting in dark conclave and guiding the whole mass of the secret societies of the world.

If it be difficult at this moment to point out the place of meeting and the members of that powerful body, its existence can be proved from past discoveries of the secret workings of the Order, and from present unity of action in numberless occurring circumstances amongst a vast multitude of men, whose essential organization consists in blind obedience to orders coming down through many degrees from an unknown source which thinks and orders for the purposes of the whole conspiracy. The great object, in order to understand the nature of such a conspiracy, is to find out the ends for which those who framed or adopted it, took it up. For instance, Infidelity, as it is now known in the world, never, it may be said, existed to any appreciable extent before the time of Voltaire. Voltaire devoted his whole life to spread Infidelity and destroy Christianity. When we see Voltaire and his disciples eagerly seize upon Freemasonry, and zealously propagate it, as a means to their ends, we may reasonably infer, it was because they judged Masonry fitting for their Infidel and anti-Christian purposes. This is further confirmed when we see Masonry adopted by all men of their principles without exception. And it becomes proved to demonstration when we see its organization seized upon as the basis of further and more complex planning for the avowed purposes of ruining Christianity and placing Atheism in its stead. French Atheism using Masonry thus perfected, produced what it aimed at during the Reign of Terror in France, which, as we shall see, is only a prelude to what it means one day to accomplish throughout the entire world.

In order to make these facts clear, the writer, so far as the form of a single lecture would allow, has given as much of the history and character of both Voltaire and Freemasonry, as might serve to show the adaptability of the latter to the designs of the former. He has spoken of the union and illuminism of Masonry through the instrumentality of Weishaupt, and has shown the immediate consequences of the organization and influence of that arch-conspirator in the first French Revolution and its outcome, the Consulate and the Empire. He deemed it a duty to dispel the glamor of false glory which many Christian writers have aided in throwing over Napoleon I, a real child of Freemasonry and Revolution, and to represent him in his true colors. For though it cannot be denied that Napoleon restored the Church, it is equally true that his half-hearted measures in favor of religion tended to deaden that strong reaction against Atheism which even Robespierre's[1] attempts could not control; while the encouragement he gave to Freemasonry caused that organization to so powerfully permeate Europe that it has since controlled the civilized world with a subtle, powerful force which nothing has been able to stay save the Catholic Church alone.

Under the headings mentioned, the author has given the salient phrases of the action of the whole dread

---

[1] EDITOR'S NOTE: Maximilien Robespierre (1758–94) was a French lawyer and statesman who played a prominent role in the French Revolution, most notably during the "Reign of Terror," which lasted from 1793 to 1794. He ordered many Frenchmen to be guillotined for supposed crimes against the Revolution and was later guillotined himself.

THE WAR OF THE ANTICHRIST

conspiracy. He has dwelt at considerable length on its efforts in Italy and in Europe generally. He has given *in extenso* documents of the dark directory which rules all the secret societies of the world. These documents give the key to that satanic policy which guides the Revolution to this day. He adopts the opinion of Eckert, Deschamps, Segur, and other grave Continental authorities, as to the fact that Lord Palmerston succeeded Nubius as Chief of the "Inner Circle,"[2] and consequently Grand Patriarch of all the secret societies of the world; and he judges this not only from the testimony of Henry Misley, one of the Alta Vendita under Nubius and Palmerston, but much more from the suicidal, revolutionary policy which Palmerston adopted when Foreign Minister of England, and which leaves that country now without an ally in the world. This policy suited the conspirators of Europe; but no man should have known better than Palmerston that it could not suit Great Britain. It was the reversal of all that the best British statesmen had adopted as safeguards against the recurrence of Bonapartism and revolution, after the peace obtained at Waterloo. But Palmerston was made a monarch to become a slave to the secret sects, and for their view he unceasingly labored, regardless of country or of any other consideration.

---

[2] EDITOR'S NOTE: The Italian Catholic historian Roberto de Mattei wrote in his biography of Blessed Pope Pius IX the following about the identity of "Nubius": "In a later and more specific study, I hope to show unpublished documents on the Alta Vendita which will reveal the identity, hitherto unknown to historians, of Nubius." Roberto de Mattei, *Blessed Pius IX*, trans. John Laughland (Leominster, UK: Gracewing, 2004), 5.

The existence of two parties in secret-society organization is a fact not generally known; but it explains many things in events daily occurring both on the Continent and at home, which would be otherwise inexplicable. It explains how ministers like Cavour[3] can sometimes—in play, of course—imprison generals like Garibaldi,[4] how Thiers[5] could crush the Commune,[6] and how Ferry can make show of being adverse to anarchists in Paris.[7] Nevertheless, the anarchists are the children of the Sovereign Directory. Their highest leaders are men of the "Inner Circle." If policy requires a revolution or an outrage, anarchists of the rank and file are led on to make it; and are generally left also to their fate—a fate, in its turn, made use of for the purposes of the general Revolution. The Inner Circle of high conspirators, in the solitude of their dark plottings, manage all and find uses for all. Politics, with them,

---

[3] EDITOR'S NOTE: Camillo Benso, Count di Cavour (1810–61) was a Piedmontese statesman whose diplomatic maneuvering helped unify most of Italy under the House of Savoy, with himself as prime minister, in 1861.

[4] EDITOR'S NOTE: Giuseppe Garibaldi (1807–82) was an Italian patriot, soldier, and revolutionary whose conquests of Sicily and Naples helped unify Italy under the royal House of Savoy in 1861.

[5] EDITOR'S NOTE: Adolphe Thiers (1797–1877) was a French statesman, journalist, and historian. He was a founder and the first president of the Third Republic, which lasted from 1870 to 1940. As president, he used ruthless military force to suppress the rebellion of the Paris Commune in 1871.

[6] EDITOR'S NOTE: The Paris Commune was a revolutionary socialist government that took over Paris from March 18 to May 28, 1871 after the defeat of France in the Franco-Prussian War.

[7] EDITOR'S NOTE: Jules Ferry (1832–93) was a French statesman and republican philosopher who promoted secularization. In 1870, he was appointed prefect of the Seine by the Government of National Defense, during which time the Paris Commune briefly took power.

are mere playthings. Upon great social movements, upon discontented populations, upon corruption, distraction, and contention, they rely to bring their one redoubted enemy, the Catholic Church, to what they call the tomb.

There are few people on earth more concerned with this fact than the Irish people.

The Irish people are now found not only in Ireland, but outside Ireland in large centers of industry, where the action of the International Association of Workmen, and other kindred working men's associations, have most influence. It must be borne in mind that the amelioration in the condition of the working man is never attempted by the International without coupling with it the strongest hatred for Christianity. Nothing proves more clearly its origin and its connection with the Supreme Directory of the Cosmopolitan Atheistic Conspiracy against religion and order than this one fact. In 1870, the society had on its rolls ten millions of members. Its numbers have yearly increased since. At the famous International Congress, held in Geneva in 1868, it formulated the following declaration, which has since been more than once acted on by its members on the Continent:

Manifesto

The object of the International Association of Workmen, as of every other Socialist Association, is to do away with the parasite and the pariah. Now, what parasite can be compared to the priest who takes away the pence of the poor and of the widow by means of lying. What outcast more miserable than the Christian Pariah.

God and Christ, these citizen-Providences have been at all times the armor of Capital and the most sanguinary enemies of the working classes. It is owing to God and to Christ that we remain to this day in slavery. It is by deluding us with lying hopes that the priests have caused us to accept all the sufferings of this earth.

It is only after sweeping away all religion, and after tearing up even to the last roots every religious idea, Christian and every other whatsoever, that we can arrive at our political and social idea.

Let Jesus look after his heaven. We believe only in humanity. It would be but to fail in all our duties were we to cease, even for a second, to pursue the monsters who have tortured us.

Down, then, with God and with Christ! Down with the despots of heaven and earth! Death to the priests! Such is the motto of our grand Crusade.

This address gives the true spirit and aim of the International League, which has emissaries everywhere striving to decoy working men into secret-society intrigues. In America it has already led Irish Catholic laborers into lamentable excesses. It has under its control some seemingly laudable benefit societies which it uses as a means to draw Catholics gradually from the influence of the Church. The necessity therefore of being prepared for its efforts must be evident to everyone.

From the general consideration of secret societies, the author turns to their action amongst ourselves. He gives the most salient features of British Freemasonry, its oaths, passwords, and signs. He shows to what extent it differs from

Continental Masonry, and how it is essentially unlawful and dangerous. He then passes to the principal point of this lecture, so far as his auditory were concerned—Fenianism.[8]

All that he had stated before, here becomes of use as explanatory of the nature of that mischievous conspiracy, which had its rise, development, and ending—if, indeed, it has ended—while the author was engaged upon the Australian mission. But he has given ample proof of its designs from admitted authorities. The history of its founders he has taken from a source that cannot be impugned, the works of the late Mr. A. M. Sullivan, of the *Nation*.[9] The other articles, on the sad ending of conspirators, and the wonderful indestructibility of Irish Faith rest upon their own merits.

A discourse which aimed at illustrating the words of our Holy Father Leo XIII[10] could not be complete without a

---

[8] EDITOR'S NOTE: According to the *Encylopedia Britannica*, a Fenian was a "member of an Irish nationalist secret society active chiefly in Ireland, the United States, and Britain, especially during the 1860s. The name derives from the Fianna Eireann, the legendary band of Irish warriors led by the fictional Finn MacCumhaill (MacCool). . . . The Irish wing of the society was sometimes called the Irish Republican Brotherhood, a name that continued to be used after Fenianism proper had virtually died out in the early 1870s. Arthur Griffith, a member of the Brotherhood, founded the Irish nationalist party Sinn Féin ("We Ourselves") in 1905."

[9] EDITOR'S NOTE: Alexander Martin Sullivan (1830–84) was an Irish politician, lawyer, and journalist.

[10] EDITOR'S NOTE: Leo XIII (1810–1903) was pope from 1878 to 1903. In light of the various revolutions that had shaken Europe throughout the nineteenth century, he attempted to reassert Catholic teaching on the state and the nature of liberty, while also making conciliatory moves with various governments. He was instrumental in developing the Church's social teaching in light of the Industrial Revolution in encyclicals such as *Rerum Novarum* (1891), which articulated the rights of both

reference to such societies as the wisdom of the great Pontiff has pointed out as fitted for Christian men. The author, therefore, speaks in favor of the excellent Temperance Society he found already in action, connected with the Catholic Institute, as a sovereign antidote against secret societies of every description, and as the best remedy for those ills he could not help witnessing when passing through Edinburgh, and other great centers of population in England and Scotland. He plainly refers to the evil which certain idle agitators bring in those cities amongst poor, good-natured, but credulous Irish Catholic working men. He believes that nine-tenths of the pabulum [insipid intellectual fare] which keeps such pernicious seducers in employment would be destroyed if Irish working men could be removed from the influence of persons who make profit out of their unfortunate drinking habits; and that misfortune of nearly every temporal kind would cease for them, if they became temperate and continued to practice those virtues which Catholic confraternities with strict sobriety as a first rule, foster. He has therefore given his aid in advocacy of such societies as are calculated to keep the Irish in England and in Scotland, and indeed everywhere, sober—a quality which, with habits of industry, economy, and thrift, enables them to live happily, and to bring up families educated, fairly provided for, and a credit, instead of a shame, to the country and the religion of their parents.

---

capital and labor. He also reasserted the supremacy of Saint Thomas Aquinas in Catholic teaching and philosophy. Finally, more than any pope prior, he warned of the errors of Freemasonry and its designs on the world, most notably in his encyclical *Humanum Genus* (1884). This encyclical inspired Monsignor Dillon's lectures, which Leo XIII himself endorsed, subsidizing their translation and printing in Italian.

The necessity of compressing a large amount of matter into the small space at his disposal, has caused many of the topics touched upon to be treated very inadequately considering their claims to attention. He has, however, given as much fact and matter as he could, even at the risk of occasionally sacrificing smoothness and ease in writing. His desire was to give within the shortest limits, as full, complete, and consecutive a view as possible of the whole subject he undertook to treat. Under any one of the headings given, a volume, and in some cases, a very large and interesting volume, could be written. Facts, however, tell for themselves, and in most instances he has left to the intelligent reader the task of drawing the inferences.

Indeed, his principal object in printing these lectures at all, and his chief hope, has been to direct the attention of those whom it most concerns to the question of secret organization *as a whole*; to point out the fact that there exists an able, vigilant body of men, trained for years in the work of conspiracy, who never cease to plot for the destruction of Christianity, and of Christian social order amongst mankind; and that the success of these men has hitherto arisen mainly from their astute and ceaseless efforts to remain concealed. The world in all its past history has never been accustomed to deal with such a body. The sworn secret society anywhere, is, what Mr. A. M. Sullivan tells us it is, in his admirable description of its action in Dublin in this time. Its policy, then, was to stifle every form of Irish public opinion except that which supported its own views. Every other expression was to be prevented by emissaries, who found their way into every popular gathering, and by secret concert, known to themselves alone, and not even so much as suspected by others, were able to make "public opinion" seem to be in favor of the policy of their chiefs. If these emissaries failed, others of the secret brotherhood menaced the adverse popular leaders with loss of business and character, with violence, and even death. With every one of these evils the secret-society men of the time threatened Mr. Sullivan. He, however, foiled their astuteness, and braved their menaces. He succeeded in escaping; but it was much more owing to the conscience remaining amongst some of the Irish Fenians than to the mercy of the organization itself.

This incident, which is related at length in Mr. Sullivan's "New Ireland," gives a true idea of the action of every secret-society organization, working, under many apparent public pretenses, for the ends of its chiefs.[11] The ruses of a bird to draw away attention from the nest of its young, is but a faint resemblance of what every secret society does to avoid detection, either of itself or of its intentions or doings. It scruples to commit no crime, not even murder, to divert suspicion, and to remain concealed. Concealment is, and has been from the beginning, the very essence of its inward organism and of its outward policy. It is vain therefore to suppose that because no visible manifestation of its presence appears, or because some evidence—always suspicious when they are shown—of its dying out, or becoming ridiculous, impotent, or dead, appear, that there is no further danger to be dreaded from its attempts. It has the cunning of the serpent, and the patience too. It can feign itself dead to save

---

[11] EDITOR'S CITATION: A. M. Sullivan, *New Ireland* (New York: Peter F. Collier, 1878).

its head from being crushed. The author of these pages was assured in Rome, that it was all nonsense to suppose that secret societies any longer existed in Ireland; that they were things of the past which Irish Faith had banished. In a few days after, however, the world was startled by the deeds of the Invincibles, led on, as was subsequently discovered, by a miscreant who had used the cloak of the most sacred practices of religion to conceal his character, and to win confederates, and then victims, to his infernal designs.

Now, if the following pages prove anything, it is that over the whole world there exists a formidable conspiracy—the War of Antichrist—carried on by a secret directory ruling every form of secret society on earth, and losing no chance of seducing men from God by first bringing them, under some pretense or other, within its ranks. It is certain that this directory will not lose sight of the Irish race in the future, any more than in the past; that most likely in the future its plans for seducing them from, or turning them, for political or other reasons, against the Church, will be laid more astutely and less visibly than ever. The methods by which these high conspirators deceive, change continually; and in the constantly recurring political agitations of Ireland, a wide field is open which they are certain to cultivate to the best advantage for the ruin of souls. Unceasing vigilance is required, therefore, to guard against their machinations and unceasing diligence in exposing their aims.

The Holy Father, in his late celebrated Bull, *Humanum Genus*, has, therefore, manifested his desire that the bishops, the clergy, and even the laity of the Church should join in exposing Freemasonry and other such societies. But without a proper knowledge of the conspiracy as a whole that cannot be done. The author attempts to give such knowledge; but he hopes that his efforts may be improved upon by others more able than himself, and that he may have the happiness before long of seeing some compendium of the whole subject in English which might form a textbook for seminarists and others to whom the future fate of the people of God in dangerous days is to be committed. All he could do in the time at his disposal was to give a popular idea of the subject. The works which he has chiefly used for this purpose are those of Cretineau Joly, Eckert, Segur, Dupanloup, and Deschamps (as edited by M. Claude Janet), together with the current information given in the *Civiltà Cattolica* and other Catholic reviews and periodicals. He believes moreover, that, as philosophical studies of the soundest kind on the basis of Saint Thomas have, through the care of the Holy Father [Pope Leo XIII], assumed their proper influence in ecclesiastical education,[12] seminarists, and others also, should study the practical growth of those Pantheistic and immoral principles to which that philosophy is opposed. The fundamental basis of Freemasonry, as perverted or "illuminated," by Weishaupt, is Pantheism; and Positivism and all the "isms" which the philosophers of the sect have since introduced, are meant ultimately to cause Pantheism and its attendant practical immorality to dominate over the earth. It is a new form of the oldest seduction: "eat the forbidden fruit and ye shall be as gods knowing good from evil" (Gen. 3:5), and is always accompanied with that other lie, of "the liar and

---

[12] EDITOR'S CITATION: Pope Leo XIII, *Aeterni Patris: On the Restoration of Christian Philosophy* (1879).

the murderer from the beginning" (John 8:44), "No, ye shall not die the death" (Gen. 3:4).

Furthermore, it must be remembered that secret societies have little dread of mere denunciation. Exposition, calm and just, is that of which they are most afraid. The masses in them are nearly always in that sad condition through deception. The light thrown vividly upon the real nature of the secret sect; the gentle, kind indulgence of the Church mourning over the ruin and yearning for the return of her children, put before them, will do wonders to win back Irish victims from secret societies. Mere abuse does no good. For the rest, prevention is better than cure; and the time seems to have arrived when in schools, in preparation for first communion, in constant, well-judged recurrence in the instructions given to the people, in lectures and articles in our Catholic newspapers, the evil of secret societies—too sure to manifest itself in many countries—should be made known to all classes of the faithful, who can thus be easily trained in such a way as to treat the secret society or any emanation from it as their ancestors treated heresy, and reject, even at the peril of their lives, the "unclean thing." Sound Catholic associations, temperance, and pious confraternities are the remedies pointed out by the Holy Father, and these will preserve the portions of the flock already untainted, and retain those whom grace and zeal may bring back to the Fold of Christ.

—Monsignor Dillon

CHAPTER 1

Introduction

"The truth is that every secret society is framed and adapted to make men the enemies of God and of His Church, and to subvert faith; and there is not one, no matter on what pretext it may be founded, which does not fall under the management of a supreme directory governing all the secret societies on earth. The one aim of this directory is to uproot Christianity, and the Christian social order as well as the Church from the world—in fact, to eradicate the name of Christ and the very Christian idea from the minds and the hearts of men. . . . I believe this secret Atheistic organization to be nothing less than the evil which we have been long warned against by Our Blessed Lord Himself, as the supreme conflict between the Church and Satan's followers. It is the commencement of the contest which must take place between Christ and Antichrist; and nothing therefore can be more necessary than that the elect of God should be warned of its nature and its aims."

—Monsignor Dillon

Monsignor Smith, Rev. Fathers, Ladies and Gentlemen,

It gives me, indeed, great pleasure to find the Catholic body in this great city possessed of such a valuable, and, I may add, magnificent block of buildings as that which forms this "Catholic Institute," and to know that over nine hundred of the Catholic young men of Edinburgh are gathered

1

together by its means for mutual improvement and for moral and religious aims. I feel proud of it as the work of my friend and fellow-student, Father Hanna, your respected pastor. I am sure his energies, which have been in other directions—in the erection and sustenance of your extensive Parochial Schools, for instance—so well employed, could not be afterwards put to better purpose than in forming and watching over such an institution. A Catholic Society founded on the spiritual lines of this Society, and enjoying its advantages in a temporal sense, is in fact, now-a-days, a necessity. It takes up and protects the Catholic boy at the most perilous and decisive period of his life—that is, when he leaves the employments and restraints of his school days to learn some trade or profession. It keeps him until manhood, well removed from those dangerous and seductive associations, so common in all large cities. It gives him rational amusement and the means of self-improvement. It causes him to frequent the sacraments, to practice prayer, to be provident, temperate, industrious, and, above all, religious. It places him in constant communication with, and therefore under, the special care of his Pastor. It is, in fact, the special attitude which our present Holy Father—whom may God long preserve to us—advises the Bishops of the Catholic Church to employ throughout the world against the poisonous influence of these secret societies, which the demon has rendered so general and so disastrous in our days. Speaking of the operative classes, Leo XIII says, in his celebrated Encyclical *Humanum Genus* of this year, "Those who sustain themselves by the labor of their own hands, besides being by their very condition most worthy above all others for charity and consolation, are also especially exposed to the allurements of men whose ways lie in fraud and deceit. Therefore, they ought to be helped with the greatest possible kindness, and be invited to join societies that are good, lest they be drawn away to others that are evil."[1]

Now, these words of the Holy Father came very forcibly to my mind when I was shown, on last Saturday, the fine hall in which we are now assembled—the library and study-rooms, and the various means of recreation and improvement attached to this building. I was specially pleased to see so many young men innocently enjoying themselves, or usefully employed, on a day, which, of all other days of the week, is the one which most invites the youth of our cities to dissipation and sin. And so it happened that when Father Hanna asked me to say "a few words"—by which, I supposed he meant the lecture advertised in this morning's papers—on this Monday evening, I could not well refuse; and as the time for preparation was very short, I determined to say "the few words" on the conflict which during this, and the last century, has taken place between the Church of Christ and Atheism. My reason was, because I knew, that Atheism, closely masked, and astutely organized, not only has sought, but still seeks the destruction of the Church, and the destruction of the souls which it is her mission to save; and as the Catholic Young Men's Society of Edinburgh is one of those beneficent associations pointed out by the Vicar of Christ as the special means of defeating the designs of Atheism, I believe I cannot do a more appropriate or indeed

---

[1] EDITOR'S CITATION: Pope Leo XIII, *Humanum Genus: On Freemasonry* (1884), no. 35.

a greater service, than by unfolding what these designs really are. In this, as in all matters of importance, "to be forewarned is to be forearmed," and it is specially necessary to be forewarned when we have to contend with an adversary who uses secrecy, fraud, and deceit.

We shall see then that all the organizations of Atheism appear at first as does their author, Satan, clothed in the raiment of angels of light, with their malignity, their Infidelity, and their ultimate designs always most carefully hidden. They come amongst all the faithful but more especially amongst young men, to seduce and to ruin them, never showing but when forced to do so, the cloven foot, and employing a million means to seem to be what they are not. It is, therefore, first of all, necessary to unmask them; and this is precisely what the Supreme Pontiff asks the pastors of the Universal Fold to do as the best means of destroying their influence. "But," he says in the Encyclical already quoted, "as it befits our pastoral office that we ourselves should point out some suitable way of proceeding, we wish it to be your rule, first of all, to tear away the mask from Freemasonry, and to let it be seen as it really is, and by instructions and pastoral letters to instruct the people as to the artifices used by societies of this kind in seducing men and enticing them into their ranks, and as to the depravity of their opinions and the wickedness of their acts."[2]

In this extract the Holy Father makes special mention of Freemasonry; but, remember, not of Freemasonry only. He speaks of "other secret societies." These other secret societies

---

[2] EDITOR'S CITATION: Pope Leo XIII, *Humanum Genus: On Freemasonry* (1884), no. 13.

are identical with Freemasonry, no matter by what name they may be called; and they are frequently the most depraved forms of Freemasonry. And though what is known in Great Britain as Freemasonry may not be so malignant as its kind is on the Continent—though it may have little or no hold at all upon the mass of Catholics in English-speaking countries, still we shall see that like every secret society in existence it is a danger for the nation and for individuals, and has hidden within it the same Atheism and hostility to Christianity which the worst Continental Freemasonry possesses. These it develops to the initiated in the higher degrees, and makes manifest to all the world in time.

The truth is that every secret society is framed and adapted to make men the enemies of God and of His Church, and to subvert faith; and there is not one, no matter on what pretext it may be founded, which does not fall under the management of a supreme directory governing all the secret societies on earth. The one aim of this directory is to uproot Christianity, and the Christian social order as well as the Church from the world—in fact, to eradicate the name of Christ and the very Christian idea from the minds and the hearts of men. This it is determined to do by every means, but especially by fraud and force; that is by first using wiles and deceit until the Atheistic conspiracy grows strong enough for measures as violent and remorseless in all countries as it exercised in one country during the first French Revolution. I believe this secret Atheistic organization to be nothing less than the evil which we have been long warned against by Our Blessed Lord Himself, as the supreme conflict between the Church and Satan's followers. It is the commencement of the contest

which must take place between Christ and Antichrist; and
nothing therefore can be more necessary than that the elect
of God should be warned of its nature and its aims.

First, we shall glance at the rise and the nature of Atheism
itself and its rapid advance amongst those sections of Christians most liable from position and surroundings to be led
astray by it; and then at the use it has made of Freemasonry
for its propagandism, and for its contemplated destruction of
Christianity. We shall see its depravity perfected by what is
called Illuminism. And we shall see that however checked it
may have been by the reaction consequent upon the excesses
of its first Revolution,[3] it has not only outlived that reaction,
but has grown wiser for doing an evil more extended and more
complete. We shall see how its chiefs have succeeded in mas-
tering and directing every kind of secret association whether
springing from itself or coming into existence by the force of
its example only; and have used, and are using them all to
its advantage. We shall see the sleepless vigilance which this
organized Atheism exercises; and thus come to know that our
best, our only resource, is to fly [from] its emissaries, and draw
nearer in affection and in effect to the teachings of the Church
and her Supreme Visible Head on earth who can never deceive
us, and whom the hosts of Satan never can deceive. We shall
see that the voice of the Vicar of Christ has been raised against
secret associations from the beginning to this hour, and that
the directions which we receive from that infallible voice can
alone save us from the wiles and deceits of a conspiracy so formidable, so active, so malignant, and so dangerous.

---

[3] EDITOR'S NOTE: Referring to the French Revolution.

CHAPTER 2

The Rise of Atheism in Europe

"The principle of private judgment introduced in apparent
zeal for the pure worship and doctrine of Christ, had ended
in leaving no part of the teaching of Christ unchallenged."

—Monsignor Dillon

IN ORDER, THEN, to comprehend thoroughly the nature of
the conspiracy, it will be necessary to go back to the opening
of the last century and contemplate the rise and advance of
the Atheism and Anti-Christianity which it now spreads rapidly through the earth. As that century opened it disclosed
a world suffering from a multitude of evils. The so-called
Reformation, which arose and continued to progress during
the two preceding centuries had well-nigh run its course. It
had ceased to be a persecuting force on the Continent, and
only for reasons of plunder continued to use the weapons of
oppression in Ireland. Scarcely a shred of the original doctrines of the Church were to be observed amongst his followers. Malignant hatred of the Spouse of Christ continued,
when the reasons alleged for the malignity had departed.
Amidst the multitude at that time calling themselves Protestants, little remained certain in Christian belief.

7

The principle of private judgment introduced in apparent zeal for the pure worship and doctrine of Christ, had ended in leaving no part of the teaching of Christ unchallenged. It had rendered His Divinity disbelieved in, and His very existence doubted, by many who yet called themselves His followers. Socinus and his nephew had succeeded in binding the various groups of Polish and German Protestants in a league where nothing was required but undying hatred and opposition to the Catholic Church.[1] Bayle threw doubt upon everything,[2] and Spinoza destroyed the little respect left for the Deity in the system of Socinus, by introducing Pantheism to the world.[3] In effect, both the Deists and the Pantheists of that period were Atheists. Whether they held that everything was God, or that God was not such a God as Christians hold Him to be, they did away with belief in the true God, and raised up an impossible being of their own imagination in His stead. In life, in conduct, and in

---

[1] EDITOR'S NOTE: Faustus Socinus (1539–1604) was an Italian theologian who developed an anti-Trinitarian theology in opposition to the Catholic Church, which later led to the development of Unitarian theology. He played a dominant role in the Minor Reformed Church (Polish Brethren) and died in Poland.

[2] EDITOR'S NOTE: Pierre Bayle (1647–1706) was a French philosopher who espoused radical skepticism and whose work *Dictionnaire Historique et Critique* ("Historical and Critical Dictionary"), published in 1697, was a precursor to the French encyclopedists of the eighteenth century, who imitated his example of weaponizing oblique criticism subversive of Christianity.

[3] EDITOR'S NOTE: Benedict de Spinoza (1632–77) was a Dutch Jewish philosopher who was one of the leading seventeenth century Rationalists and a Pantheist. He was excommunicated by the Amsterdam synagogue as a heretic, and all its members were prohibited from having any relationship with him, or reading any of his works, the most famous of which was his treatise *Ethics* (1677).

adoration of God, they were practical Atheists, and soon manifested that hatred for the truth which the Atheist is sure to possess. Their theories made headway early in the century throughout Central Europe and England. Bolingbroke,[4] Shaftesbury,[5] and the elite amongst the statesmen and literary aristocracy of the reign of Queen Anne were Infidels. Tindal, Collins, Woolston, Toland, and Chubbs were as advanced as Tom Paine was, later on, in the way of Atheism.[6] But however much England and Germany had advanced their Protestantism to what was called Free-thinking, both were soon destined to be eclipsed in that sad progress by Catholic and monarchical France. France owes this evil pre-eminence to one individual, who, though largely assisted in his road to ruin by Bayle, and subsequently by association with English Infidels, had yet enough of innate wickedness in himself to outstrip them all. That individual was Voltaire.[7]

---

[4] EDITOR'S NOTE: Henry Saint John, First Viscount Bolingbroke (1678–1751), was a prominent Tory politician during the reign of Queen Anne of England who held very unorthodox religious opinions, and frequently wrote on philosophical, theological, and moral subjects.

[5] EDITOR'S NOTE: Anthony Ashley Cooper, Third Earl of Shaftesbury (1671–1713) was an English politician and philosopher, and one of the most prominent Deists of the eighteenth century.

[6] EDITOR'S NOTE: Matthew Tindal (1657–1733), Anthony Collins (1676–1729), Thomas Woolston (1668–1733), John Toland (1670–1722), and Thomas Chubb (1679–1747) were all English (except Toland, who was Irish) Deists and "freethinkers."

[7] EDITOR'S NOTE: Voltaire (1694–1778) was a French philosopher who was one of the foremost ideologues of the "Enlightenment" and a frequently vociferous critic of the Catholic Church and its doctrines.

CHAPTER 3

Voltaire

*"For Christ he had but one feeling—eternal, contemptuous
hatred. His watchword, the concluding lines of all his letters to
his infidel confederates, was for fifty years 'e'crasons nous l'infame,'
'let us crush the wretch,' meaning Christ and his cause."*

—Monsignor Dillon

I SHALL HAVE to occupy your attention, for some little
time, with the career of this abandoned, unhappy, but most
extraordinary man. It was in his day and by his means that
Atheism became perfected, generalized, and organized for
the destruction of Christianity, Christian civilization, and all
religion. He was the first, and remains still, the greatest of its
Apostles. There is not one of its dark principles which he did
not teach and advocate; and from his writings, and by their
means, the intellectual and every other form of war against
the Catholic Church and the cause of Christ are carried on
to this day and will be to the end.

His real name was Francis Mary Arouet, but, for some
reason which has never been clearly explained, he chose
to call himself Voltaire. He was the son of good parents,
and by position and education should have been an excellent Catholic. He was trained by the very Jesuits whom

he afterwards so hated and persecuted. He was destined for the profession of the law, and made good progress in literary studies.

But the corruption of the age in which he lived soon seized upon him, overmastered him, and bore him along in a current which in his case did not end in vice only, but in vice which sought its own justification in Infidelity. From the beginning, the fool said in his heart "there is no God" [Ps. 14:1], and in the days of Voltaire the number of these fools was indeed infinite. Never before was vice so rampant in countries calling themselves Christian. If the Gospel was preached at all in that age it was certainly to the poor; for the rich, as a rule—to which there were, thank God, many exceptions—seemed so sunk in vice as not to believe in a particle of it. The Courts of Europe were, in general, corrupt to the core; and the Court of the Most Christian King was perhaps the most abandoned, in a wide sense, of them all. The Court of Catherine of Russia[1] was a scene of unblushing lewdness. The Court of Frederick of Prussia[2] was so corrupt, that it cannot be described without doing violence to decency, and even to humanity. The Regent Orleans and Louis XV had carried license to such an extent as to render the Court of Versailles a veritable pandemonium. The vices

---

[1] EDITOR'S NOTE: Catherine the Great (1729–96) was the empress of Russia from 1762 to 1796. Catherine was considered somewhat of a devotee of the "Enlightenment," and during her reign, Russia was recognized as a great European power. She extended Russia's territory to include Crimea and much of Poland.

[2] EDITOR'S NOTE: Frederick the Great (1712–86), or Frederick II, was the king of Prussia who made it the greatest military power on the European continent. He was known for being an adherent of the "Enlightenment."

of royalty infected the nobles and all others who were so unfortunate as to be permitted to frequent Courts.

Vice, in fact, was the fashion, and numbers of all classes, not excepting the poorest, wallowed in it. As a consequence, the libertines of the period hated the Church, which alone, amidst the universal depravity, raised her voice for purity. They took up warmly, therefore, the movements which, within or without her pale, were likely to do her damage. With a sure instinct they sided in France with Gallicanism and Jansenism;[3] and they welcomed the new Infidelity which came over from England and Germany, with unconcealed gladness. Voltaire appeared in French society at this most opportune moment for the advancement of their views. Witty, sarcastic, gay, vivacious, he soon made his way amongst the voluptuaries who then filled Paris. His conduct and habit of ridiculing religion and royalty brought him, however, into disfavor with the government, and at the age of twenty-three we find him in the Bastille.

Liberated from this prison [a second time] in 1726, but only on condition of exile, he crossed over to England, where he finally adopted those Infidel and anti-Christian principles which made him, for the half century through which he afterwards lived, what Cretineau-Joly very justly calls "the most perfect incarnation of Satan that the world ever

---

[3] EDITOR'S NOTE: Gallicanism advocated the independence of the Church in France from the papacy. Jansenism was a heresy that grew out of the ideas of Cornelius Otto Jansen (1585–1638), a theologian at the University of Leuven (Louvain) and later the bishop of Ypres, who emphasized predestination at the expense of free will. It was officially condemned by Pope Clement XI on September 8, 1713, in the papal bull *Unigenitus Dei Filius*.

saw."[4] The Society of Freemasons was just then perfected in London, and Voltaire at the instance of his Infidel associates joined one of its lodges; and he left England, where he had been during the years 1726–27 and '28, an adept in both Infidelity and Freemasonry. He returned to the Continent with bitterness rankling in his breast against monarchical government which had imprisoned and exiled him, against the Bastille where he was immured, and, above all, against the Catholic Church and her Divine Founder. Christ and His Church condemned his excesses, and to the overthrow of both he devoted himself with an ardor and a malignity more characteristic, certainly, of a demon than of a man.

A master of French prose hardly ever equaled and never perhaps excelled, and a graceful and correct versifier, his writings against morality and religion grew into immense favor with the corrupt reading-public of his day. He was a perfect adept in the use of ridicule, and he employed it with remorseless and blasphemous force against everything pure and sacred. He had as little respect for the honor or welfare of his country as he had for the sanctity of religion. His ruffian pen attacked the fair fame of the Maid of Orleans[5] with as

---

[4] ORIGINAL FOOTNOTE: *L'Eglise Romaine en face de la Révolution*, par J. Crétineau-Joly, ouvrage composé sur des documents inédits et orné des portraits de Leurs Saintetés Les Papes Pie VII. Et Pie IX. dessinés per Stall. Paris: Henri Plon, Libaire-éditeur, Rue Garancière, 8—1861.

[5] EDITOR'S NOTE: The "Maid of Orleans" refers to Saint Joan of Arc (c. 1412–31), who was a French national hero for leading French armies to victory against the English at Orleans in the Hundred Years' War. She was a peasant girl who believed she was guided by God and was later burned at the stake as a heretic. Her local judges ignored her desire to appeal to the pope, and she was later acquitted of heresy and declared a saint.

little scruple as it cast shame upon the consecrated servants of Christ. For Christ he had but one feeling—eternal, contemptuous hatred. His watchword, the concluding lines of all his letters to his infidel confederates, was for fifty years *e'crasons nous l'infame*, "let us crush the wretch," meaning Christ and his cause.[6] This he boasted was his *delenda est Carthago*. And he believed he could succeed. "I am tired," said he, "of hearing it said that twelve men sufficed to establish Christianity, and I desire to show that it requires but one man to pull it down." A lieutenant of police once said to him that, notwithstanding all he wrote, he should never be able to destroy Christianity. "That is exactly what we shall see," he replied. Voltaire was never weary of using his horrible watch-word.

Upon the news of the suppression of the Jesuits reaching him, he exclaimed: "See, one head of the hydra has fallen. I lift my eyes to heaven and cry 'crush the wretch.'" We have from himself his reason for using these blasphemous words. He says, "I finish all my letters by saying '*Ecrasons l'infame, ecrasez l'infame.*' 'Let us crush the wretch, crush the wretch,' as Cato[7] used one time to say, *Delenda est Carthago*, Carthage

---

[6] EDITOR'S NOTE: The American founding father and second US president, John Adams (1735–1826), observed in an August 24, 1815 letter to Thomas Jefferson that this phrase was used by Frederick the Great, Voltaire, and d'Alembert to refer to the destruction of "the Pope and the Catholic Church and Hierarchy." He repeated this in a January 7, 1817 letter to his grandson, John Adams Smith, noting that the "wretch" was "the Pope and his Hierarchy."

[7] EDITOR'S NOTE: Marcus Porcius Cato (234–149 BC) was a Roman statesman and senator who was a prominent conservative. He served as a censor, the purpose of which was to preserve Rome's ancient customs. His famous phrase, *Carthago delenda est*, was uttered during the debates leading up to Rome's Third Punic War with Carthage.

must be destroyed." Even at a time when the miscreant protested the greatest respect for religion to the Court of Rome,
he wrote to Damilaville:[8] "We embrace the philosophers,
and we beseech them to inspire for the wretch all the horror
which they can. Let us fall upon the wretch ably. That which
most concerns me is the propagation of the faith of truth,
and the making of the wretch vile, *Delenda est Carthago*."

Certainly his determination was strong to do so; and he
left no stone unturned for that end. He was a man of amazing industry; and though his vanity caused him to quarrel
with many of his confreres, he had in his lifetime a large
school of disciples, which became still more numerous after
his death.

He sketched out for them the whole mode of procedure
against the Church. His policy as revealed by the correspondence of Frederick II, and others with him,[9] was not to
commence an immediate persecution, but first to suppress
the Jesuits and all religious orders, and to secularize their
goods; then to deprive the Pope of temporal authority, and
the Church of property and state recognition. Primary and
higher-class education of a lay and Infidel character was to be
established, the principle of divorce affirmed, and respect for
ecclesiastics lessened and destroyed. Lastly, when the whole
body of the Church should be sufficiently weakened and
Infidelity strong enough, the final blow was to be dealt by
the sword of open, relentless persecution. A reign of terror

[8] EDITOR'S NOTE: Étienne Noël Damilaville (1723–68) was a French
government official, man of letters, and friend of "Enlightenment" philosophers Voltaire, Diderot, and d'Alembert.
[9] EDITOR'S NOTE: See Monsignor Dillon's original footnote, with rele-
vant correspondence, in appendix I provided at the end of this chapter.

was to spread over the whole earth, and to continue while a Christian should be found obstinate enough to adhere to Christianity. This, of course, was to be followed by a Universal Brotherhood without marriage, family, property, God, or law, in which all men would reach that level of social degradation aimed at by the disciples of Saint-Simon,[10] and carried into practice whenever possible, as attempted by the French Commune.[11]

In the carrying out of his infernal designs against religion and society, Voltaire had as little scruple in using lying and hypocrisy as Satan himself is accredited with. In his attacks upon religion he falsified history and fact. He made a principle of lying, and taught the same vice to his followers. Writing to his disciple Theriot, he says: "Lying is a vice when it does evil. It is a great virtue when it does good. Be therefore more virtuous than ever. It is necessary to lie like a devil, not timidly and for a time, but boldly and always."[12]

He was also, as the school he left behind has been ever since, a hypocrite. Infidel to the heart's core, he could, whenever it suited his purpose, both practice, and even feign a zeal for religion. On the expectation of a pension from the King, he wrote to M. Argental, a disciple of his, who reproached him with his hypocrisy and contradictions in conduct: "If I had a hundred thousand men, I know well what I would do; but as I have not got them, I will go to communion at

---

[10] EDITOR's NOTE: Henri de Saint-Simon (1760–1825) was a French social theorist and one of the founders of Christian socialism. He asserted that a brotherhood of man would result from the scientific organization of industry and society.

[11] EDITOR's NOTE: See footnote 6 of the preface.

[12] ORIGINAL CITATION: Oeuvres, t. 52, p. 326.

Easter, and you may call me a hypocrite as long as you like."
And Voltaire, on getting his pension, went to communion
the year following.[13] It is needless to say that he was in life,
as well as in his writings, immoral as it was possible for a
man to be. He lived without shame and even ostentatiously
in open adultery. He laughed at every moral restraint. He
preached libertinage and practiced it. He was the guest and
the inmate of the Court of Frederick of Prussia, where crime
reached proportions impossible to speak of. And lastly, coward, liar, hypocrite, and panderer to the basest passions of
humanity, he was finally, like Satan, a murderer if he had the
power to be so. Writing to Damilaville, he says:

> The Christian religion is an infamous religion, an
> abominable hydra which must be destroyed by a hun-
> dred invisible hands. It is necessary that the philoso-
> phers should course through the streets to destroy it as
> missionaries course over earth and sea to propagate it.
> They ought to dare all things, risk all things, even to be
> burned, in order to destroy it. Let us crush the wretch!
> Crush the wretch!

His doctrine thus expressed found fatal effect in the French
Revolution, and it will obtain effect whenever his disciples
are strong enough in men and means to act. I have no doubt
his teachings have led to all the revolutions of this century,
and will lead to the final attack of Atheism on the Church.
Nor was his hatred confined to Catholicism only. Christians
of every denomination were marked out for destruction by

---

[13] EDITOR'S NOTE: See Monsignor Dillon's original footnote, with rele-
vant correspondence, in appendix II provided at the end of this chapter.

him; and our separated Christian brethren, who feel glad
at seeing his followers' triumph over the Church, might
well ponder on these words of his: "Christians," he says,
"of every form of profession, are beings exceedingly injurious, fanatics, thieves, dupes, imposters, who lie together
with their gospels, enemies of the human race." And of the
system itself he writes: "The Christian religion is evidently
false, the Christian religion is a sect which every good man
ought to hold in horror. It cannot be approved of even by
those to whom it gives power and honor." In fact, since his
day, it has been a cardinal point of policy with his followers to take advantage of the unfortunate differences between
the various sects of Christians in the world and the Church,
in order to ruin both; for the destruction of every form of
Christianity, as well as Catholicism, was the aim of Voltaire,
and remains as certainly the aim of his disciples. They place,
of course, the Church and the Vicar of Christ in the first line
of attack, well knowing that if the great Catholic unity could
be destroyed, the work of eradicating every kind of separated
Christianity would be easy.

In dealing, therefore, with such a foe as modern Atheism, so powerfully organized, as we shall see it to be, Protestants as well as Catholics should guard against its wiles and
deceits. They should, at least, regarding questions such as
the religious education of rising generations, the attempted
secularization of the Sabbath and state-established Christian
Institutions, and the recognition of religion by the State, all
of which the Atheism of the world now attempts to destroy,
present an unbroken front of determined union. Nothing
less, certainly, can save even the Protestantism, the national,

Christian character of Great Britain and her colonies from impending ruin.

Although Voltaire was as confirmed and malignant a hater of Christ and of Christianity as ever lived, still he showed from time to time that his own professed principles of Infidelity were never really believed in by himself. In health and strength he cried out his blasphemous "crush the wretch!" but when the moment came for his soul to appear before the judgment-seat of "the wretch," his faith was shown, and his vaunted courage failed him.

The miscreant always acted against his better knowledge. His life gives us many examples of this fact. I will relate one for you. When he broke a blood vessel on one occasion, he begged his assistants to hurry for the priest. He confessed, signed with his hand a profession of faith, asked pardon of God and the Church for his offenses, and ordered that his retraction should be printed in the public newspapers; but, recovering, he commenced his war upon God anew, and died refusing all spiritual aid, and crying out in the fury of despair and agony, "I am abandoned by God and man." Dr. Fruchen, who witnessed the awful spectacle of his death, said to his friends, "Would that all who had been seduced by the writings of Voltaire had been witness of his death, it would be impossible to hold out, in the face of such an awful spectacle."[14] But that spectacle was forgotten, and consequently, before ten years passed, the world saw the effects of his works.

---

[14] ORIGINAL FOOTNOTE: See *Le Secret de la Franc-Maçonnerie*, par Monsigneur Amand Joseph Fava, Eveque de Grenoble. Lille, 1883, p. 38.

Speaking of the French Revolution, Condorcet,[15] in his "Life of Voltaire," says of him, "He did not see all that which he accomplished, but he did all that which we see. Enlightened observations prove to those who know how to reflect that the first author of that Great Revolution was without doubt Voltaire."

I have thus far spoken of Voltaire and his teachings in order to introduce with greater clearness the important subject to which I ask the favor of your attention this evening. It never was the intention of this man to let his teachings die, or beat the air, so to speak, with mere words. He determined that his fatal gospel should be perpetuated, and should bring forth as speedy as possible its fruits of death. Even in his lifetime, we have evidence that he constantly conspired with his associates for this end, and that with them he concocted in secret both the means by which his doctrines should reach all classes in Europe, and the methods by which civil order and Christianity might be best destroyed. Sainte-Beuve[16] writes of him and of his, in the *Journal des Debats*, 8 November, 1852:

> All the correspondence of Voltaire and d'Alembert is ugly. It smells of the sect, of the conspiracy of the Brotherhood, of the secret society. From whatever point it is viewed it does no honor to men who make a principle of lying, and who consider contempt of

---

[15] EDITOR'S NOTE: Marie-Jean-Antoine-Nicolas de Caritat, marquis de Condorcet (1743–94), was a French "Enlightenment" philosopher who advocated the indefinite perfectibility of man.

[16] EDITOR'S NOTE: Charles Augustin Sainte-Beuve (1804–69) was a French literary historian and critic, and a well-known public intellectual of the nineteenth century.

their kind the first condition necessary to enlighten them. "Enlighten and despise the human race." A sure watchword this, and it is theirs. "March on always sneering, my brethren, in the way of truth." That is their perpetual refrain.

But not only did he and his thus conspire in a manner which might seem to arise naturally from identical sentiments and aims, but what was of infinitely greater consequence, the demon, just as their sad gospel was ripe for propagation, called into existence the most efficacious means possible for its extension amongst men, and for the wished-for destruction of the Church, of Christian civilization, and of every form of existing Christianity. This was the spread amongst those already demoralized by Voltaireanism, of Freemasonry and its cognate systems of secret Atheistic organization.

This is the point upon which I am most anxious to fix your attention this evening.

Appendix I (footnote 9)

To show how early the confederates of Voltaire had determined upon the gradual impoverishment of the Church and the suppression of the religious orders, the following letters from Frederick II will be of use. In the first dated 13th August, 1775, the Monarch writes to the then very aged "Patriarch of Ferney," who had demanded the secularization of the Rhine ecclesiastical electorates and other episcopal benefices in Germany, as follows:

All you say concerning our German bishops is but too true; they grow fat upon the tithes of Sion. But you know, also, that in the Holy Roman Empire the ancient usage, the Bull of Gold, and other antique follies, cause abuses established to be respected. If we wish to diminish fanaticism, we must not touch the bishops. But, if we manage to diminish the monks, especially the mendicant orders, the people will grow cold and less superstitious, they will permit the powers that be, to dispose of the bishops in the manner best suited to the good of each State. This is the only course to follow. To undermine silently and without noise the edifice of infatuation is to oblige it to fall of itself. The Pope, seeing the situation in which he finds himself, is obliged to give briefs and bulls as his dear sons demand of him. The power founded upon the ideal credit of the faith loses in proportion as the latter diminishes. If there were now found at the head of nations some ministers above vulgar prejudices, the Holy Father would become bankrupt. Without doubt posterity will enjoy the advantage of being able to think freely.

Again, this curious compound of warrior, despot, Protestant free-thinker, poet, and mocker, writes to Voltaire on the 8th September, 1775:

It is to Bayle,[17] your predecessor, and to you, without doubt, that the glory is due of that revolution which has taken place in minds, but, to say the truth, it is not complete. The devotees have their party, and never will that be crushed except by a greater force.

---

[17] EDITOR'S NOTE: See footnote 2 of chapter 2.

It is from the governments that the sentence must go forth. . . . Without doubt this will be done in time, but neither you nor I will be spectators of an event so much desired. . . .

I have remarked [he says, also] and others with me, that the places where there are most convents and monks are those wherein the people are most given to superstition. It is not doubtful that if we could succeed in destroying these asylums of fanaticism, the people would shortly grow indifferent and lukewarm regarding the things which form at present the objects of their veneration. It would be necessary then to destroy the cloisters, or at least to commence to diminish their number. The moment is arrived because the French Government and that of Austria are so indebted that they have exhausted the resources of industry without being able to pay their debts. The list of rich abbeys and of convents, with a good rent-roll, is seducing. In representing to them the evil which the cenobites do the population of their States, as well as the abuse of the great number of religious who fill their provinces, and, in the meantime, the facility of paying a part of their debts, by applying to that purpose the treasures of communities which have no natural succession, I think they could be brought to determine upon commencing that reform. It is to be presumed that after having enjoyed the secularization of some benefices their avidity would soon swallow up the rest. Every Government, which determines upon that operation, will desire the spread of philosophers and be a partisan of all the books which attack popular superstitions and the false zeal of hypocrites, who wish to oppose them. Behold a little project which I wish to submit for the examination of the Patriarch of Ferney. It is for him, as the Father of the Faithful, to rectify and to execute it. The Patriarch may demand of me, perhaps, what is to be done with the bishops. I answer that it is not yet the time to touch them, that it is necessary to commence by destroying those who inflame with fanaticism the hearts of the people. When the people shall have grown cold the bishops will become little boys, whom the Sovereigns will dispose of in the course of time at their good pleasure.

Appendix II (footnote 13)

In 1768 Voltaire wrote as follows to the Marquis de Villevielle:

No, my dear Marquis, no, the modern Socrates will not drink the hemlock. The Socrates of Athens was, between you and me, a pitiless caviler, who made himself a thousand enemies and who braved his judges very foolishly.

Our modern philosophers are more adroit. They have not the foolish and dangerous vanity to put their names to their works. Theirs are the invisible hands which pierce fanaticism from one end of Europe to the other with the arrows of truth. Damilaville recently died. He was the author of 'Christianism unveiled,' and many other writings. No one ever knew him. His friends preserved the secret of his name as long as he lived with a fidelity worthy of philosophy. No one yet knows who is the author of the work given under the name of Pieret. In Holland, during the last two years, they have printed more than sixty volumes against superstition. The authors of them are absolutely unknown, although they could boldly proclaim themselves. The Italian who has written the "Reform of Italy," has not cared to present his work to the Pope, but his book has a prodigious effect. A thousand pens write, and a hundred thousand voices arise against abuses and in favor of tolerance. Be assured that the revolution which has taken place in minds during the past twelve years has served, and not a little, to drive the Jesuits from so many States, and to strongly encourage princes to strike at the idol of Rome which caused them all to tremble at another epoch. The people are very stupid, and, nevertheless, the light has penetrated even to them. Be very sure, for example, that there are not twenty persons in Geneva who do not abjure Calvin as well as the Pope, and that there are philosophers even in the shops of Paris.

I shall die consoled in seeing the true religion, that of the heart, established on the ruins of affectations. I have never preached but the adoration of one God, beneficence, and indulgence. With these sentiments I brave the devil who does not exist and the true devils who exist only too much.

CHAPTER 4

Freemasonry

"He gave its members…the title of Freemasons, and invented the allegory of the Temple of Solomon, now so much used by Masonry of every kind, and which meant the original state of man supposed to be a commonwealth of equality with a vague Deism as its religion. This temple, destroyed by Christ for the Christian order, was to be restored by Freemasonry after Christ and the Christian order should be obliterated by conspiracy and revolution."

—Monsignor Dillon

FREEMASONRY, WE MUST remember always, appeared generally and spread generally, too, in the interests of all that Voltaire aimed at, when it best suited his purpose. The first lodge established in France under the English obedience was in 1727. Its founder and first master was the celebrated Jacobite, Lord Derwentwater. It had almost immediate acceptance from the degenerate nobility of France, who, partly because of the influence of English and Scotch Jacobite nobles, and partly because of its novelty, hard swearing, and mystery, joined the strange institution. Its lodges were soon in every considerable city of the realm.

The philosophers and various schools of Atheists, however, were the first to enter into and to extend it. For them

27

it had special attractions and special uses, which they were not slow to appreciate and to employ. Now, though it very little concerns us to know much of the origin of this society, which became then and since so notorious throughout the world, still, as that origin throws some light on its subsequent history, it will not be lost time to glance at what is known, or supposed to be known, about it.

Mgr. Segur,[1] Bishop of Grenoble, who devoted much time to a study of Freemasonry, is persuaded that it was first elaborated by Faustus Socinus,[2] the nephew of the too celebrated Laelius Socinus, the heresiarch and founder of the sect of Unitarians or, as they are generally called after him, Socinians. Both were of the ancient family of the Sozini of Sienna. Faustus, like many of his relatives, imbibed the errors of his uncle, and in order to escape the vigilance of the Inquisition, to which both Italy and Spain owed much of the tranquility they enjoyed in these troublesome times, he fled to France. While in that country at Lyons, and when only twenty years of age, he heard of the death of his uncle at Zurich, and went at once to that city to obtain the papers and effects of the deceased. From the papers he found that Laelius had assisted at a conference of Heretics at Vicenza in 1547, in which the destruction of Christianity was resolved upon, and where resolutions were adopted for the renewal of Arianism—a system of false doctrine calculated to sap the very foundations of existing Faith by attacking the Trinity and the Incarnation. Feller, an authority of considerable weight, in his reference to this conference, says:

---

[1] ORIGINAL FOOTNOTE: Opus cit. p. 15.
[2] EDITOR'S NOTE: See footnote 1 of chapter 2.

In the assembly of Vicenza they agreed upon the means of destroying the religion of Jesus Christ, by forming a society which by its progressive successes brought on, towards the end of the eighteenth century, an almost general apostasy. When the Republic of Venice became informed of this conspiracy, it seized upon Julian Trevisano and Francis de Rugo, and strangled them. Ochinus and the others saved themselves. The society thus dispersed became only the more dangerous, and it is that which is known to-day under the name of Freemasons.

For this information Feller refers us to a work entitled "The Veil Removed," *Le Voile Levé*, by the Abbé Le Franc, a victim of the reign of terror in 1792. The latter tells us that the conspirators whom the severity of the Venetian Republic had scattered, and who were Ochinus, Laelius Socinus, Peruta, Gentilis, Jacques Chiari, Francis Lenoir, Darius Socinus, Alicas, and the Abbé Leonard, carried their poison with them, and caused it to bear fruits of death in all parts of Europe.

The success of Faustus Socinus in spreading his uncle's theories was enormous. His aim was not only to destroy the Church, but to raise up another temple into which any enemy of orthodoxy might freely enter. In this temple every heterodox belief might be held. It was called Christian but was without Christian faith, or hope, or love. It was simply an astutely planned system for propagating the ideas of its founders; for a fundamental part of the policy of Socinus, and one in which he well instructed his disciples, was to associate either to Unitarianism or to the confederation formed at Vicenza, the rich, the learned, the powerful, and the influential of the world. He feigned an equal esteem for Trinitarians and anti-Trinitarians, for Lutherans and Calvinists. He praised the undertakings of all against the Church of Rome, and working upon their intense hatred for Catholicism, caused them to forget their many "isms" in order to unite them for the destruction of the common enemy. When that should be effected, it would be time to consider a system agreeable to all. Until then, unity of action inspired by hatred of the Church should reign amongst them.

He therefore wished that all his adherents should, whether Lutheran or Calvinist, treat one another as brothers; and hence his disciples have been called at various times "United Brethren," "Polish Brothers," "Moravian Brothers," "Brother Masons," and finally "Freemasons." Monsignor Segur informs us, on the authorities before quoted, as well as upon that of Bergier, and the learned author of a work entitled, *Les Franc Maçons Ecrasés*—the Abbé Lerudan—printed at Amsterdam, as early as the year 1747, that the real secret of Freemasonry consisted, even then, in disbelief in the Divinity of Christ, and a determination to replace that doctrine, which is the very foundation of Christianity, by Naturalism or Rationalism. Socinus having established his Sect in Poland, sent emissaries to preach his doctrines stealthily in Germany, Holland, and England. In Germany, Protestants and Catholics united to unmask them. In Holland they blended with the Anabaptists, and in England they found partisans amongst the Independents and various other sects into which the people were divided.

The Abbé Lefranc believes that Oliver Cromwell[3] was a Socinian, and that he introduced Freemasonry into England. Certainly, Cromwell's sympathies were not for the Church favored by the monarch he supplanted, and were much with the Independents. If he was a Socinian, we can easily understand how the secret society of Vicenza could have attractions for one of his anti-Catholic and ambitious sentiments. He gave its members in England, as Monsignor Fava tells us, the title of Freemasons, and invented the allegory of the Temple of Solomon, now so much used by Masonry of every kind, and which meant the original state of man supposed to be a commonwealth of equality with a vague Deism as its religion. This temple, destroyed by Christ for the Christian order, was to be restored by Freemasonry after Christ and the Christian order should be obliterated by conspiracy and revolution. The state of Nature was the "Hiram" whose murder Masonry was to avenge; and which, having previously removed Christ, was to resuscitate Hiram, by re-building the temple of Nature as it had been before.[4]

---

[3] EDITOR'S NOTE: Oliver Cromwell (1599–1658) was an English soldier and statesman who led parliamentary forces to victory in the English Civil Wars against the royalist forces of Charles I. He abolished the monarchy and declared himself "Lord Protector" of England, Scotland, and Ireland from 1653 to 1658—the first and only time that England was a "republic."

[4] EDITOR'S NOTE: The "Hiramic Legend" is one of the key allegories of Freemasonry. It is supposedly connected to Hiram, king of Tyre, and his role in building Solomon's Temple in Jerusalem, who is referenced in the Bible (see, for example, 2 Sm 5; 1 Kgs 5, 7, 9, 10; and 1 Chr 14). The masonic allegory claims the messenger he sent to assist Solomon in building the Temple was Hiram Abiff, who was assassinated. They also associate this legend with that of Jacques de Molay, the leader of the Knights Templar who was burned at the stake for heresy in 1314 for

Monsignor Segur, moreover, connects modern Freemasonry with the Jews (see editor's note) and Templars, as well
as with Socinus. There are reasons which lead me to think
that he is right in doing so. The Jews for many centuries previous to the Reformation had formed secret societies for their
own protection and for the destruction of the Christianity
which persecuted them, and which they so much hated. The
rebuilding of the Temple of Solomon was the dream of their
lives. It is unquestionable that they wished to make common
cause with other bodies of persecuted religionists. They had
special reason to welcome with joy such heretics as were cast
off by Catholicism. It is, therefore, not at all improbable that
they admitted into their secret conclaves some at least of
the discontented Templars, burning for revenge upon those
who dispossessed and suppressed the Order. That fact would
account for the curious combination of Jewish and conven-
tual allusions to be found in modern Masonry.[5]

Then, as to its British History, we have seen that numbers of the secret brotherhood of Socinus made their way
to England and Scotland, where they found rich friends,
and, perhaps, confederates. I have, therefore, no doubt but
that the Abbé Lefranc is correct when he says that Cromwell was connected with them. At least, before he succeeded
in his designs, he had need of some such secret society, and
would, no doubt, be glad to use it for his purposes. But it is
not so clear that Cromwell was the first, as Lefranc thinks,

(according to them) not revealing the secrets of Freemasonry. Freemasons see their murderers as allegories for the forces of superstition and
intolerance, and the Freemasons' task as avenging their deaths.

[5] EDITOR'S NOTE: See Monsignor Dillon's original footnote in appendix I provided at the end of this chapter.

to blend that brotherhood with the real Freemasons. The ancient guild of working masons had existed in Great Britain and in Europe for many centuries previous to his time. They were like every other guild of craftsmen—a body formed for mutual protection and trade offices. But they differed from other tradespeople in this, that from their duties they were more cosmopolitan, and knew more of the ceremonies of religion at a period when the arts of reading and writing were not very generally understood. They travelled over every portion of England and Scotland, and frequently crossed the Channel, to work at the innumerable religious houses, castles, fortifications, great abbeys, churches, and cathedrals which arose over the face of Christendom in such number and splendor in the middle and succeeding ages. To keep away interlopers, to sustain a uniform rate of wages, to be known amongst strangers, and, above all, amongst foreigners of their craft, signs were necessary; and these signs could be of value only in proportion to the secrecy with which they were kept within the craft itself. They had signs for those whom they accepted as novices, for the companion mason or journeyman, and for the masters of the craft. In ages when a trade was transmitted from father to son, and formed a kind of family inheritance, we can very well imagine that its secrets were guarded with much jealousy, and that its adepts were enjoined not to communicate them to anyone, not even to their wives, lest they become known to outsiders.

The masons were, if we except the clockmakers and jewelers, the most skilled artisans of Europe. By the cunning of their hands they knew how to make the rough stone speak out the grand conceptions of the architects of the middle ages; and often, the delicate foliage and flowers and statuary of the fanes [temple or shrine] they built, remind us of the most perfect eras of Greek and Roman sculpture. So closely connected with religion and religious architecture as were these "Brothers Masons," "Friars," "Fra," or "Free Masons," they shared to a large extent in the favor of the Popes. They obtained many and valuable charters. But they degenerated. The era of the so-called Reformation was a sad epoch for them. It was an era of Church demolition rather than of Church building. Wherever the blight of Protestantism fell, the beauty and stateliness of Church architecture became dwarfed, stunted, and degraded, whenever it was not utterly destroyed. The need of Brother Masons had passed, and succeeding Masons began to admit men to their guilds who won a living otherwise than by the craft.

In Germany their confraternity had become a cover for the reformers, and Socinus, seeing it as a means for advancing his Sect—a method for winning adepts and progressing stealthily without attracting the notice of Catholic government—would desire no doubt to use it for his purposes. We have to this day the statute the genuine Freemasons of Strasbourg framed in 1462, and the same revised as late as 1563, but in them there is absolutely nothing of heresy or hostility to the Church. But there is a curious document called the Charter of Cologne dated 1535, which, if it be genuine, proves to us that there existed at that early period a body of Freemasons having principles identical with those professed by the Masons of our own day. It is to be found in the archives of the Mother Lodge of Amsterdam which also preserves the act of its own constitution under the date of 1519. It reveals the existence of lodges of kindred intent in London, Edinburgh, Vienna, Amsterdam, Paris, Lyons, Frankfurt, Hamburg, Antwerp, Rotterdam, Madrid, Venice, Goriz, Koenigsberg, Brussels, Dantzig, Magdeburg, Bremen, and Cologne; and it bears the signatures of well-known enemies of the Church at that period, namely—Hermanus or Herman de Weir, the immoral and heretical Archbishop-Elector of Cologne, placed for his misdeeds under the ban of the Empire; De Coligny, leader of the Huguenots of France; Jacob d'Anville, Prior of the Augustinians of Cologne, who incurred the same reproaches as Archbishop Herman; Melanchthon, the Reformer; Nicholas Van Noot, Carlton, Bruce, Upson, Banning, Vireaux, Schroeder, Hoffman, Nobel, De la Torre, Doria, Uttenbow, Falck, Huissen, Wormer. These names reveal both the country and the celebrity of all the men who signed the document. It was, possibly, a society like theirs, which the Venetian Government broke up and scattered in 1547, for we find distinct mention of a lodge existing at Venice in 1535.

However this may be, Freemason lodges existed in Scotland from the time of the Reformation. One of them is referred to in the Charter of Cologne, and doubtless had many affiliations. In Scotland, as in other Catholic countries, the Templars were suppressed; and there, if nowhere else, that Order had the guilds of working masons under its special protection. It is therefore possible, as some say, that the knights coalesced with these Masons, and protected their own machinations with the aid of the secrets of the craft.

But while this and all else stated regarding the connection of the Templars with Masonry may be true, there is no real evidence that it is so. Much is said about the building of the Temple of Solomon; and that the Hiram killed, and whose death the craft is to avenge, is James [Jacques] Molay, the Grand Master, executed in the barbarous manner of his age for supposed complicity in the crimes with which the Templars were everywhere charged. There is tall talk about such things in modern Masonry, and a great deal of the absurd and puerile ritual in which the sect indulges when conferring the higher grades, is supposed to have reference to them.

But the Freemasonry with which we have to deal, however connected in its origin with the Templars, with Socinus, with the conspirators of Cologne, or those of Vicenza, or with Cromwell, received its modern characteristics from Elias Ashmole, the Antiquary, and the provider, if not the founder, of the Oxford Museum.[6] Ashmole was an alchemist and an astrologer, and imbued consequently with a love for the jargon and mysticism of that strange body so busied about the philosopher's stone and other Utopias. The existing lodges of the Freemasons had an inexpressible charm for Ashmole, and in 1646 he, together with Colonel Mainwaring, became members of the craft. He perfected it, added various mystic symbols to those already in use and gave partly a scriptural, partly an Egyptian form to its jargon and ceremonies.

---

[6] EDITOR'S NOTE: Elias Ashmole (1617–92) was an English antiquary, politician, astrologer, and alchemist. He established the Ashmolean Museum, or, in full, the Ashmolean Museum of Art and Archaeology, by donating his collection of artifacts to Oxford University in 1677. The museum was opened to the public in 1683.

The Rosecroix, Rosicrucian degree, a society formed after the idea of Bacon's *New Atlantis*,[7] appeared; and the various grades of companion, master, secret master, perfect master, elect, and Irish master, were either remodeled or newly formed, as we know them now. Charles I was decapitated in 1649, and Ashmole being a Royalist to the core, soon turned English Masonry from the purposes of Cromwell and his party, and made the craft, which was always strong in Scotland, a means to upset the Government of the Protector and to bring back the Stuarts. Now "Hiram" became the murdered Charles, who was to be avenged instead of James [Jacques] Molay, and the reconstruction of the Temple meant the restoration of the exiled House of Stuart. On the accession of Charles II the craft was, of course, not treated with disfavor; and when the misfortunes of James II drove him from the throne, the partisans of the House of Stuart had renewed recourse to it as a means of secret organization against the enemy.

To bring back the Pretender, the Jacobites formed a Scotch and an English and an Irish constitution. The English constitution embraced the Mother Lodge of York and that of London, which latter separated from York, and with a new spring of action started into life as the Grand Lodge of London in 1717. The Jacobite nobles brought it to France chiefly to aid their attempts in favor of the Stuarts. They opened a lodge called the "Amity and Fraternity," in Dunkirk, in 1721, and

---

[7] EDITOR'S NOTE: Francis Bacon (1561–1626) was an English lawyer, statesman, and philosopher, whose *New Atlantis* (posthumously published in 1626) was an unfinished Utopian novel that envisioned a new society in which knowledge and science, centered on an ideal college he named "Salomon's House" (or "Solomon's House"), reigned supreme.

in 1725 the Lord Derwentwater opened the famous Mother
Lodge of Paris. Masonry soon spread to Holland (1730),
to Germany in 1736, to Ireland in 1729, and afterwards to
Italy, Spain and Europe generally. All its lodges were placed
under the Grand Lodge of England, and remained so for
many years.

I mention these facts and dates in order to let you see that
precisely at the period when Freemasonry was thus extending abroad, the Infidelity, which had been introduced by
Bayle and openly advocated by Voltaire, was being dissemi-
nated largely amongst the corrupt nobility of France and of
Europe generally. It was, as we have already seen, a period
of universal license in morals with the great in every country, and the members of the Grand Lodge in England were
generally men of easy virtue whose example was agreeable to
Continental libertines.

Voltaire found that the Masonry to which he had been
affiliated in London was a capital means of diffusing his doctrines among the courtiers, the men of letters, and the public
of France. It was like himself, the incarnation of hypocrisy and lying. It came recommended by an appearance
of philanthropy and of religion. Ashmole gave it the open
Bible, together with the square and compass. It called the
world to witness that it believed in God, "the great Architect
of the Universe." It had "an open eye," which may be taken
for God's all-seeing providence, or for the impossibility of a
sworn Mason escaping his fate if he revealed the secrets of
the craft or failed to obey the orders he was selected to carry
out. It made members known to each other, just as did the
ancient craft, in every country, and professed to take charge

of the orphans and widows of deceased brethren who could not provide for them.

But, in its secret conclaves and in its ascending degrees, it had means to tell the victim whom it could count upon, that the "Architect" meant a circle, a nothing;[8] that the open Bible was the universe; and that the square and compass was simply the fitness of things—the means to make all men "fraternal, equal, and free" in some impossible Utopia it promised but never gave. In the recesses of its lodges, the political conspirator found the men and the means to arrive at his ends in security. Those who ambitioned office found there the means of advancement. The old spirit breathed into the fraternity by Socinus, and nourished so well by the heretical libertines of the England and Germany of the seventeenth century, and perfected by the Infidels of the eighteenth, was master in all its lodges. Banquets, ribald songs and jests, reveling in sin, constituted from the beginning a leading feature in its life. Lodges became the secure home for the *roué* [sic], the spendthrift, the man of broken fortunes, the Infidel, and the depraved of the upper classes.

Such attractive centers of sin, therefore, spread over Europe with great rapidity. They were encouraged not only by Voltaire, but by his whole host of Atheistic writers, philosophers, encyclopedists, revolutionists, and rakes. The scoundrels of Europe found congenial employment in them; and before twenty years elapsed from their first introduction the lodges were a power in Europe, formidable by the union which subsisted between them all, and by the wealth, social position, and unscrupulousness of those who formed their

---

[8] ORIGINAL FOOTNOTE: See chapter 21, "Freemasonry with Ourselves."

brotherhood. The principles fashionable—and indeed alone tolerated—in them all, before long, were the principles of Voltaire and of his school. This led in time to the Union and "Illuminism" of Masonry.

Appendix I (footnote 5)

M. Gougenot-Demousseaux, in his work on the Jew (see editor's note), Judaism, and the Judaization of Christian people (Paris 1869), has brought together a great number of indications on the relations of the high chiefs of Masonry with Judaism. He thus concludes:

> Masonry, that immense association, the rare initiates of which, that is to say, the real chiefs of which, whom we must be careful not to confound with the nominal chiefs, live in a strict and intimate alliance with the militant members of Judaism, princes and imitators of the high cabal. For that elite of the order—these real chiefs whom so few of the initiated know, or whom they only know for the most part under a *nom de guerre*, are employed in the profitable and secret dependence of the cabalistic Israelites. And this phenomenon is accomplished, thanks to the habits of rigorous discretion to which they subject themselves by oaths and terrible menaces; thanks also to the majority of Jewish members which the mysterious constitution of Masonry seats in its sovereign counsel.

M. Cretineau-Joly gives a very interesting account of the correspondence between Nubius and an opulent German Jew who supplied him with money for the purposes of his dark intrigues against the Papacy. The Jewish connection with modern Freemasonry is an established fact everywhere manifested in its history. The Jewish formulas employed by Masonry, the Jewish traditions which run through its ceremonial, point to a Jewish origin, or to the work of Jewish contrivers. It is easy to conceive how such a society could be thought necessary to protect them from Christianity in power. It is easy also to understand how the one darling object of their lives is the rebuilding of the Temple. Who knows but behind the Atheism and desire of gain which impels them to urge on Christians to persecute the Church and to destroy it, there lies a hidden hope to reconstruct their Temple, and at the darkest depths of secret society plotting there lurks a deeper society still which looks to a return to the land of Judah and to the re-building of the Temple of Jerusalem. One of the works which Antichrist will do, it is said, is to reunite the Jews, and to proclaim himself as their long looked-for Messiah. As it is now generally believed that he is to come from Masonry and to be of it, this is not improbable, for in it he will find the Jews the most inveterate haters of Christianity, the deepest plotters, and the fittest to establish his reign.

CHAPTER 5

The Union and "Illuminism" of Masonry

"The state of nature, goods and the sexes in common, no God, and instead of God a hatred for everything sustaining the idea of God, formed about the sum total of the happiness which they desired to see reign in a world where people should be reduced to a level resembling that of wild cattle in the American prairies."

—Monsignor Dillon

WITH THE AID of Voltaire, and of his party, Freemasonry rapidly spread amongst the higher classes of France and wherever else in Europe the influence of the French Infidels extended. It soon after obtained immense power of union and propagandism. In France and everywhere else it had an English, a Scotch, and a local obedience. These had separate constitutions and officers, even separate grades, but all were identical in essence and in aim. A brother in one was a brother in all. However, it seemed to the leaders that more unity was needed, and aided by the adhesion of the Duke of Chartres, subsequently better known as the Duke of Orleans, the infamous Philippe Égalité,[1] who was

---

[1] EDITOR'S NOTE: Louis Philippe II, Duke of Orleans (1747–93), was a

Grand Master of the Scotch Masonic Body in France, the French Masons in the English obedience desiring independence of the Mother Lodge of England, separated and elected him the first Grand Master of the since celebrated Grand Orient of France. Two years after this, the execrable "Androgyne" lodges for women, called "Lodges of Adoption" were established, and had as Grand Mistress over them all the Duchess of Bourbon, sister of Égalité.[2] The Infidels, by extending these lodges for women, obtained an immense amount of influence, which they otherwise never could attain. They thus invaded the domestic circle of the Court of France and of every Court in Europe. Thus, too, the royal edicts, the decrees of Clement XII and Benedict XIV against Freemasonry,[3] and the efforts of conscientious officers, were rendered completely inoperative. After the death of Voltaire, the extension of Freemasonry became alarming; but no State effort could then stop its progress. It daily grew more powerful and more corrupt. It began already to extend its influence into every department of state. Promotion in the army, in the navy, in the public service, in the law, and even to the fat benefices *in commendam* ["to commend"] of the Church, became impossible

---

French nobleman who supported the Revolution, and changed his name to "Philippe Égalité," after the motto of the French Revolution, "*Liberté, Égalité, Fraternité*" ["Liberty, Equality, Brotherhood"].

[2] EDITOR'S NOTE: Bathilde d'Orleans (1750–1822) was a French princess who supported the Revolution and had the nickname *Citoyenne Vérité* ("*Citizeness Truth*").

[3] EDITOR'S NOTE: Pope Clement XII condemned Freemasony in the papal bull *In Eminenti Apostolatus* (1738), and Pope Benedict XIV likewise condemned it in the bull *Providas Romanorum* (1751).

without its aid;[4] and at this precise juncture, when the political fortunes of France were, for many reasons, growing desperate, two events occurred to make the already general and corrupt Freemasonry still more formidable. These were the advent of the Illuminism of Saint-Martin in France,[5] and that of Adam Weishaupt in Germany,[6] and the increased corruption introduced principally by means of women-Freemasons.

A Portuguese Jew, named Martinez Pasqualis,[7] was the first to introduce Illuminism into the Lodge of Lyons, and his system was afterwards perfected in wickedness by Saint-Martin, from whom French Illuminism took its name. Illuminism meant the extreme extent of immorality, Atheism, anarchy, levelling, and bloodshed, to which the principles of Masonry could be carried. It meant a universal conspiracy against the Church and established order. It constituted a degree of advancement for all the lodges, and powerfully aided to make them the centers of revolutionary intrigue and of political manipulation which they soon became in the hands of men at once sunk in Atheism and moral corruption.

An idea of these lodges may be obtained from a description given of that of Ermanonville, by M. Le Marquis de

---

[4] EDITOR'S NOTE: See Monsignor Dillon's original footnote in appendix I provided at the end of this chapter.
[5] EDITOR'S NOTE: Louis-Claude de Saint-Martin (1743–1803) was a French philosopher and leading illuminist of the eighteenth century.
[6] EDITOR'S NOTE: Adam Weishaupt (1748–1830) was a German philosopher and professor of canon law.
[7] EDITOR'S NOTE: Martinez de Pasqualis (c. 1727–74) was a theurgist and theosopher who founded the French branch of illuminism in 1754.

Lefroi, in *Dictionnaire des Erreurs Societies*, quoted by Deschamps, vol. ii, page 93.

"It is known," he says, "that the Chateau de Ermanonville belonging to the Sieur Girardin, about ten leagues from Paris, was a famous haunt of Illuminism. It is known that there, near the tomb of Jean-Jacques, under the pretext of bringing men back to the age of nature, reigned the most horrible dissoluteness of morals. Nothing can equal the turpitude of morals which reigns amongst that horde of Ermanonville. Every woman admitted to the mysteries became common to the brothers, and was delivered up to the chance or to the choice of these true 'Adamites.'"[8] Barruel in his *Memoires sur le Jacobinisme*, vol. iv. p. 334, says "that M. Leseure, the father of the hero of La Vendee, having been affiliated to a lodge of this kind, and having, in obedience to the promptings of conscience, abandoned it, was soon after poisoned." He himself declared to the Marquis de Montron that he fell a victim to "that infamous horde of the Illuminati."

The Illuminism of Saint-Martin was simply an advance in the intensity of immorality, Atheism, secrecy, and terror, which already reigned in the lodges of France. It planned a deeper means of revolution and destruction. It became in its hidden depths a lair in which the Atheists of the period could mature their plans for the overthrow of the existing order of things to their own best advantage. It gave itself very captivating names. Its members were "Knights of Beneficence," "Good Templars," "Knights of St. John," etc.

---

[8] Editor's Note: The Adamites were an ancient heretical group who advocated nudity for men and women in their religious ceremonies.

They numbered, however, amongst them, the most active, daring, and unscrupulous members of Masonry. They set themselves at work to dominate over and to control the entire body. They had no system, any more than any other sort of Masons, to give the world instead of that which they determined to pull down. The state of nature, goods and the sexes in common, no God, and instead of God a hatred for everything sustaining the idea of God, formed about the sum total of the happiness which they desired to see reign in a world where people should be reduced to a level resembling that of wild cattle in the American prairies. This was the Illumination they destined for humanity; yet such was the infatuation inspired by their immoral and strange doctrines that nobles, princes, and monarchs of the period, including Frederick II[9] of Prussia and the silly Joseph II of Austria,[10] admitted to a part of their secrets, were the tools and the dupes, and even the accomplices, of these infamous conspirators.

Appendix I (footnote 4)

Before the celebrated "Convent" of Wilhelmsbad[11] there was a thorough understanding between the Freemasons of

---

[9] EDITOR'S NOTE: See footnote 2 of chapter 3.

[10] EDITOR'S NOTE: Joseph II (1741–90) was Holy Roman emperor from 1765 to 1790, during which time he was co-ruler with his mother, Maria Theresa, from 1765 to 1780, and the sole ruler of the Austrian Hapsburg dominions from 1780 to 1790. He was an "enlightened despot" who, with limited success, introduced numerous political, legal, administrative, economic, and ecclesiastical reforms.

[11] EDITOR'S NOTE: See chapter 7, *The Convent of Wilhelmsbad.*

the various Catholic countries of Continental Europe. This
was manifested in the horrible intrigues which led to the
suppression of the Society of Jesus in France, Spain, Portugal, Germany, and Naples; and which finally compelled
Clement XIV to dissolve the great body by ecclesiastical
authority. No doubt the Jesuits had very potent enemies
in the Jansenists, the Gallicans, and in others whose party
spirit and jealousy were stronger than their sense of the real
good of religion. But without the unscrupulous intrigues of
the Infidels of Voltaire's school banded into a compact active
league by the newly-developed Freemasonry, the influence
of the sects of Christians hostile to the Order could never
effect an effacement so complete and so general. Anglican
lodges, we must remember, appeared in Spain and Portugal
as soon as in France. One was opened in Gibraltar in 1726,
and one in Madrid in 1727. This latter broke with the
mother lodge of London in 1779, and founded lodges in
Barcelona, Cadiz, Valladolid, and other cities. There were
several lodges at work in Lisbon as early as 1735. The Duke
of Choiseul, a Freemason, with the aid of the abominable
de Pompadour,[12] the harlot of the still more abominable
Louis XV, succeeded in driving the Jesuits from France. He
then set about influencing his brother Masons, the Count
De Aranda, Prime Minister of Charles III of Spain, and the
infamous Carvalho-Pombal, the *alter ego* of the weak King
of Portugal, to do the same work in the Catholic States
of their respective sovereigns. The Marquis de L'Angle, a

---

[12] EDITOR'S NOTE: Madame de Pompadour (1721–64) was a female
member of the French court and the official chief mistress of King Louis
XV from 1745 to 1751.

French Freemason Atheist, and friend of Choiseul, thus writes of De Aranda:

> He is the only man of which Spain can be proud of at this moment. He is the sole Spaniard of our days whom posterity will place on its tablets. It is he whom it will love to place on the front of all its temples, and whose name it will engrave on its escutcheon together with the names of Luther, of Calvin, of Mahomet, of William Penn, and of Jesus Christ! It is he who desired to sell the wardrobe of the saints, the property of virgins, and to convert the cross, the chandeliers, the patens, etc., into bridges and inns and main roads.

We cannot be surprised at what De Aranda attempted after this testimony. He conspired with Choiseul to forge a letter as if from the General of the Jesuits, Ricci, which purported to prove that the King's mother was an adulteress, and that the King had no claim to the Spanish throne. Secretly, therefore, an order was obtained from the weak Monarch, and on a given day and hour the Jesuits in all parts of the Spanish dominions were dragged from their homes, placed on board ships, and cast on the shores of the Pontifical States in a condition of utter destitution. A calumny as atrocious and unfounded enabled Pombal to inflict a worse fate on the Jesuits of Portugal and its dependencies. Charles III ordered Panucci, another Masonic enemy of the Jesuits, to banish the members of the society from Naples, where his son reigned. Geiser writes to Voltaire that the half-fool Joseph II was initiated in the mysteries of Masonry and accordingly the Jesuits, notwithstanding the sympathies of the Empress

Mary Theresa, fell in Austria. The world was left thus free for the Masonic philosophers to compass the destruction which they planned at Wilhelmsbad and effected in the Revolution eight years afterwards.

CHAPTER 6

The Illuminism of Adam Weishaupt

*"But the hatred for God and all form of worship, and the
determination to found a universal republic on the lines of
Communism, was on the part of Weishaupt a settled sentiment.
. . . Weishaupt employed, for fifty years after the death of
Voltaire, his whole life and energies in the one work of perfecting
secret associations to accomplish by deep deceit, and by force
when that should be practical, the ruin of the existing order
of religion, civilization, and government, in order to plant
in its stead his own system of Atheism and Socialism."*

—Monsignor Dillon

BUT THE ILLUMINISM of Lyons was destined soon to have a
worldwide and ineradicable hold on the Masonry of the world
by means of an adept far more able than Saint-Martin[1] or any
of his associates. This was Adam Weishaupt, a Professor of
Canon Law in the University of Munich. I shall detain you a
while to consider this remarkable individual who, more than
any of the Atheists that have arisen in Masonry, has been the
cause of the success of its agencies in controlling the fate of

---

[1] EDITOR'S NOTE: See footnote 5 of chapter 5.

the world since his day. Had Weishaupt not lived, Masonry may have ceased to be a power after the reaction consequent on the first French Revolution. He gave it a form and character which caused it to outlive that reaction, to energize it to the present day, and which will cause it to advance until its final conflict with Christianity must determine whether Christ or Satan shall reign on this earth to the end.

Voltaire's will to do God and man injury was as strong as that of Weishaupt. His disciples, d'Alembert,[2] Diderot,[3] Damilaville,[4] Condorcet,[5] and the rest, were as fully determined as he was, to eradicate Christianity. But they desired in its stead a system with only a mitigated antipathy for monarchy, and which might have tolerated for a long time such kings as Frederick of Prussia,[6] and such Empresses as Catherine of Russia.[7] But the hatred for God and all form of worship, and the determination to found a universal republic on the lines of Communism, was on the part of Weishaupt a settled sentiment. Possessed of a rare power of organization, an education in law which made him a pre-eminent teacher in its highest faculty, an extended

---

[2] EDITOR'S NOTE: Jean le Rond d'Alembert (1717–83) was a French "Enlightenment" philosopher, mathematician, physicist, and music theorist who is most famous for his being a co-contributor to the *Encyclopédie*, originally published in 1751, which laid out a catalogue of "Enlightenment" thought.

[3] EDITOR'S NOTE: Denis Diderot (1713–84) was a French "Enlightenment" philosopher, most famous for being one of the co-contributors of the *Encyclopédie*.

[4] EDITOR'S NOTE: See footnote 8 of chapter 3.

[5] EDITOR'S NOTE: See footnote 15 of chapter 3.

[6] EDITOR'S NOTE: See footnote 2 of chapter 3.

[7] EDITOR'S NOTE: See footnote 1 of chapter 3.

knowledge of men and things, a command over himself, a repute for external morality, and finally, a position calculated to win able disciples, Weishaupt employed, for fifty years after the death of Voltaire, his whole life and energies in the one work of perfecting secret associations to accomplish by deep deceit, and by force when that should be practical, the ruin of the existing order of religion, civilization, and government, in order to plant in its stead his own system of Atheism and Socialism.

He found contemporary Masonry well adapted for his ends. His object was to extend it as far as possible as a means of seducing men away from Christianity. He well knew that Masonry and the Church were in mortal conflict, and that the moment a man became a Mason, he, that instant, became excommunicated; he lost the grace of God; he passed into a state of hostility to the Church; he ceased to approach the Sacraments; he was constituted in a state of rebellion; he forfeited his liberty to unknown superiors; he took a dreadful oath—perhaps many—not to reveal the secrets then, or at any after time, to be committed to his keeping; and finally, he placed himself amongst men, all of whom were in his own position, and in whose society it was possible and easy for the astute disciples of Weishaupt to lead him farther on the road to ruin.

Weishaupt's view, then, was first to entice men into Masonry—into the lowest degree. A great gain for evil was thus at once obtained. But a man, though in Masonry, may not be willing to become an Atheist and a Socialist, for some time at least. He may have in his heart a profound conviction that a God existed, and some hope left of returning to that God at or before his death. He may have entered Masonry for purposes of ambition, for motives of vanity, from mere lightness of character. He may continue his prayers, and refuse, if a Catholic, to give up the Mother of God and some practice of piety loved by him from his youth. But Masonry was a capital system to wean a man gradually away from all these things. It did not at once deny the existence of God, nor at once attack the Christian Dispensation. It commenced by giving the Christian idea of God an easy, and, under semblance of respect, an almost imperceptible shake. It swore by the name of God in all its oaths. It called him, however, not a Creator, only an architect—the great Architect of the universe. It carefully avoided all mention of Christ, of the Adorable Trinity, of the Unity of the Faith, or of any faith. It protested a respect for the convictions of every man, for the idolatrous Parsee [a Zoroastrian], for the Mahommedan [a Muslim], for the Heretic, the Schismatic, the Catholic. By-and-by, it gave, in higher degrees, a ruder shock to the belief in the Deity and a gradual inducement to favor Naturalism. This it did gradually, imperceptibly, but effectually.

Now, to a man who meditated the vast designs of social and religious destruction contemplated by Weishaupt, Masonry, especially the Masonry of his period, was the most effective means that could be conceived. In its midst, therefore, he planted his disciples, well versed in his system. These consisted of three classes, each class having subdivisions, and all of which were high degrees of Masonry. The first class of Illuminati was that of preparation. It consisted of two degrees, namely, the degree of Novice and that of Minerval [sic]. The Minervals formed the great body of the order, and were under the direction of certain chiefs, who themselves were subjected to other agencies invisible to those instructed by themselves. Weishaupt instructed the teachers of the Minervals to propose each year to their scholars some interesting questions, to cause them to write themes calculated to spread impiety amongst the people, such as burlesques on the Psalms, pasquinades[8] on the Prophets, and caricatures of personages of the Old Testament after the manner of Voltaire and his school.

It is surprising with what exactitude these Minervals follow out the instructions of Weishaupt to this day. At this moment, in London, under the eyes of the Lord Chancellor, pamphlets, with hideous woodcuts, ridiculing David, "the man after God's own heart," are weekly published. One of these, which was handed to me in a public place, had a woodcut representing the "meek Monarch of Judea," with a head just severed from a human body in one hand, and the sword that did the deed in the other. Another represented him amidst a set of ridiculous figures dancing. From this we can easily judge that illuminated Masonry is at work somewhere even in London, and that the Masonry in high quarters is blind to its excesses, exactly as happened in France a few years before the French Revolution. Now these Minervals, if they manifested what the German Masons called "religionary" inclinations, might indeed receive the first three Masonic degrees, but they were not to be further promoted in Illuminism. They were relegated to the rank

---

8   EDITOR'S NOTE: A satire or lampoon.

and file of Masonry, who were of use in many ways for the movement, but they were never to be trusted with the real secret. The teacher, without seeming to do so, was ordered to encourage, but not to applaud publicly, such blasphemies as the Minervals might make use of in their essays. They were to be led on, seemingly by themselves, in the ways of irreligion, immorality, and Atheism, until ripe for further promotion in evil progress. Finally, in the advanced grades of Illuminated Major and Minor, and in those of Scotch Knight and Epopte [sic] or Priest they were told the whole secret of the Order as follows, in a discourse by the initiator:

> Remember [he said] that from the first invitations which we have given you, in order to attract you to us, we have commenced by telling you that in the projects of our Order there did not enter any designs against religion. You remember that such an assurance was again given to you when you were admitted into the ranks of our novices, and that it was repeated when you entered into our Minerval Academy. Remember also how much from the first grades we have spoken to you of morality and virtue, but at the same time how much the studies which we prescribed for you and the instructions which we gave you rendered both morality and virtue independent of all religion; how much we have been at pains to make you understand, while making to you the eulogy of religion, that it was not anything else than those mysteries, and that worship degenerated in the hands of the priest. You remember with what art, with what simulated respect,

we have spoken to you of Christ and of his Gospel;
but in the grades of greater Illuminism, of Scotch
Knight, and of Epopte [sic] or Priest, how we have
known to form from Christ's Gospel that of our reason, and from its morality that of nature, and from
its religion that of nature, and from religion, reason,
morality, and nature, to make the religion, and the
morality of the rights of man, of equality, and of liberty. Remember that while insinuating to you the different parts of this system, we have caused them to
bud forth from yourselves as if your own opinions.
We have placed you on the way; you have replied to
our questions very much more than we did to yours.
When we demanded of you, for example, whether the
religions of peoples responded to the end for which
men adopted them; if the religion of Christ, pure and
simple, was that which the different Sects professed
today, we know well enough what to hold. But it was
necessary to know to what point we had succeeded to
cause our sentiments to germinate in you. We have
had very many prejudices to overcome in you, before
being able to persuade you that the pretended religion
of Christ was nothing else than the work of priests, of
imposture, and of tyranny. If it be so with that religion so much proclaimed and admired, what are we to
think of other religions? Understand, then, that they
have all the same fictions for their origin, that they
are all equally founded on lying, error, chimera, and
imposture. Behold our secret!

The turns and counter-turns which it was necessary
to make; the eulogies which it was necessary to give
to the pretended secret schools; the fable of the Freemasons being in possession of the veritable doctrine;
and our Illuminism today, the sole inheritor of these
mysteries, will no longer astonish you at this moment.
If, in order to destroy all Christianity, all religion, we
have pretended to have the sole true religion, remember that the end justifies the means, and that the wise
ought to take all the means to do good, which the
wicked take to do evil. Those which we have taken to
deliver you, those which we take to deliver one day the
human race from all religion, are nothing else than a
pious fraud which we reserve to unveil some day in the
grade of Magus or Philosopher Illuminated.[9]

The above extract will serve to show you what manner of
man Weishaupt was, and the quality of the teaching he
invented. His organization—for the perfection of which he
deeply studied the constitution of the then suppressed Society of Jesus—contemplated placing the thread of the whole
conspiracy, destined to be controlled by the Illuminati, in
the hands of one man, advised by a small council. The Illuminati were to be in Masonry and of Masonry, so as to move
amongst its members secretly. They were so trained that they
could obtain the mastery in every form of secret society, and
thus render it subservient to their own Chief. Their fidelity
to him was made perfect by the most severe and complex
system of espionage. The Chief himself was kept safe by his

---

[9]   ORIGINAL CITATION: Segur: *Le Secret de la Franc-Maçonnerie*, p. 49.

position, his long training, and by his council. It thus happened that no matter to what office or position the Illuminati attained, they had to become subservient to the general aims of the Order.

Weishaupt, after being deprived of his professorship in Bavaria, found an asylum with the Prince of Coburg-Gotha, where he remained in honor, affluence and security, until his death in 1830. He continued all his life the Chief of the Illuminati, and this fact may account, in large measure, for the fidelity with which the Illuminati of the Revolution, the Directory, Consulate, the Empire, the Restoration, and the Revolution of 1830, invariably carried out his program of perpetual conspiracy for the ends he had in view. It may also account for the strange vitality of the spirit of the Illuminati in Italy, Switzerland, Germany, and Spain, and of its continuance through the "Illuminated" reigns of Nubius and Palmerston, the successors of Weishaupt to our own day. This we shall see further on; but, meanwhile, we shall glance at the first step of Weishaupt to rule over Masonry through his disciples. This was by calling together the famous "General Council" of Freemasonry, known as the Convent of Wilhelmsbad.

CHAPTER 7

The Convent of Wilhelmsbad

*"I will not tell you the secrets which I bring, but I can say that
a conspiracy is laid so secret and so deep that it will be very
difficult for monarchy and religion not to succumb to it."*

—Monsignor Dillon, quoting the Count de Virene

FROM ITS RISE Freemasonry appears as a kind of dark parody of the Church of Christ. The names taken by its dignitaries, the form of its hierarchy, the designations affected by its lodges and "obediences," the language of its rituals, all seem to be a kind of aping after the usages of Christianity.

When Saint-Martin[1] wished to spread his Illuminism in France, he managed to have a meeting of deputy Masons from all the lodges in that country. This was designated the "Convent of the Gauls"; and Lyons, the place of its meeting, was called "The Holy City."

Weishaupt had more extended views. He meant to reach all humanity by means of Masonry, and looked for a "Convent" far more general than that of Lyons. When, therefore, he had matured his plans for impregnating the Masonry of the world with his infernal system, he began to cast about for

---

[1] EDITOR'S NOTE: See footnote 5 of chapter 5.

means to call that Convent. The Illuminism of Saint-Martin was in full sympathy with him, but it could not effect his purpose. What he wanted was, that a kind of General Council of the Masonry extended at the time throughout the earth, should be called together; and he hoped that, by adroitly manipulating the representatives whom he knew would be sent to it by the lodges of every nationality of Masons, his own Illuminism might be adopted as a kind of high, arch, or hidden Masonry throughout its entire extent.

He succeeded in his design, and in 1781, under the official convocation of the Duke of Brunswick,[2] acting as Supreme Grand Master, deputies from every country where Freemasonry existed were summoned to meet at Wilhelmsbad in council. They came from every portion of the British Empire; from the newly formed United States of America; from all the Nations of Continental Europe, every one of which, at that period, had lodges; from the territories of the Grand Turk, and from the Indian and Colonial possessions of France, Spain, Portugal, and Holland. The principal and most numerous representatives were, however, from Germany and France. Through the skillful agency of the notorious Baron Knigge, and another still more astute adept of his, named Dittfort, Weishaupt completely controlled this Council. He further caused measures to be there concerted which in a few years led to the French Revolution, and

---

[2] EDITOR'S NOTE: Charles William Ferdinand, Duke of Brunswick (1735–1806), was the Prince of Brunswick-Wolfenbüttel (one of the states of the Holy Roman Empire) and Duke of Brunswick-Lüneburg, and a military commander. He was married to Princess Augusta, who was a sister of King George III of Great Britain, and considered an "enlightened despot" along the lines of Frederick II.

afterwards handed Germany over to the French revolutionary Generals acting under the Girondins, the Jacobins, and
the Directory. I would wish, if time permitted, to enter at
length into the proofs of this fact. It will suffice, however, for
my present purpose, to state that more than sufficient evidence of it was found by the Bavarian Government, which
had, some five years later, to suppress the Illuminati, and that
one of the members of the convent, the Count de Virene,
was struck with such horror at the depravity of the body that
he abandoned Illuminism and became a fervent Catholic.
He said to a friend: "I will not tell you the secrets which I
bring, but I can say that a conspiracy is laid so secret and so
deep that it will be very difficult for monarchy and religion
not to succumb to it." It may be also of use to remark that
many of the leaders of the French Revolution, and notably
most of those who lived through it, and profited by it, were
deputy Masons sent from various lodges in France to the
Convent of Wilhelmsbad.

CHAPTER 8

Cabalistic Masonry or Masonic Spiritism

"Necromancy is a characteristic of Antichrist, of whom
we read, 'that he will show great signs and wonders so as
to deceive, if that were possible, even the elect.' He will be
when he comes both a Cromwell and a Cagliostro."

—Monsignor Dillon

BEFORE PROCEEDING FURTHER with the history of Freemasonry, I shall stay a moment to consider a very remarkable feature in its strange composition, without which it scarcely ever appears.

The world was never without wizards, witches, necromancers, jugglers, and those who really had, or through imposture, pretended to have, intercourse with demons. Masonry in its various ramifications is the great continuator of this feature of a past which we had thought departed forever. Spirit-rapping, table-turning, medium-imposture, etc., distinguish its adepts in Protestant countries and in Catholic ones. We have almost incredible stories of the intercourse with the devil and his angels, which men like the Carbonari of Italy maintain. However, from the very beginning Freemasonry has had a kind of peculiar dark mysticism connected with it.

It loves to revel in such mysteries as the secret conclaves that the Jews used to practice in the countries in which they were persecuted, and which were common among those unclean heretics, the Bulgarians, the Gnostics, the Albigenses, and the Waldenses. The excesses alleged against the Templars were also accompanied by secret signs and symbols which Masonry adopted. But whatever may have been the extent of this mysticism in Masonry before, a spurious kind of spiritism became part of its very essence since the advent of the celebrated Cagliostro,[1] who travelled all over Europe under the instructions of Weishaupt, and founded more lodges than did any individual Freemason then or since.

The real name of this arch-imposter was Balsamo. He was an inveterate sorcerer, and in his peregrinations [long meandering journeys] in the East, picked up from every source the secrets of alchemy, astrology, jugglery, legerdemain, and occult science of every kind about which he could get any information. Like the Masonry to which he became affiliated at an early period, he was an adept at acting and speaking a lie. He suited Weishaupt, who, though knowing him to be an imposter, nevertheless employed for him the diffusion of Illuminism. Accompanied by his no less celebrated wife, Lorenza, he appeared in Venice as the Marquis Pelligrini, and subsequently traversed Italy, Germany, Spain, England, the Netherlands, and Russia. In the latter country he amassed, at the Court of Catherine II,[2] an immense fortune. In France,

---

[1] EDITOR'S NOTE: Alessandro Cagliostro (1743–95) was the alias of Italian occultist and magician Giuseppe Balsamo who frequented the royal courts of Europe.

[2] EDITOR'S NOTE: See footnote 1 of chapter 3.

assisted by the efforts of the Illuminati, he was received as a kind of demigod, and called the divine Cagliostro. He established new lodges in all parts of the country. At Bordeaux he remained eleven months for this purpose. In Paris he established lodges for women of a peculiarly cabalistic and impure kind, with inner departments horribly mysterious. At the reception of members he used rites and ceremonies exactly resembling the absurd practices of spirit mediums, who see and speak to spirits, etc., and introduced all that nonsense with which we are made now familiar by his modern followers. He claimed the power of conferring immortal youth, health, and beauty, and what he called moral and physical regeneration, by the aid of drugs and Illuminated Masonry. He was the father and the founder of the existing rite of Misraim—the Egyptian rite in Masonry. The scoundrel became involved in the celebrated case of the "Diamond Necklace,"[3] and was sent to the Bastille, from which he managed to pass to England, where, in 1787, he undertook to foretell the destruction of the Bastille, and of the Monarchy of France, the Revolution, and—but here he miscalculated—the advent of a Prince who would abolish *Lettres de Cachet*,[4] convoke the States General, and establish the worship of Reason. All these

---

[3] EDITOR'S NOTE: The "Affair of the Diamond Necklace" refers to an event in the court of King Louis XVI of France from 1784 to 1785 in which Queen Marie Antoinette was falsely accused of deciding to purchase, but then refusing to pay for, an expensive diamond necklace. While the queen was innocent, the incident served to encourage disillusionment with monarchy in France in the days leading up to the French Revolution.

[4] EDITOR'S NOTE: Letters signed by the king and one of his ministers containing orders that could not be appealed. They were most often used to authorize someone's imprisonment.

measures were resolved on at Wilhelmsbad, and Cagliostro of course knew that well. His only miscalculation was regarding the Prince Grand Master. The Revolution went on a little too far for the wretched [Philippe] Égalité,[5] who ended his treason to his house by losing his head at the guillotine. As to Cagliostro, he made his way to Rome, where the Inquisition put an end to his exploits upon detecting his attempts at Illuminism. His secret powers could not deliver him from prison. He died there miserably, in 1795, after attempting to strangle a poor Capuchin whom he asked for as a confessor, and in whose habit he had hoped to escape. This impostor is of course made a martyr to the Inquisition accordingly.

Masonry does much to disown Cagliostro; but with a strange inconsistency it keeps the Egyptian rite founded by him, and clings to mysticism of the debased kind he introduced. It is wonderful how extremes thus meet—how men who make it a sign of intellectual strength to deny the existence of the God that made them bow down stupidly and superstitiously before devils, real or imaginary. Necromancy is a characteristic of Antichrist, of whom we read, "that he will show great signs and wonders so as to deceive, if that were possible, even the elect" [Matt. 24:24]. He will be when he comes both a Cromwell[6] and a Cagliostro.

---

[5] EDITOR'S NOTE: See footnote 1 of chapter 5.
[6] EDITOR'S NOTE: See footnote 3 of chapter 4.

Chapter 9

The French Revolution

*"What Freemasonry did in France, it now labors, with
greater caution, to effect on some future day throughout the
entire world. It then submitted, with perfect docility, to a
great military leader, who arose out of its own work and
principles. Such another leader will finally direct its last efforts
against God and man. That leader will be Antichrist."*

—Monsignor Dillon

I MAY HERE remark that the conspiracy of the Illuminati, and
of Freemasonry generally, was far from being a secret to many
of the Courts of Europe. But, then, just as at the present
moment, it had friends, female as well as male, in every court.
These baulked the wholesome attempts of some rulers to stay
its deadly intrigues against princes, governments, and all order,
as well as against its one grand enemy, the Church of Jesus
Christ. The Court of Bavaria found out, as I have said, but
only by an accident, a part of the plans of the Illuminati, and
gave the alarm; but, strange to say, that alarm was unheeded
by the other Courts of Europe, Catholic as well as Protestant.
A Revolution was expected, but, as now, each Court hoped
to stave off the worst consequences from itself, and to profit
by the ruin of its neighbors. The voice of the Holy Father was

raised against Freemasonry again and again. Clement XII,[1] Benedict XIV, and other Pontiffs condemned it. The Agents and Ministers of the Holy See gave private advice and made urgent appeals to have the evil stopped while yet the powers of Europe could do so. These were all baffled, and the Court of the Grand Monarch and every Court of Continental Europe slept in the torpor of a living death, until wakened to a true sense of danger at a period far too late to remedy the disasters which irreligion, vice, stupidity, and recklessness hastened.

The lodges of the Illuminati in France meanwhile carried on the conspiracy. They had amassed and expended immense sums in deluging the country with immoral and Atheistic literature. Mirabeau,[2] in his *Monarchie Prussienne*,[3] published before the Revolution, thus speaks of these sums:

> Masonry in general, and especially the branch of the Templars, produced annually immense sums by means of the cost of receptions and contributions of every kind. A part of the total was employed in the expenses

---

[1] EDITOR'S NOTE: In the original publication, this was "Clement VIII," which was in all likelihood a typo. Monsignor Dillon was doubtlessly referring to Pope Clement XII, who issued the first papal condemnation of Freemasonry in the papal bull *In Eminenti* in 1738, and is cited by Pope Leo XIII in *Humanum Genus* (1884), which originally inspired Monsignor Dillon's lectures.

[2] EDITOR'S NOTE: Honoré-Gabriel Riqueti, Comte de Mirabeau (1749–91), was a French politician and orator who played a significant role in the National Assembly that governed France in the early days of the French Revolution. He died before the Revolution entered its more radical phase, but during his time, he was considered a voice of moderation and a supporter of constitutional monarchy.

[3] ORIGINAL CITATION: Vol. 6, page 67. EDITOR'S CITATION: Mirabeau's 1788 book, *De la monarchie Prussienne sous Frédéric le Grand* ["Of the Prussian Monarchy Under Frederick the Great"].

of the order, but another part, much more considerable, went into a general fund, of which no one, except the first amongst the brethren, knew the destination.

Cagliostro,[4] when questioned before the Holy Roman Inquisition, "confessed that he led his sumptuous existence thanks to the funds furnished him by the Illuminati. He also stated that he had a commission from Weishaupt to prepare the French Lodges to receive his direction."[5]

Discontent was thus sown broadcast amongst every class of the population. Masonic Lodges multiplied, inspired by the instructed emissaries of the remorseless Weishaupt. And the direct work of Freemasonry in subsequent events is manifest not only in the detailed prophecy of Cagliostro, founded on what he knew was decided upon; but is still more clearly evidenced by a second convent, held by the French Illuminati, where everything was arranged for the Revolution. The men prominent in this conclave were the men subsequently most active in every scene that followed. Mirabeau, Lafayette,[6] Fouchè,[7] Talleyrand,[8]

---

[4] EDITOR'S NOTE: See footnote 1 of chapter 8.

[5] ORIGINAL CITATION: See Deschamps, v., p. 129.

[6] EDITOR'S NOTE: Marquis de Lafayette (1757–1834) was a French aristocrat and soldier who fought with the Continental Army in America against the British, and was a leading advocate for constitutional monarchy during the French Revolution.

[7] EDITOR'S NOTE: Joseph Fouchè (1759–1820) was a French statesman who served in various capacities under the revolutionary and Napoleonic regimes. He was infamous for his vicious suppression of the Lyon insurrection in 1793 during the Reign of Terror.

[8] EDITOR'S NOTE: Charles-Maurice de Talleyrand (1754–1838) was a French statesman and diplomat who held office during the French Revolution, under Napoleon, during the restoration of the Bourbon monarchy, and under King Louis Philippe I.

Danton,[9] Marat,[10] Robespierre,[11] Cambacérès,[12] and in fact every foremost name in the subsequent convulsions of the country were not only Illuminati, but foremost amongst the Illuminati.[13] Some disappeared under their own guillotine; others outlived the doom of their fellows. Constantly, the men of the whole conspiracy had understandings and relations with each other. Weishaupt, at the safe distance of Coburg-Gotha, gave them his willing aid and that of the German Freemasons. This concert enabled them to float on every billow which the troubled sea of the Revolution caused to swell; and if they did not succeed in making France and all Europe a social ruin, such as that contemplated at Wilhelmsbad, it was from want of power, not from want of will. Position and wealth made many of them desire to conserve what the Revolution threw into their hands. But they remained under all changes of fortune Freemasons, as they

---

[9] Editor's Note: Georges Danton (1759–94) was a French revolutionary whose oratory is often credited for overthrowing the French monarchy and helping to establish the First Republic in 1792. He later resisted some of the more radical tendencies of the Committee of Public Safety during the Reign of Terror, for which he himself was guillotined.

[10] Editor's Note: Jean-Paul Marat (1743–93) was a French politician, physician, journalist, and radical leader of the Montagnard faction during the French Revolution. He was famously assassinated in his bath by a young woman who belonged to the more conservative Girondin faction, Charlotte Corday.

[11] Editor's Note: See footnote 1 of the preface.

[12] Editor's Note: Jean-Jacques-Régis de Cambacérès, Duke de Parme (1753–1824), was a French statesman and lawyer who served as a consul with Napoleon and then as archchancellor of the First Empire. He was instrumental in formulating the Napoleonic Code, also known as the Civil Code, in 1804.

[13] Editor's Note: See Monsignor Dillon's original footnote in appendix I provided at the end of this chapter.

and their successors are to this day. Perhaps, under the influence of oaths, of secret terror, and of the Sect, they dare not remain long otherwise. One or two individuals may drop aside; but some fatality or necessity keeps the leaders Illuminati always. They as a whole body remain ever the same, and recoil before political adversity, only to gather more strength for a future attack upon religion and order still wider and more fatal than the one which preceded it. They are not at any time one whit less determined to plunge the world into the anarchy and bloodshed they created at the French Revolution, than they were in 1789. On this point let one of themselves speak:

> I have been able to trace these attempts, made, through a course of fifty years, under the specious pretext of enlightening the world by the torch of philosophy, and of dispelling the clouds of civil and religious superstition which keep the nations of Europe in darkness and slavery. I have observed these doctrines gradually diffusing and mixing with all the different systems of Free Masonry; till, at last, *An Association has been formed* for the express purpose of *rooting out all the religious establishments, and overturning all the existing governments of Europe.* I have seen this Association exerting itself zealously and systematically, till it has become almost irresistible: and I have seen that the most active leaders in the French Revolution were members of this Association, and conducted their first movements according to its principles, and by means of its instructions and assistance, *formally*

requested and obtained: And lastly, I have seen that this Association still exists, still works in secret, and that not only several appearances among ourselves show that its emissaries are endeavoring to propagate their detestable doctrines among us, but that the Association has Lodges in Britain corresponding with the mother Lodge at Munich ever since 1784.

If all this were a matter of mere curiosity, and susceptible of no good use, it would have been better to have kept it to myself, than to disturb my neighbors with the knowledge of a state of things which they cannot amend. But if it shall appear that the minds of my countrymen are misled in the very same manner as were those of our continental neighbors—if I can show that the reasonings which make a very strong impression on some persons in this country are the same which actually produced the dangerous association in Germany; and that they had this unhappy influence solely because they were thought to be sincere, and the expressions of the sentiments of the speakers—if I can show that this was all a cheat, and that the Leaders of this Association disbelieved *every word* that they uttered, and every doctrine that they taught; and that their real intention was to abolish *all* religion, overturn every government, and make the world a general plunder and a wreck—[if I can show, that the principles which the Founder and Leaders of this Association held forth as the perfection of human virtue, and the most powerful and efficacious for forming the minds of men, and

making them good and happy, had no influence on
the Founder and Leaders themselves, and that they
were, almost without exception, the most insignifi-
cant, worthless, and profligate of men]; I cannot but
think that such information will make my countrymen hesitate a little, and receive with caution, and
even distrust, addresses and instructions which flatter
our self-conceit.[14]

I have quoted these words of Robison to show that as early as
1797 the connection between Freemasonry and the French
Revolution was well understood. Since then Louis Blanc,
and other Masonic writers, have gloried in the fact. "Our
end," said the celebrated Alta Vendita, to which I shall have
to refer presently, "is that of Voltaire and the French Revolution." In fact, what Freemasonry did in France, it now
labors, with greater caution, to effect on some future day
throughout the entire world. It then submitted, with perfect
docility, to a great military leader, who arose out of its own
work and principles. Such another leader will finally direct
its last efforts against God and man.

That leader will be Antichrist.

Appendix I (footnote 13)

It is commonly believed that the encyclopedists and philosophers were the only men who overturned by their writings

---

[14] ORIGINAL FOOTNOTE: Extracts from *Proofs of a Conspiracy*, by John
Robison, A.M., Professor of Natural Philosophy and Secretary to the
Royal Society of Edinburgh—The Third Edition, corrected, 1789. (pp.
11-13). EDITOR'S CITATION: We verified the text using a later edition of

altar and throne at the time of the Revolution. But, apart
from the facts that these writers were to a man Freemasons,
and the most daring and plotting of Freemasons, we have
abundant authority to prove that other Freemasons were
everywhere even more practically engaged in the same work.
Louis Blanc,[15] who will be accepted as an authority on this
point, thus writes:

> It is of consequence to introduce the reader into the
> mine which at that time was being dug beneath thrones
> and altars by revolutionists, very much more profound
> and active than the encyclopedists: an association
> composed of men of all countries, of all religions, of
> all ranks, bound together by symbolic bonds, engaged
> under an inviolable oath to preserve the secret of their
> interior existence. They were forced to undergo ter-
> rific proofs while occupying themselves with fantastic
> ceremonies, but otherwise practiced beneficence and
> looked upon themselves as equals though divided in
> three classes, apprentices, companions, and masters.
> Freemasonry consists in that. Now, on the eve of the
> French Revolution, Freemasonry was found to have
> received an immense development. Spread through-
> out the entirety of Europe, it seconded the medita-
> tive genius of Germany, agitated France silently, and

---

the same work, with the portion surrounded by double brackets included by us, but not originally by Monsignor Dillon. The source was John
Robison, *Proofs of a Conspiracy Against all the Religions and Governments
of Europe* (Philadelphia: T. Dobson, No. 41, South Second Street, and
W. Cobbet, No. 25, North Second Street, 1798), 12–13.

[15] EDITOR'S NOTE: Louis Blanc (1811–82) was a French socialist politician and historian.

presented everywhere the image of a society founded on principles contrary to those of civil society.

Monsignor Segur writes on this:

> See to what a point the reign of Jesus Christ was menaced at the hour the Revolution broke out. It was not France alone that it agitated, but the entirety of Europe. What do I say? The world was in the power of Masonry. All the lodges of the world came in 1781 to Wilhelmsbad by delegates from Europe, Asia, Africa, and America; from the most distant coasts discovered by navigators, they came, zealous apostles of Masonry. . . . They all returned penetrated with the Illuminism of Weishaupt, that is Atheism, and animated with the poison of incredulity with which the orators of the Convent had inspired them. Europe and the Masonic world were then in arms against Catholicity. Therefore, when the signal was given, the shock was terrible, terrible especially in France, in Italy, in Spain, in the Catholic nations which they wished to separate from the Pope and cast into schism, until the time came when they could completely de-Christianize them. This accounts well for the captivities of Pius VI and Pius VII. The Cardinals were dispersed, the Bishops torn from their Sees, the pastors separated from their flocks, the religious orders destroyed, the goods of the Church confiscated, the churches overturned, the convents turned into barracks, the sacred vessels stolen and melted down by sacrilegious avidity, the bells turned into money and cannons, scaffolds

erected everywhere, and victims in thousands, in hecatombs, especially from amongst the clergy; in one word, all the horrors summed up in the "Revolution," and the end, which was the great unerring power of all its actions, namely, to see Christ cast down from His altars to make way for the goddess called Reason.

CHAPTER 10

Napoleon and Freemasonry

*"Freemasonry welcomes, as we have seen, the Mahommedan,
the Indian, the Chinese, and the Buddhist, as well as the
Christian and the Jew. It designs to conquer all, as a means of
bringing all into the one level of Atheism and Communism.
. . . A universal monarchy is, in their idea, the most
efficacious means for arriving at a universal republic."*

—Monsignor Dillon

THE LEADER WHO arose out of the first French Revolution,
and whose military and diplomatic fame is still fresh in the
recollection of many of the present generation—that leader
was Napoleon Bonaparte.[1] In the days of his greatest prosperity, nothing was so distasteful to him as to be reminded of his
Jacobin past. He then wished to pose as another Charlemagne,[2]

---

[1] EDITOR'S NOTE: Napoleon Bonaparte (1769–1821) was a French soldier and statesman who rose to prominence during the French Revolution. He led many successful campaigns during the Revolutionary Wars
and eventually declared himself emperor of the French, reigning from
1804 to 1814. After his defeat at the Battle of Waterloo in 1815, he was
exiled by the British to the remote Atlantic island Saint Helena, where
he would eventually die.
[2] EDITOR'S NOTE: Charlemagne (747–814), sometimes known as
"Charles the Great," was a member of the Carolingian dynasty, king of
the Franks, and was coronated by Pope Leo III on Christmas day, 800,

or Rudolph of Hapsburg.[3] He wished to be considered the friend of religion, and of the Catholic religion in particular. He did something for the restoration of the Church in France, but it was as little as he could help. It, perhaps, prevented a more wholesome and complete reaction in favor of the true religious aspirations of the population. It was done grudgingly, parsimoniously, and meanly. And when it had been done, Napoleon did all he could to undo its benefits. He soon became the persecutor—the heartless, cruel, ungrateful persecutor of the Pontiff—and an opponent to the best interests of religion in France, and in every country which had the misfortune to fall under his sway.

The reason for all this was, that Napoleon had commenced his career as a Freemason, and a Freemason he remained in spirit and in effect to the end of his life. It is known that he owed his first elevation to the Jacobins, and that his earliest patron was Robespierre.[4] His first campaign in Italy was characterized by the utmost brutality which could gratify Masonic hatred for the Church. He suppressed the abodes of the consecrated servants of God, sacked churches, cathedrals, and sanctuaries, and reduced the Pope to the direst extremities. His language was the reflex of his acts and of his heart. His letters breathe everywhere the spirit of advanced Freemasonry, gloating over the wounds it had been able to inflict upon the Spouse of Christ.

---

as Holy Roman emperor—the first emperor to rule from western Europe since the fall of the Roman Empire in AD 476. His empire united the majority of western and central Europe.

[3] EDITOR'S NOTE: Rudolf I of Germany (1218–91) was the first king of Germany and Holy Roman emperor from the House of Hapsburg.

[4] EDITOR'S NOTE: See footnote 1 of the preface.

Yet this adventurer has, with great adroitness, been able to pass with many, and especially in Ireland, as a good Catholic. Because he was the enemy of England, or rather that England led by the counsels of Pitt and Burke[5] constituted herself the implacable enemy of the Revolution of which he was the incarnation and continuation, many opposed to England for political reasons, regard Bonaparte as a kind of hero. No one can doubt the military genius of the man, nor indeed his great general ability; but he was in all his acts what Freemasonry made him. He was mean, selfish, tyrannical, cruel. He was reckless of blood. He could tolerate or use the Church while that suited his policy. But he had from the beginning to the very end of his career that thorough indifference to her welfare, and want of belief in her doctrines, which an early and life-long connection with the Illuminati inspired.

Father Deschamps writes of him:

> Napoleon Bonaparte was in effect an advanced Free-mason, and his reign has been the most flourishing epoch of Freemasonry. During the reign of terror the Grand Orient ceased its activity. The moment Napoleon seized power the lodges were opened in every place.

I have said that the revolutionary rulers in France were all Illuminati—that is Freemasons of the most pronounced

---

[5]   EDITOR'S NOTE: William Pitt the Younger (1759–1806) was a British Tory statesman who served as prime minister from 1783 to 1801, and again from 1804 to 1806. Edmund Burke (1729–97) was an Anglo-Irish statesman, economist, and philosopher who served as a member of Parliament from 1766 to 1794, famously authoring *Reflections on the Revolution in France*, in which he condemned the French Revolution.

type—whose ultimate aim was the destruction of every existing religion and form of secular government, in order to found
an atheistic, social republic, which would extend throughout
the world and embrace all mankind. Freemasonry welcomes,
as we have seen, the Mahommedan, the Indian, the Chinese,
and the Buddhist, as well as the Christian and the Jew. It
designs to conquer all, as a means of bringing all into the
one level of Atheism and Communism. When, therefore, its
Directory, in their desire to get rid of Napoleon, planned the
expedition to Egypt and Asia, they meant the realization of
a part of this program, as well as the removal of a troublesome rival. A universal monarchy is, in their idea, the most
efficacious means for arriving at a universal republic. Once
obtained, the dagger with which they removed Gustavus III
of Sweden,[6] or the guillotine by which they rid France of
Louis XVI,[7] can at any moment remove Caesar and call in
Brutus. They are not the men to recoil before deeds of blood
for the accomplishment of their purposes.

Now Napoleon, who was, as Father Deschamps informs
us, a member of the lodge of the Templars, the extreme Illuminated lodge of Lyons, and had given proof of his fidelity
to Masonry in Italy, was the very man to extend the rule of
Republicanism throughout Asia. He appeared in Egypt with
the same professions of hypocritical respect for the Qur'an,
the Prophet, and Mahometanism, as he afterwards made
when it suited his policy for Catholicism. His address to the

---

[6]   EDITOR'S NOTE: Gustav III (1746–92) was the King of Sweden from
1771 until his assassination in 1792.
[7]   EDITOR'S NOTE: Louis XVI (1754–93) was the king of France from
1774 to 1792. He was beheaded as a traitor to the Revolution on January 21, 1793.

people of Egypt will prove this. It ran as follows, with true Masonic hypocrisy:

> Cadis, Chieks [Shieks], Imans, tell the people that we are the friends of true Mussulmen [Muslims]; that we respect more than the Mamelukes do, God, His Prophet, and the [Qur'an]. Is it not we who have destroyed the Pope, who wished that war should be made against the Mussulman? Is it not we who have destroyed the Knights of Malta, because these madmen thought that God willed them to make war upon the Mussulman? Is it not we who have been, in all ages the friends of the Grand Seigneur—may God fulfil his desires—and the enemy of his enemies. God is God, and Mahomet is his Prophet! Fear nothing above all for the religion of the Prophet, which I love.[8]

---

[8] EDITOR'S CITATION: The text of the *Proclamation to the Egyptians* issued by Napoleon in July 1798 is similar to, but somewhat different than, the text cited by Monsignor Dillon. It runs as follows:

> People of Egypt: You will be told by our enemies, that I am come to destroy your religion. Believe them not. Tell them that I am come to restore your rights, punish your usurpers, and raise the true worship of Mahomet. Tell them that I venerate, more than do the Mamelukes, God, His prophet, and the Koran. Tell them that all men are equal in the sight of God; that wisdom, talents, and virtue alone constitute the difference between them. And what are the virtues which distinguish the Mamelukes, that entitle them to appropriate all the enjoyments of life to themselves? If Egypt is their farm, let them show their lease, from God, by which they hold it. Is there a fine estate? It belongs to the Mamelukes. Is there a beautiful slave, a fine horse, a good house? All belong to the Mamelukes. But God is just and merciful, and

The cool hypocrisy of this address is manifested by a proclamation he made on that occasion to his own soldiers. The same proclamation also shows the value we may place on his protestations of attachment to, and respect for, the usages of Christianity. The following is a translation of it:

> Soldiers! the peoples with whom we are about to live are Mahommedan. The first article of their faith is this: "There is no God but God, and Mahomet is his Prophet." Do not contradict them. Act with them as you have acted with the Jews and with the Italians. Have the same respect for their Muftis and their Imans, as you have had for Rabbis and Bishops. Have for the ceremonies prescribed by the Alkoran [Qur'an], for the Mosques, the same tolerance you had for Convents, for Synagogues, and for the religion of Moses and of Jesus Christ.[9]

He hath ordained that the Empire of the Mamelukes shall come to an end. Thrice happy those who shall side with us; they shall prosper in their fortune and their rank. Happy they who shall be neutral; they will have time to become acquainted with us, and will range themselves upon our side. But woe, threefold woe, to those who shall arm for the Mamelukes and fight against us! For them there will be no hope; they shall perish.

Source: Tom Holmberg, "Napoleon's Addresses: The Egyptian Campaign," *The Napoleon Series*, January 2003, https://www.napoleon-series .org/research/napoleon/speeches/c_speeches2.html.

[9]   EDITOR'S CITATION: The text cited by Monsignor Dillon comes from Napoleon's *Proclamation to the Troops on Embarking for Egypt*, from June 1798.

Source: Tom Holmberg, "Napoleon's Addresses: The Egyptian Campaign," *The Napoleon Series*, January 2003, https://www.napoleon-series .org/research/napoleon/speeches/c_speeches2.html

We read in the correspondence of Napoleon I, published by order of Napoleon III,[10] what he thought of this proclamation at the very end of his career:

> After all, it was not impossible that circumstances might have brought me to embrace Islam [he said at St. Helena]. Could it be thought that the Empire of the East, and perhaps the subjection of the whole of Asia, was not worth a turban and pantaloons, for it was reduced to so much solely. We would lose only our breeches and our hats. I say that the army, disposed as it was, would have lent itself to that project undoubtedly, and it saw in it nothing but a subject for laughter and pleasantry. Meanwhile, you see the consequences. I took Europe by a back stroke. The old civilization was beaten down, and who then thought to disturb the destinies of our France and the regeneration of the world? Who had dared to undertake it? Who could have accomplished it?

Neither prosperity nor adversity changed Napoleon. He was a sceptic to the end. He said at St. Helena to Las Cases:

> Everything proclaims the existence of a God—that is not to be doubted—but all our religions are evidently the children of men. Why do these religions cry down one another, combat one another? Why has that been in all ages, and all places? It is because men are always men. It is because the Priests have always insinuated, slipped in lies and fraud everywhere.

---

[10] Original Citation: t. v., pp. 185, 191, 241.

Nevertheless [he continued], from the moment that I had the power, I had been eager to re-establish religion. I used it as the base and the root. It was in my eyes the support of good morality, of true principles, of good manners. I am assuredly far from being an Atheist; but I cannot believe all that they teach me in spite of my reason, under penalty of being deceitful and hypocritical. To say whence I come, what I am, where I go, is above my ideas. And nevertheless all that *is*, I am the watch which exists and does not know itself.

No doubt [he commented], but my spirit of mere doubt was, in my quality of Emperor, a benefit for the people. Otherwise how could I equally favor sects so contrary, if I had been dominated over by one alone? How could I preserve the independence of my thoughts and of my movements under the suggestions of a confessor who could govern me by means of the fear of hell? What an empire could not a wicked man, the most stupid of men, under that title of confessor, exercise over those who govern nations? I was so penetrated with these truths that I preserved myself well to act in such a manner, that, in as far as it lay in me, I would educate my son in the same religious lines in which I found myself.

Two months later the ex-Emperor said that from the age of thirteen he had lost all religious faith. Thiers[11] says that when Napoleon intended to proclaim himself Emperor, he wished to give the Masons a pledge of his principles, and that he did

---

[11] EDITOR'S NOTE: See footnote 5 of the preface.

this by killing the Duke d'Enghien.[12] He said, "They wish to destroy the Revolution in attacking it in my person. I will defend it, for I am the Revolution. I, myself—I, myself. They will so consider it from this day forward, for they will know of what we are capable."

A less brave but still more accomplished relative of his, Napoleon III, in his *Idees Napoleoniennes*, says:

> The Revolution dying, but not vanquished, left to Napoleon the accomplishments of its last designs. Enlighten the nations it would have said to him. Place upon solid bases the principal result of our efforts. Execute in extent that which I have done in depth. Be for Europe what I have been for France. That grand mission Napoleon accomplished even to the end.

When Napoleon obtained power, it was we know principally by means of the Illuminated Freemason Talleyrand.[13] By him and his confederates of the Illuminati, he was recalled from Egypt and placed in the way of its attainment. His brothers were—every one of them—deep in the secrets of the Sect. Its supreme hidden directory saw that a reaction had set in, which if not averted, would speedily lead to the return of the exiled Bourbons, and to the disgorgement of ill-gotten goods on the part of the revolutionists. As a lesser evil, therefore, and as a means of forwarding the unification of Europe which they had planned by his conquests, they placed supreme power in the hands of Bonaparte, and urged

---

[12] ORIGINAL CITATION: *Histoire du Consulat et de l'Empire*, iv. p. 14.

[13] EDITOR'S NOTE: See Monsignor Dillon's original footnote in appendix I provided at the end of this chapter. Also, see footnote 8 of chapter 9.

him on in his career, watching, at the same time, closely, their own opportunities for the development of the deadly designs of the Sect. Then, they obtained the first places in his Empire for themselves. They put as much mischief into the measures of relief given to conscience as they could. They established a fatal supremacy for secularism in the matter of education. They brought dissension between the Pope and the Emperor. They caused the second confiscation of the States of the Church. They caused and continued to the end the imprisonment of Pius VI.[14] They were at the bottom of every attack made by Napoleon while Emperor upon the rights of the Church, the freedom and independence of the Supreme Pontiff, and the well-being of religion.

But the chief mistake of Napoleon was the encouragement he gave to Freemasonry. It served his purpose admirably for a while, that is so long as he served the present and ultimate views of the conspiracy; for a conspiracy Masonry ever was and ever will be. Even if Cambacérès,[15] Talleyrand,[16] Fouchè,[17] and the old leaders of the Illuminati, whom he had taken into his confidence and richly rewarded, should be satisfied, there was a mass of others whom no reward could conciliate, and who, filled with the spirit of the Sect, were sure to be ever on the lookout for the means to advance the designs of Weishaupt and his inner circle. That inner

---

[14] EDITOR's NOTE: The original manuscript said Pius VII, but likely meant Pius VI (1717–99), who was pope from 1775 to 1799. He was taken prisoner by France in 1798 after refusing to renounce his temporal authority. He died as an exile in the French town of Valence.

[15] EDITOR's NOTE: See footnote 12 of chapter 9.

[16] EDITOR's NOTE: See footnote 8 of chapter 9.

[17] EDITOR's NOTE: See footnote 7 of chapter 9.

circle never ceased its action. It held the members of the Sect, whom it not only permitted but assisted to attain high worldly honors, completely in its power, and hence in absolute subjection. For them as well as for the humblest member of the secret conclave, the poisoned *aqua tofana*[18] and the dagger were ready to do the work of certain death should they lack obedience to those depraved fanatics of one diabolical idea, who were found worthy to be selected by their fellow conspirators to occupy the highest place of infamy and secret power. These latter scattered secretly amidst the rank and file of the lodges, hundreds of Argus-eyed, skilled plotters, who kept the real power of inner or high Masonry in the hands of its hidden masters.

Masonry from this secret vantage ground ceaselessly conspired during the Empire. It assisted the conquest of the victor of Austerlitz and Jena;[19] and if Deschamps, who quotes from the most reliable sources, is to be trusted, it actually did more for these victories than the great military leader himself. Through its instrumentality the resources of the enemies of Napoleon were never at hand, the designs of the Austrian and other generals opposed to him were thwarted, treason was rife in their camps, and information fatal to their designs was conveyed to the French commander. Masonry

---

[18] EDITOR'S NOTE: A strong poison originally created in Sicily around 1630.

[19] EDITOR'S NOTE: The Battle of Austerlitz—also known as the Battle of the Three Emperors—took place near the town of Austerlitz in the Austrian Empire on December 2, 1805. It resulted in a French victory over the Russian and Austrian Empires. The Battle of Jena-Auerstedt took place near the river Saale in modern Germany on October 14, 1806. It resulted in a French victory over Frederick William III of Prussia. Both battles were won by Napoleon Bonaparte.

was then on his side, and as now the secret resources of the Order, its power of hidden influence and espionage were placed at the disposal of the cause it served.

But when Masonry had reason to fear that Napoleon's power might be perpetuated; when his alliance with the Imperial Family of Austria, and above all, when the consequence of that alliance, an heir to his throne, caused danger to the universal republic it could otherwise assure itself of at his death; when, too, he began to show a coldness for the sect, and sought means to prevent it from the propagandism of its diabolical aims, then it became his enemy, and his end was not far off.[20] Distracting councils prevailed in his cabinet. His opponents began to get information regarding his movements, which he had obtained previously of theirs. Members of the sect urged on his mad expedition to Moscow. His resources were paralyzed; and he was, in one word, sold by secret, invisible foes into the hands of his enemies. In Germany, Weishaupt and his party, still living on in dark intrigue, prepared secretly for his downfall. His generals were beaten in detail. He was betrayed, hoodwinked, and finally led to his deposition and ruin. He then received with a measure, pressed down and overflowing, and shaken together, the gratitude of the father of lies, incarnate in Freemasonry, in the Illuminati, and kindred Atheist secret societies. Banished to Elba he was permitted to return to France only in order to meet the fate of an outcast and a prisoner upon the rock of St. Helena, where he died abandoned and persecuted by the dark Sect which had used, abused, and betrayed him.

---

[20] EDITOR'S NOTE: See Monsignor Dillon's original footnote in appendix II provided at the end of this chapter.

So it has continued, as we shall see, to use, to abuse, and to betray every usurper or despot whom it lures into its toils. We shall now glance at its action, the action of Freemasonry after the fall of Napoleon.

Appendix I (footnote 13)

Alexander Dumas in his *Memoires de Garibaldi*, first series, p. 34, tells us:

> Illuminism and Freemasonry, these two great enemies of royalty, and the adopted device of both of which was L.P.D., *lilia pedibus destrue* ["tread the lilies underfoot"], had a grand part in the French Revolution.
>
> Napoleon took Masonry under his protection. Joseph Napoleon was Grand Master of the Order, Joachim Murat [sic] second Master adjoint. The Empress Josephine being at Strasbourg, in 1805, presided over the fete [sic] for the adoption of the lodge of True Chevaliers of Paris. At the same time Eugene de Beauharnais was Venerable of the lodge of St. Eugene in Paris. Having come to Italy with the title of Viceroy, the Grand Orient of Milan named him Master and Sovereign Commander of the Supreme Council of the thirty-second grade, that is to say, accorded him the greatest honor which could be given him according to the Statutes of the Order. Bernadotte was a Mason. His son Oscar was Grand Master of the Swedish lodge. In the different lodges of Paris were successively initiated, Alexander, Duke of Wurtemburg; the Prince Bernard of Saxe-Weimar, even the Persian Ambassador,

Askeri Khan. The President of the Senate, Count de Lacipede, presided over the Grand Orient of France, which had for officers of honor the Generals Kellerman, Messina, and Soult. Princes, Ministers, Marshals, Officers, Magistrates, all the men, in fine, remarkable for their glory or considerable by their position, ambitioned to be made Masons. The women even wished to have their lodges into which entered Mesdames de Vaudemont, de Carignan, de Gerardin, de Narbonne and many other ladies.

Frere Clavel, in his picturesque history of Freemasonry, says that:

Of all these high personages the Prince Cambacérès was the one who most occupied himself with Masonry. He made it his duty to rally to Masonry all the men in France who were influential by their official position, by their talent, or by their fortune. The personal services which he rendered to many of the brethren, the *eclat* which he caused to be given to the lodges in bringing to their sittings by his example and invitations all those illustrious amongst the military and judicial professions and others, contributed powerfully to the fusion of parties and to the consolidation of the imperial throne. In effect under his brilliant and active administration the lodges multiplied *ad infinitum*. They were composed of the elect of French society. They became a point of reunion for the partisans of the existing and of passed regimes. They celebrated in them the feasts of the Emperor. They read in them the bulletins of his victories before they were made public by the press, and able men organized the enthusiasm which gradually took hold of all minds.

Appendix II (footnote 20)

Deschamps says that it was at this period that the order of the Templars (for Masonry is divided into any amount of rites which exercise one over the other a kind of influence in proportion to the members of the inner grades which they contain) was resuscitated in France. It publicly interred one of its members from the Church of St. Antoine. The funeral oration of Jacques Molay was publicly pronounced. Napoleon permitted this. The danger his permission created was foreseen, and M. de Maistre writes:

> A very remarkable phenomenon is that of the resuscitation of Freemasonry in France, so far, that a brother has been interred solemnly in Paris with all the attributes and ceremonies of the order. The Master who reigns in France does not leave it to be even suspected that such a thing can exist in France without his leave. Judging from his known character and from his ideas upon secret societies, how then can the thing be explained? Is he the Chief, or dupe, or perhaps the one and the other of a society which he thinks he knows, and which mocks him.

Illustrating these remarks we have the comments of M. Bagot in his *Codes des Franc-Maçons*, p. 183:

The Imperial Government took advantage of its omnipotence, to which so many men, so many institutions, yielded so complacently, in order to dominate over Masonry. The latter became neither afraid nor revolted. What did it desire in effect? To extend its empire—it permitted itself to become subject to despotism in order to become sovereign.

This gives us the whole reason why Masonry first permitted Napoleon to rule, then to reign, then to conquer, and finally to fall.

CHAPTER 11

Freemasonry after the
Fall of Napoleon

"There is nothing which Freemasonry dreads more than light. It is the one thing it cannot stand. Therefore, it has always taken care to provide itself with adepts and allies able to disarm public suspicion in its regard. Should outsiders endeavor to find out its real character and aims, it takes refuge at once under the semblance of puerility, of harmless amusement, of beneficence, or even of half-witted simplicity. It is content to be laughed at, in order not to be found out. But it is for all its puerility the same dangerous foe to Christianity, law, legitimacy, and order, which it proved itself to be before and during the first French Revolution, and which it will continue to be until the world has universal reason to know the depth, the malignity, and the extent of its remorseless designs."

—Monsignor Dillon

IT WOULD BE very interesting, if we had the time, to enter into the many intrigues of that very same body of Illuminati who had planned and executed the Revolution, then created successively the Directory, the Consulate, and the Empire in France, as they now posed in a new capacity as friends to the return of Monarchy in Europe generally. This they did for the purposes of the Freemasons, and in order to keep the power they wielded so long in their own hands, and in the hands of their party.

Now, I wish you to note, that Weishaupt, the father of the Illuminati, and the fanatical and deep director of all its operations, was even then living in power and security at Coburg-Gotha, and that his wily confederates were ministers in every court of Europe. Then, as now, the invincible determination with which they secreted their quality from the eyes of monarchs as well as of the general public, enabled them to pose in any character or capacity without fear of being detected as Freemasons, or at least as Illuminati. Since the reign of Frederick the Great,[1] they filled the Court of Berlin. Many minor German Princes continued to be Freemasons. The Duke of Brunswick[2] was the central figure in the first Masonic conspiracy, and though, with the hypocrisy common to the Sect, he issued a declaration highly condemnatory of his fellows, it is generally believed that he remained to the end attached to the "regeneration of humanity" in the interests of Atheism. The Court of Vienna was more or less Masonic since the reign of the wretched Joseph II.[3] Alexander of Russia was educated by La Harpe, a Freemason, and at the very period when called upon to play a principal part in the celebrated "Holy Alliance,"[4] he

---

[1]   EDITOR'S NOTE: See footnote 2 of chapter 3.

[2]   EDITOR'S NOTE: See footnote 2 of chapter 7.

[3]   EDITOR'S NOTE: See footnote 10 of chapter 5.

[4]   EDITOR'S NOTE: The Holy Alliance was an alliance spearheaded by Tsar Alexander I of Russia between Russia, Austria, and Prussia after the final defeat of Napoleon in 1815. It was formed on September 26, 1815, and its ostensible purpose was to promote the role of Christianity in national affairs.

was under the hidden guidance of others of the Illuminati. Fessler,[5] an apostate Austrian religious, the Councilor [sic] of Joseph II, after having abjured Christianity, remained, while professing a respect for religion, its most determined enemy. He founded what is known as the Tugendbund, a society by which German Freemasonry put on a certain Christian covering, in order more securely to outlive the reaction against Atheism, and to de-Christianize the world again at a better opportunity. The Tugendbund refused to receive Jews, and devised many other means to deceive Christians to become substantially Freemasons without incurring Church censures or going against ideas then adverse to the old Freemasonry, which, nevertheless, continued to exist as satanic as ever under Christian devices.

In France, the Illuminati of the schools of Wilhelmsbad and Lyons continued their machinations without much change of front, though they covered themselves with that impenetrable secrecy which the sect has found so convenient for disarming public suspicion while pursuing its aims. Possessing means of deceiving the outside world, and capable of using every kind of hypocrisy and ruse, the Freemasons of both France and Germany plotted at this period with more secure secrecy and success than ever. There is nothing which Freemasonry dreads more than light. It is the one thing it cannot stand. Therefore, it has always taken care to provide itself with adepts and allies able to disarm public suspicion in its regard. Should outsiders endeavor to find out its real character and aims, it takes refuge at once under the semblance of

---

[5] EDITOR'S NOTE: Ignaz Aurelius Fessler (1756–1839) was a Hungarian Freemason, churchman, politician, and historian.

puerility, of harmless amusement, of beneficence, or even of half-witted simplicity. It is content to be laughed at, in order not to be found out. But it is for all its puerility the same dangerous foe to Christianity, law, legitimacy, and order, which it proved itself to be before and during the first French Revolution, and which it will continue to be until the world has universal reason to know the depth, the malignity, and the extent of its remorseless designs.[6]

At the period of the reaction against Bonaparte it seems to have taken long and wise counsel. When Talleyrand[7] found that Weishaupt and the inner Masonry no longer approved of Napoleon's autocracy, he managed very adroitly that the Emperor should grow cold with him. He was thus free to take adverse measures against his master, and to prepare himself for the coming change. The whole following of Bonaparte recruited from the Illuminati were ready to betray him. They could compass the fall of the tyrant, but the difficulty for them was to find one suitable to put in his place. It was decreed in their highest council that whosoever should come upon the throne of France, should be as far removed as possible from being a friend to Catholicity or to any principle sustaining true religion. They therefore determined that, if at all possible, no member of the ancient House should reign; and as soon as the allied sovereigns who were for the most part non-Catholic, had crushed Napoleon, these French Masons demanded the Protestant and Masonic King of Holland for King in France. This failing,

---

[6] EDITOR's NOTE: See Monsignor Dillon's original footnote in appendix I provided at the end of this chapter.

[7] EDITOR's NOTE: See footnote 8 of chapter 9.

they contrived by Masonic arts to obtain the first places in the Provisional Government which succeeded Napoleon. They endeavored to make the most of the inevitable, and to rule the incoming Louis XVIII,[8] in the interests of their sect, and to the detriment of the Church and of Christianity.

Notwithstanding the fact that they had shown open hostility to himself and to his house, Louis XVIII, strange to say, favored the Illuminati. Talleyrand was made minister, and the other advanced Freemasons of the Empire—Sieyès,[9] Cambacérès,[10] Fouchè,[11] and the rest—obtained place and power. These men at once applied themselves to subvert the sentiment of reaction in favor of the monarchy and of religion. Soon, Louis XVIII gave the world the sad spectacle of a man prepared at their bidding to cut his own throat. He dissolved a Parliament of ultra-loyalists because they were too loyal to him. The Freemasons took care that his next Parliament should be full of its own creatures. They also wrung from the King, under the plea of freedom of the press, permission to deluge the country anew with the infidel and immoral publications of Voltaire, and his confederates, and

---

[8] EDITOR'S NOTE: Louis XVIII (1755–1824) was the king of France *de jure* beginning in 1795, but *de facto* from 1814 to 1824 after the initial fall of Napoleon, who returned from exile for a hundred days, and was finally defeated at the Battle of Waterloo in 1815. His reign initiated what is known as the Bourbon Restoration, the return of the House of Bourbon to the French monarchy.

[9] EDITOR'S NOTE: Emmanuel Joseph Sieyès (1748–1836) was a French Catholic *abbé* (term of honor), clergyman, and political writer. He was one of the chief political theorists of the French Revolution and held offices in the French Consulate (1799–1804) and the First Empire (1804–1815).

[10] EDITOR'S NOTE: See footnote 12 of chapter 9.

[11] EDITOR'S NOTE: See footnote 7 of chapter 9.

with newspapers and periodicals, which proved disastrous to his house, to royalty, and to Christianity, in France. These led before long to the attempt upon the life of the Duke of Berry, to the revolution against Charles X,[12] to the elevation of the son of the Grand Master, Egalité, as Constitutional King, and to all the revolutionary results that have since distracted and disgraced unfortunate France.

But much as Freemasonry effected in that country, it was not there but in peaceful Italy that its illuminated machinations produced the worst and most widespread fruits of death. We shall see this by a brief review of the Freemasonry which formed the kindred secret societies in Europe.

Appendix I (footnote 6)

At the Council of Verona, held by the European sovereigns in 1822, to guard their thrones and peoples from the revolutionary excesses which threatened Spain, Naples, and Piedmont, the Count Haugwitz, Minister of the King of Prussia, who then accompanied his master, made the following speech:

> Arrived at the end of my career, I believe it to be my duty to cast a glance upon the secret societies whose power menaces humanity today more than ever. Their history is so bound up with that of my life that I

---

[12] EDITOR'S NOTE: Charles X (1757–1836) was the king of France from 1824 to 1830. He was unable to harmonize the Bourbon tradition of the divine right of kings with France's more democratic post-Revolution spirit. He abdicated in 1830, eventually living in exile in Prague.

cannot refrain from publishing it once more and from giving some details regarding it.

My natural disposition, and my education, having excited in me so great a desire for information that I could not content myself with ordinary knowledge, I wished to penetrate into the very essence of things. But shadow follows light, thus an insatiable curiosity develops itself in proportion to the efforts which one makes to penetrate further into the sanctuary of science. These two sentiments impelled me to enter into the society of Freemasons.

It is well known that the first step which one makes in the order is little calculated to satisfy the mind. That is precisely the danger to be dreaded for the inflammable imagination of youth. Scarcely had I attained my majority, when, not only did I find myself at the head of Masonry, but what is more, I occupied a distinguished place in the chapter of high grades. Before I had the power of knowing myself, before I could comprehend the situation in which I had rashly engaged myself, I found myself charged with the superior direction of the Masonic reunions of a part of Prussia, of Poland, and of Russia. Masonry was, at that time, divided into two parts, in its secret labor. The first place in its emblems, the explanation of the philosopher's stone: Deism and non-Atheism was the religion of these Sectaries. The central seat of their labors was at Berlin, under the direction of the Doctor Zumdorf. It was not the same with the other part of which the Duke of Brunswick was the apparent chief. In open conflict between themselves, the two parties gave each other the hand in order to obtain the dominion of the world, to conquer thrones, to serve themselves with Kings as an order, such was their aim. It would be superfluous to explain to you in what manner, in my ardent curiosity, I came to know the secrets of the one party and of the other. The truth is, the secret of the two Sects is no longer a mystery for me. That secret is revolting.

It was in the year 1777, that I became charged with the direction of one part of the Prussian lodges, three or four years before the Convent of Wilhelmsbad and the invasion of the lodges by Illuminism. My action extended even over the brothers dispersed throughout Poland and Russia. If I did not myself see it, I could not give myself even a plausible explanation of the carelessness with which Governments have been able to shut their eyes to such a disorder, a veritable state within a State. Not only were the chiefs in constant correspondence, and employed particular cyphers, but even they reciprocally sent emissaries one to another. To exercise a dominating influence over thrones, such was our aim, as it had been of the Knight Templars.

I thus acquired the firm conviction that the drama commenced in 1788 and 1789, the French Revolution, the regicide with all its horrors, not only was then resolved upon, but was even the result of these associations and oaths, etc.

Of all my contemporaries of that epoch there is not one left. . . . My first care was to communicate to

William III all my discoveries. We came to the conclusion that all the Masonic associations, from the most humble even to the very highest degrees, could not do otherwise than employ religious sentiments in order to execute plans the most criminal, and make use of the first in order to cover the second. This conviction, which His Highness Prince William held in common with me, caused me to take the firm resolution of renouncing Masonry.

CHAPTER 12

Kindred Societies in Europe

"The Atheistic conspiracy, guided now by old, experienced revolutionists, saw also that the conservatism of the world which they had to destroy in order to dominate in its stead, could not be undermined without first taking away the foundation of Christian civilization upon which it rested, and which unquestionably, even for Christian schismatics and heretics, was the temporal and the spiritual authority of the Pope."

—Monsignor Dillon

WE HAVE SEEN that the use made of Freemasonry by the Atheists of the last century was a very elastic one. As it came from England it had all the qualities required by the remorseless revolutionists, who so eagerly and so ably employed it for their purposes. Its hypocritical professions of Theism, of acceptation of the Bible, and of beneficence; its terrible oaths of secrecy; its grotesque and absurd ceremonial, to which any meaning from the most silly to the deepest and darkest could be given; its ascending degrees, each one demanding additional secrets, to be kept not only from outsiders, but from the lower degrees; the death penalty for indiscretion or disobedience; the system of mystery capable of any extension; the hidden hierarchy; in a word, all its qualities could be improved and elaborated at will by the Infidels of the Continent who had made British Masonry their own.

Soon the strict subjection of all subordinate lodges to whatever Grand Orient or Mother Lodge they spring from, and on which they depend, and, above all, the complete understanding between the directors of the Masonic "powers," that is of the different rites into which the Masonry is divided, placed its entire government in a select ruling body, directed in turn by a small committee of the ablest conspirators, elected by and known to that body alone. The whole rank and file of Masonry receive their orders at present from this inner body, who are unknown to the mere masons of the lodges. The members of the committee deputed by the lodges are able to testify to the fact of the authenticity of the orders. Those who rule from the hidden recesses take care that these deputies shall be men worthy of confidence. A lodge, therefore, has its masters, it officers, and management; but its orders come through a channel that appears to be nothing, whereas it is everything in the movement of the whole mass. Thus it happens that the master of a lodge or the grand master of a province, or of a nation, whose high-sounding titles may make him seem to outsiders to be everything, is in reality often nothing at all in the actual government of Masonry. The real power rests with the hidden committee of direction, and confidential agents, who move almost invisibly amongst the officers and members of the lodges. These hidden agents of iniquity are vigilant spies, secret "wire pullers," who are seldom promoted to any office, but content themselves with the real power which they are selected to use with dexterity and care.

It was through this system that Weishaupt obtained the adoption of illuminated Masonry at the convent of Wilhelmsbad. Through the machinations of Knigge he obtained from the delegates there assembled the approval of his plan that the ultimate end of Freemasonry and all secret plotting should be:

1. Pantheism—a form of Atheism which flatters Masonic pride.
2. Communism of goods, women, and general concerns.
3. That the means to arrive at these ends should be the destruction of the Church, and of all forms of Christianity; the obliteration of every kind of supernatural belief; and,
4. Finally, the removal of all existing human governments to make way for a universal republic in which the Utopian ideas of complete liberty from existing social, moral, and religious restraint, absolute equality, and social fraternity, should reign.

When these ends should be attained, but not till then, the secret work of the Atheistic Freemasons should cease.

At the convent of Wilhelmsbad, Weishaupt had the means taken to carry out this determination. There Masonry became one organized Atheistic mass, while being still permitted to assume many fantastic shapes. The Knights Rosicrucian, the Templars, the Knights of Beneficence, the Brothers of Amity were strictly united to Illuminated Masonry. All could be reached through Masonry itself. All were placed under the same government. Masonry was made more elastic than ever. When, as in the cases of Ireland and Poland, an enslaved nationality should be found, which the supreme Invisible Directory wished to revolutionize, and when, at the same time, the existing respect for the words of the Vicar of Christ made Masonry hateful, a secret political society was ordered to be formed on the plan of Freemasonry, but with some other name. It too put on, after the example of Masonry itself, the semblance of zeal and respect for religion, but it was bound to have horrible oaths, ascending degrees, centers, the terrible death penalty for indiscretion or treason, to be, in essence, and in every sense, if not in name, a society identical with Freemasonry. The supreme direction of the Revolution was to contrive by sure means to have adepts high and powerful in its management; and the society was, even if founded to defend the Catholic religion, thus sure, sooner or later, to diverge from the Church and to become hostile to religion and to its ministers.

The Atheistic revolutionists of the Continent in the last century learned to perfection the art to effect this; and hence the ready assistance which men who were murdering priests in Paris and throughout France and Italy gave to the Catholics of Ireland in 1798. Was it to relieve the Catholics of Ireland from persecution, while they themselves were to a far more frightful extent oppressing the Catholic Church, the Catholic priesthood, Catholic religious, and Catholic people, for no other reason than the profession of the Catholic faith in France and Italy? By no means. They, at the very time, had already corrupted Irishmen. Some of these were open Infidels and others were Jacobite Freemasons of no particular attachment to any form of Christianity. They shared in Napoleon's indifference to religion, and were as ready to profess zeal for their Catholic fellow countrymen, as he and his soldiers were ready to profess "love" for the [Qur'an] and the Prophet in Egypt, or for St. Januarius in Naples.

But they and their leaders in Black Masonry knew that once they could unite even the very best and truest Catholic men in Ireland into a secret society on such lines as I have described, they would soon find an entrance for Atheism into the country. They would not be wanting in means to win recruits by degrees from the best-intentioned Catholics so bound by oaths, and so subjected to hidden influences. They were adepts at proselytism, especially amongst those who gave up liberty and will to unknown masters. If Irishmen, few indeed, thank God, but still Irishmen and Catholics, had lost their faith in France at the period of the Revolution, what could save the Irish Catholics in Ireland from the efforts and example of French and Irish Atheistic liberators? Catholics suffered terribly under the Protestant domination, but they nobly kept their faith through the whole of that dreadful period. Their condition was bad during the penal days, but if the French had obtained the mastery, even for a decade, at the Revolution, it would be worse, I believe, for the Faith and liberty of Irish Catholics, than the previous two centuries of heretical persecution. Providence, moved by the prayers of God's Mother, of St. Patrick, and of the innumerable host of Irish Saints and Martyrs, no doubt, saved the country; and the agency of the Atheists of France was carried to work the mischief it intended for Ireland upon other Catholic lands. It forced its tyranny very soon upon Italy, Spain, Portugal,

Switzerland, and the Rhenish provinces of Germany. That was bad enough, but it was not all. When the French revolutionary armies had departed from these countries, after the fall of Bonaparte, they left a deadly scourge that could not be removed behind them. That was the system of Atheistic organization of which we have been speaking, and which was not slow in producing its malignant fruits.

In Catholic Italy, where the scourge of the Revolution fell most heavily, the misfortune happened thus: The discontent consequent upon the multitude of political parties in that country gave the secret machinators of the Weishaupt school a splendid opportunity of again renewing their intrigues; while the miserable government of the Bourbons in France, in permitting Freemasonry to flourish, afforded its supreme direction an opportunity to assist them in many ways. Public opinion in Germany was unripe for any Atheism unless veiled under the hypocritical pretenses of the Tugendbund.[1]

In Italy, however, though religion was strong amongst all classes, the division of the country into small principalities caused the hopes of the revolutionists to be more sanguine than anywhere else, and the opportunity of dealing a blow at the Temporal Power of the Pope under the national pretext of a united Italy, was too great a temptation for the Supreme Masonic Directory to resist. Besides, it could not be forgotten by them, that in making past efforts the power of the Pope was the principal cause of their many failures. They

---

[1] EDITOR'S NOTE: The Tugendbund, or "League of Virtue," was a quasi-Masonic secret society established in 1808 after Napoleon's defeat of the Prussians at the Battle of Jena-Auerstedt. Its purpose was to revive Prussian national spirit after this defeat. See chapter 11.

rightly judged that the complete destruction of his temporal authority was essential to Atheism, and the first and most necessary step to their ultimate views upon all Christianity, and for the subjugation of the world to their sway. The Temporal Power was the stronghold, the rallying point of every legitimate authority in Europe. With a sure instinct of self-preservation, the Schismatical Lord of Russia, the Evangelical King of Prussia, the Protestant Governments of England, Denmark, and Sweden, as well as the ancient legitimate Catholic dynasties of Portugal, Austria, Bavaria, and Spain had determined at the Congress of Vienna on the restoration of the temporal dominions of the Pope.[2] The Conservatives of Europe, whether Catholic, Protestant, or Schismatic, felt that while the States of the Church were preserved intact to the Head of the Catholic religion, their own rights would remain unquestioned—that to reach themselves his rights should be first assailed.

The Atheistic conspiracy, guided now by old, experienced revolutionists, saw also that the conservatism of the world which they had to destroy in order to dominate in its stead, could not be undermined without first taking away the foundation of Christian civilization upon which it rested, and which unquestionably, even for Christian schismatics and heretics, was the temporal and the spiritual authority of the Pope. Having no idea of a divine preservation of the

---

[2] EDITOR'S NOTE: The Congress of Vienna assembled from September 1814 (after Napoleon's first abdication) to June 9, 1815 (shortly before Napoleon's final defeat at Waterloo). Its purpose was to reorganize Europe after the Napoleonic Wars, and produced what was up to that point the most comprehensive treaty ever seen in Europe. The European configuration reached by the congress lasted for more than forty years.

Christian religion, they judged that the destruction of the
Temporal Power would lead inevitably to the destruction of
the spiritual; and as experience proved that it would be useless to attempt to destroy both altogether, they then set all
their agencies at work to destroy the Temporal Power first.

They therefore determined to create and ferment to the
utmost extent a political discontent amongst the populations of the different states into which the Italian Peninsula was divided. Now this was a difficult task in the face of
the experience which the Italian people had gained of the
revolutions and constant political changes brought by the
French from the first attempt of the Republic to the last of
the Empire. The Congress of Vienna restored most of the
ancient Italian States as well as the States of the Church to
the legitimate rulers. Peace and prosperity beyond what had
been known for years began to reign in the Peninsula. The
mass of the people were profoundly contented. They were
more Catholic than ever, notwithstanding all that the revolutionary agents of France did to pervert them.

But there remained a dangerous fraction amidst the population not at all satisfied with the change which had so
much improved the nation generally. This fraction consisted
of those individuals and their children who benefited by the
revolutionary regime. They were the men who made themselves deputies in Rome, Naples, and elsewhere, and by the
aid of French revolutionary bayonets seized upon Church
property and became enriched by public spoliation. These
still remained revolutionary to the core. Then, there was the
interest effected by their party. And finally, there was that
uneasy class, educated by the many cheap universities of the

country in too great number, the sons of advocates and other professional men, who, tinged with liberalism, easily became the prey of the designing men who still remained addicted to the principles and were leagued in the secret organizations of Weishaupt and his fellow Atheists. Even one of these youths corrupted and excited to ambition by the adroit manipulation of these emissaries of Satan, still active, though more imperceptible than ever, would be sufficient to kindle a flame amongst his fellows capable of creating a wide discontent.

Aided then by such elements, already at hand for their purposes, Weishaupt and his hidden Directory determined to kindle such a flame of Revolution in Italy as, in its effects, should, before long, do more harm to religion and order than even the French Revolution had caused in its sanguinary but brief career. They effected this by the formation, on the darkest lines of "illuminated" Masonry, of the terrible Sect of the Carbonari.

CHAPTER 13

The Carbonari

"It [the Carbonari] considered, with that wisdom peculiar to the children of darkness, that the conspiracy against the Holy See was the conspiracy in permanence. It employed its principal intrigues against the State, the surroundings, and the very person of the Pontiff. It had hopes, by its manipulations, to gain eventually, even the Pope himself, to betray the Christian cause, and then it well knew the universe would be placed at its feet."

—Monsignor Dillon

IN THIS SECT, the whole of the hitherto recognized principles of organized Atheism were perfected and intensified. In it, from the commencement, a cunning hypocrisy was the means most used as the best calculated to lead away a people Catholic to the very core.

The first of the Carbonari of which we have any distinct notice appeared at a season when Atheism, directed by Weishaupt, was busy in forming everywhere secret associations for apparently no purpose other than political amelioration. He determined to try upon the peasantry of Italy the same arts which the French had intended for the Catholic peasantry of Ireland. The United Irishmen[1] were banded

---

[1] EDITOR'S NOTE: The Society of United Irishmen was founded in Oc-

together to demand amongst other things, Catholic Emancipation. Never had a people greater reason to rise against oppression than the Catholics of Ireland of that period. They were urged on to do so, however, by leaders who, in many instances, were not Catholic, and who had no political grievance, and whose aim was the formation in Ireland of an independent republic ruled, of course, by themselves, on the model of the one which was established then in France. That seemed to the Catholic the only way to get out of the heretical domination which had for such a lengthened period oppressed his country.

Now, the Carbonari of Italy were at first formed for a purpose identical with that of the United Irishmen. They conspired to bring back their national independence ruined by the French, the freedom of their religion, and their rightful Bourbon sovereign. With them it was made an indispensable obligation that each member should be not only a Catholic, but a Catholic going regularly to the Sacraments. They took for their Grand Master, Jesus Christ our Lord. But, as I have said before, it is impossible for a secret society having a death penalty for breach of secret, having ascending degrees, and bound to blind obedience to hidden masters, to remain any appreciable length of time without falling under the domination of the Supreme Directory of organized Atheism. It was so with Carbonarism, which, having started on the purest Catholic and loyal lines, soon ended in

tober 1791 during the French Revolution. Their goal was to achieve Roman Catholic emancipation and parliamentary reform. In 1794, the Society began negotiating with Revolutionary France for military aid, and later planned a rebellion against the British in 1798, which failed.

being the very worst kind of secret society which Infidelity had then formed on the lines of Masonry.

Very soon, Italian adepts in black Masonry invaded its ranks, the loudest in the protestation of religion and loyalty. Equally soon, these skilled, experienced, and unscrupulous veterans in dark intrigue obtained the mastery in its supreme direction, won over proselytes from fit conspirators, and had the whole association in their power. It was then easy to find abundant pretexts to excite the passions of the rank and file, to kindle hopes from revolution, to create political dissatisfaction, and to make the whole body of the Sect what it has actually become. Italian genius soon outstripped the Germans in astuteness; and as soon, perhaps sooner, than Weishaupt passed away, the supreme government of all the secret societies of the world was exercised by the Alta Vendita or highest lodge of the Italian Carbonari. The Alta Vendita ruled the blackest Freemasonry of France, Germany, and England; and until Mazzini[2] wrenched the scepter of the dark Empire from that body, it continued with consummate ability to direct the revolutions of Europe.

It [the Carbonari] considered, with that wisdom peculiar to the children of darkness, that the conspiracy against the Holy See was the conspiracy in permanence. It employed its principal intrigues against the State, the surroundings, and the very person of the Pontiff. It had hopes, by its

---

[2] EDITOR'S NOTE: Giuseppe Mazzini (1805–72) was a Genoese revolutionary, propagandist, and one of the founders of the secret revolutionary society known as "Young Italy" in 1832. He was one of the champions of Italian unity, known as the *Risorgimento*, which is Italian for "rising again." He was an uncompromising republican and completely rejected monarchy.

manipulations, to gain eventually, even the Pope himself, to betray the Christian cause, and then it well knew the universe would be placed at its feet. It left unmeasured freedom to the lodges of Masonry to carry on those revolutions of a political kind, which worked out the problems of the sect upon France, Spain, Italy, and other countries. It kept still greater movements to itself. The permanent instruction of this body to its adepts will give you an idea of its power, its policy, and its principles. It says—(proceed to next chapter)

CHAPTER 14

Permanent Instruction
of the Alta Vendita

"That which we ought to demand, that which we should seek and
expect, as the Jews expected the Messiah, is a Pope according to
our wants. . . . Seek out the Pope of whom we give the portrait.
You wish to establish the reign of the elect upon the throne of the
prostitute of Babylon? Let the clergy march under your banner
in the belief always that they march under the banner of the
Apostolic Keys. You wish to cause the last vestige of tyranny and
of oppression to disappear? Lay your nets like Simon Barjona.
Lay them in the depths of sacristies, seminaries, and convents,
rather than in the depths of the sea, and if you will precipitate
nothing you will give yourself a draught of fishes more miraculous
than his. The fisher of fishes will become a fisher of men. You
will bring yourselves as friends around the Apostolic Chair. You
will have fished up a Revolution in Tiara and Cope, marching
with Cross and banner—a Revolution which needs only to be
spurred on a little to put the four quarters of the world on fire."

—*Permanent Instruction of the Alta Vendita*

[THE TEXT OF the *Permanent Instruction of the Alta Vendita*
reads as follows]:

Ever since we have established ourselves as a body of action, and that order has commenced to reign in the bosom of the most distant lodge, as in that one nearest the center of action, there is one thought which has profoundly occupied the men who aspire to universal regeneration. That is the thought of the enfranchisement of Italy, from which must one day come the enfranchisement of the entire world, the fraternal republic, and the harmony of humanity. That thought has not yet been seized upon by our brethren beyond the Alps. They believe that revolutionary Italy can only conspire in the shade, deal some strokes of the poniard to *sbirri*[1] and traitors, and tranquilly undergo the yoke of events which take place beyond the Alps for Italy, but without Italy. This error has been fatal to us on many occasions. It is not necessary to combat it with phrases which would be only to propagate it. It is necessary to kill it by facts. Thus, amidst the cares which have the privilege of agitating the minds of the most vigorous of our lodges, there is one which we ought never to forget.

The Papacy has at all times exercised a decisive action upon the affairs of Italy. By the hands, by the voices, by the pens, by the hearts of its innumerable bishops, priests, monks, nuns, and people in all latitudes, the Papacy finds devotedness without end ready for martyrdom, and that to enthusiasm. Everywhere, whenever it pleases to call upon them, it has friends ready to die or lose all for its cause. This is an immense

---

[1]   EDITOR'S NOTE: Italian slang for the police.

leverage which the Popes alone have been able to appreciate to its full power, and as yet they have used it only to a certain extent. Today there is no question of reconstituting for ourselves that power, the prestige of which is for the moment weakened. Our final end is that of Voltaire and of the French Revolution, the destruction forever of Catholicism and even of the Christian idea which, if left standing on the ruins of Rome, would be the resuscitation of Christianity later on. But to attain more certainly that result, and not prepare ourselves with gaiety of heart for reverses which adjourn indefinitely, or compromise for ages the success of a good cause, we must not pay attention to those braggarts of Frenchmen, those cloudy Germans, those melancholy Englishmen, all of whom imagine they can kill Catholicism, now with an impure song, then with an illogical deduction; at another time, with a sarcasm smuggled in like the cottons of Great Britain. Catholicism has a life much more tenacious than that. It has seen the most implacable, the most terrible adversaries, and it has often had the malignant pleasure of throwing holy water on the tombs of the most enraged. Let us permit, then, our brethren of these countries to give themselves up to the sterile intemperance of their anti-Catholic zeal. Let them even mock at our Madonnas and our apparent devotion. With this passport we can conspire at our ease, and arrive little by little at the end we have in view.

Now the Papacy has been for seventeen centuries inherent to the history of Italy. Italy cannot breathe or move without the permission of the Supreme Pastor. With him she has the hundred arms of Briareus, without him she is condemned to a pitiable impotence. She has nothing but divisions to foment, hatreds to break out, and hostilities to manifest themselves from the highest chain of the Alps to the lowest of the Apennines. We cannot desire such a state of things. It is necessary, then, to seek a remedy for that situation. The remedy is found. The Pope, whoever he may be, will never come to the secret societies. It is for the secret societies to come first to the Church, in the resolve to conquer the two.

The work which we have undertaken is not the work of a day, nor of a month, nor of a year. It may last many years, a century perhaps, but in our ranks the soldier dies and the fight continues.

We do not mean to win the Popes to our cause, to make them neophytes of our principles, and propagators of our ideas. That would be a ridiculous dream, no matter in what manner events may turn. Should cardinals or prelates, for example, enter, willingly or by surprise, in some manner, into a part of our secrets, it would be by no means a motive to desire their elevation to the See of Peter. That elevation would destroy us. Ambition alone would bring them to apostasy from us. The needs of power would force them to immolate us. That which we ought to demand, that which we should seek and expect, as the Jews expected the Messiah, is a Pope according to our wants. Alexander VI, with all his private crimes, would not suit us, for he never erred in religious matters. Clement XIV, on the contrary, would suit us from head to foot. Borgia was a libertine, a true sensualist of the eighteenth century strayed into the fifteenth. He has been anathematized, notwithstanding his vices, by all the voices of philosophy and incredulity, and he owes that anathema to the vigor with which he defended the Church. Ganganelli[2] gave himself over, bound hand and foot, to the ministers of the Bourbons, who made him afraid, and to the incredulous who celebrated his tolerance, and Ganganelli is become a very great Pope. He is almost in the same condition that it is necessary for us to find another, if that be yet possible. With that we should march more surely to the attack upon the Church than with the pamphlets of our brethren in France, or even with the gold of England. Do you wish to know the reason? It is because by that we should have no more need of the vinegar of Hannibal, no more need of the powder of cannon, no more need even of our arms: We have the little finger of the successor of St. Peter engaged in the plot, and that little finger is of more value for our crusade than all the Innocents, the Urbans, and the St. Bernards of Christianity.

We do not doubt that we shall arrive at that supreme term of all our efforts; but when? but how? The unknown does not yet manifest itself. Nevertheless, as nothing should separate us from the plan traced out; as, on the contrary, all things should tend

---

[2] EDITOR'S NOTE: "Ganganelli" was the surname of Pope Clement XIV (1705–74), who reigned from 1769 to 1774.

to it—as if success were to crown the work scarcely sketched out tomorrow—we wish in this instruction which must rest a secret for the simple initiated, to give to those of the Supreme Lodge, councils with which they should enlighten the universality of the brethren, under the form of an instruction or memorandum. It is of special importance, and because of a discretion, the motives of which are transparent, never to permit it to be felt that these counsels are orders emanating from the Alta Vendita. The clergy is put too much in peril by it, that one can at the present hour permit oneself to play with it, as with one of these small affairs or of these little princes upon which one need but blow to cause them to disappear.

Little can be done with those old cardinals or with those prelates, whose character is very decided. It is necessary to leave them as we find them, incorrigible, in the school of Consalvi, and draw from our magazines of popularity or unpopularity the arms which will render useful or ridiculous the power in their hands. A word which one can ably invent and which one has the art to spread amongst certain honorable chosen families by whose means it descends into the cafes and from the cafes into the streets; a word can sometimes kill a man. If a prelate comes to Rome to exercise some public function from the depths of the provinces, know presently his character, his antecedents, his qualities, his defects above all things. If he is in advance, a declared enemy, an Albani, a Pallotta, a Bernetti, a Delia Genga, a Riverola, envelope him in all the snares which you can place beneath his feet; create for him one of those reputations which will frighten little children and old women; paint him cruel and sanguinary; recount, regarding him, some traits of cruelty which can be easily engraved in the minds of people. When foreign journals shall gather for us these recitals, which they will embellish in their turn (inevitably because of their respect for truth), show, or rather cause to be shown, by some respectable fool those papers where the names and the excesses of the personages implicated are related. As France and England, so Italy will never be wanting in facile pens which know how to employ themselves in these lies so useful to the good cause. With a newspaper, the language of which they do not understand, but in which they will see the name of their delegate or judge, the people have no need of other proofs. They are in the infancy of liberalism; they believe in liberals, as, later on, they will believe in us, not knowing very well why.

Crush the enemy whoever he may be; crush the powerful by means of lies and calumnies; but especially crush him in the egg. It is to the youth we must go. It is that which we must seduce; it is that which we must bring under the banner of the secret societies. In order to advance by steps, calculated but sure, in that perilous way, two things are of the first necessity. You ought to have the air of being simple as doves, but you must be prudent as the serpent. Your fathers, your children, your wives themselves, ought always to be ignorant of the secret which you carry in your bosoms. If it pleases you, in order the better to deceive the inquisitorial eye, to go often to confession, you are as by right authorized to preserve the most absolute silence regarding these things. You know that the least revelation, that the slightest indication escaped from you in the tribunal of penance, or elsewhere, can bring on great calamities and that the sentence of death is already pronounced upon the revealer, whether voluntary or involuntary.

Now then, in order to secure to us a Pope in the manner required, it is necessary to fashion for that Pope a generation worthy of the reign of which we dream. Leave on one side old age and middle life, go to the youth, and, if possible, even to infancy. Never speak in their presence a word of impiety or impurity. *Maxima debetur puero reverentia* ["The greatest respect is due the young"]. Never forget these words of the poet,[3] for they will preserve you from licenses which it is absolutely essential to guard against for the good of the cause. In order to reap profit at the home of each family, in order to give yourself the right of asylum at the domestic hearth, you ought to present yourself with all the appearance of a man grave and moral. Once your reputation is established in the colleges, in the gymnasiums, in the universities, and in the seminaries—once that you shall have captivated the confidence of professors and students, so act that those who are principally engaged in the ecclesiastical

---

[3]   EDITOR'S NOTE: This Latin phrase comes from the Roman poet Juvenal's *Satire XIV*.

state should love to seek your conversation. Nourish their souls with the splendors of ancient Papal Rome. There is always at the bottom of the Italian heart a regret for Republican Rome. Excite, enkindle those natures so full of warmth and of patriotic fire. Offer them at first, but always in secret, inoffensive books, poetry resplendent with national emphasis; then little by little you will bring your disciples to the degree of cooking desired. When upon all the points of the ecclesiastical state at once, this daily work shall have spread our ideas as the light, then you will be able to appreciate the wisdom of the counsel in which we take the initiative.

Events, which in our opinion, precipitate themselves too rapidly, go necessarily in a few months' time to bring on an intervention of Austria. There are fools who in the lightness of their hearts please themselves in casting others into the midst of perils, and, meanwhile, there are fools who at a given hour drag on even wise men. The revolution which they meditate in Italy will only end in misfortunes and persecutions. Nothing is ripe, neither the men nor the things, and nothing shall be for a long time yet; but from these evils you can easily draw one new chord, and cause it to vibrate in the hearts of the young clergy. That is the hatred of the stranger. Cause the German to become ridiculous and odious even before his foreseen entry. With the idea of the Pontifical supremacy, mix always the old memories of the wars of the priesthood and the Empire. Awaken the smoldering passions of the

Guelphs and the Ghibellines, and thus you will obtain for yourselves the reputation of good Catholics and pure patriots.

That reputation will open the way for our doctrines to pass to the bosoms of the young clergy, and go even to the depths of convents. In a few years the young clergy will have, by the force of events, invaded all the functions. They will govern, administer, and judge. They will form the council of the Sovereign. They will be called upon to choose the Pontiff who will reign; and that Pontiff, like the greater part of his contemporaries, will be necessarily imbued with the Italian and humanitarian principles which we are about to put in circulation. It is a little grain of mustard which we place in the earth, but the sun of justice will develop it even to be a great power, and you will see one day what a rich harvest that little seed will produce.

In the way which we trace for our brethren there are found great obstacles to conquer, difficulties of more than one kind to surmount. They will be overcome by experience and by perspicacity; but the end is beautiful. What does it matter to put all the sails to the wind in order to attain it. You wish to revolutionize Italy? Seek out the Pope of whom we give the portrait. You wish to establish the reign of the elect upon the throne of the prostitute of Babylon? Let the clergy march under your banner in the belief always that they march under the banner of the Apostolic Keys. You wish to cause the last vestige of tyranny and of oppression to disappear? Lay your nets like Simon

Barjona. Lay them in the depths of sacristies, semi-naries, and convents, rather than in the depths of the sea, and if you will precipitate nothing you will give yourself a draught of fishes more miraculous than his. The fisher of fishes will become a fisher of men. You will bring yourselves as friends around the Apostolic Chair. You will have fished up a Revolution in Tiara and Cope, marching with Cross and banner—a Revolution which needs only to be spurred on a little to put the four quarters of the world on fire.

Let each act of your life tend then to discover the Philosopher's Stone. The alchemists of the middle ages lost their time and the gold of their dupes in the quest of this dream. That of the secret societies will be accomplished for the most simple of reasons, because it is based on the passions of man. Let us not be dis-couraged then by a check, a reverse, or a defeat. Let us prepare our arms in the silence of the lodges, dress our batteries, flatter all passions the most evil and the most generous, and all lead us to think that our plans will succeed one day above even our most improbable calculations.

This document reveals the whole line of action followed since by the Italian Revolutionists. It gives also a fair insight into tactics with which other European countries have been made familiar by Freemasonry generally.

But we are in possession of what appears to me a still more striking document, written for the benefit of the Pied-montese lodges of the Carbonari, by one of the Alta Ven-dita, whose pseudonym was Piccolo Tigre—Little Tiger. I may here mention that the custom of taking these fanciful appellations has been common to the secret societies from the very beginning. Arouet became Voltaire, the notorious Baron Knigge was called Philo, Baron Dittfort was called Minos, a custom adopted by the principal chiefs of the dark Atheistic conspiracy then and since. The first leader or grand chief of the Alta Vendita was a corrupt Italian nobleman who took the name of Nubius. From such documents as he, before his death, managed, in revenge for being sacrificed by the party of Mazzini,[4] as we shall see, to have communicated to the authorities of Rome; or which were found by the vigilance of the Roman detective police; we find that his funds, and the funds for carrying on the deep and dark conspiracy in which he and his confederates were engaged, came chiefly from rich German Jews. Jews, in fact, from the commencement, played always a prominent part in the conspiracies of Atheism. They do so still.

Piccolo Tigre, who seems to have been the most active agent of Nubius, was a Jew. He travelled under the appearance of an itinerant banker and jeweler. This character of moneylender or usurer disarmed suspicion regarding himself and such of his confederates as he had occasion to call upon in his peregrinations [long meandering journeys]. Of course he had the protection of the Masonic body everywhere. The most desperate revolutionists were generally the most desperate scoundrels otherwise. They were gamblers, spendthrifts, and the very class with which a usurious Jew would be expected to have money dealings. Piccolo Tigre thus travelled safely, and brought safely to the superior lodges of

---

4   EDITOR'S NOTE: See footnote 2 of chapter 13.

the Carbonari such instructions as the Alta Vendita thought proper to give.

In the document referred to, which I shall now read for you, it will be seen how anxious the Secret Directory were to make use of the common form of Masonry notwithstanding the contempt they had for the *bons vivants* who only learned from the craft how to become drunkards and liberals. Beyond the Masons, and unknown to them, though formed generally from them, lay the deadly secret conclave which, nevertheless, used and directed them for the ruin of the world and of their own selves. The next chapter contains a translation of the document, or "instructions," as it was called, addressed by Piccolo Tigre to the Piedmontese lodges of the Carbonari.

CHAPTER 15

Letter of Piccolo Tigre

*"Content yourselves to prowl about the Catholic sheepfold,
but as good wolves seize in the passage the first lamb who
offers himself in the desired conditions. . . . It is of absolute
necessity to de-Catholicize the world. . . . The Revolution
in the Church is the Revolution en permanence. It is the
necessary overthrowing of thrones and dynasties."*

—*Letter of Piccolo Tigre*

[THE TEXT OF the *Letter of Piccolo Tigre* reads as follows]:

In the impossibility in which our brothers and friends
find themselves, to say, as yet, their last word, it has
been judged good and useful to propagate the light
everywhere, and to set in motion all that which aspires
to move. For this reason we do not cease to recommend to you, to affiliate persons of every class to every
manner of association, no matter of what kind, *only
provided that mystery and secrecy should be the dominant characteristics.* All Italy is covered with religious
confraternities, and with penitents of diverse colors.
Do not fear to slip in some of your people into the
very midst of these flocks, led as they are by a stupid

devotion. Let our agents study with care the *personnel* of these confraternity men, and they will see that little by little, they will not be wanting in a harvest. Under a pretext the most futile, but never political or religious, create by yourselves, or, better yet, cause to be created by others, associations, having commerce, industry, music, the fine arts, etc., for object [sic].[1] Reunite in one place or another—in the sacristies or chapels even—these tribes of yours as yet ignorant: put them under the pastoral staff of some virtuous priest, well known, but credulous and easy to be deceived. Then infiltrate the poison into those chosen hearts; infiltrate it in little doses, and as if by chance. Afterwards, upon reflection, you will yourselves be astonished at your success.

The essential thing is to isolate a man from his family, to cause him to lose his morals. He is sufficiently disposed by the bent of his character to flee from household cares, and to run after easy pleasures and forbidden joys. He loves the long conversations of the *café* and the idleness of shows. Lead him along, sustain him, give him an importance of some kind or other; discreetly teach him to grow weary of his daily labors, and by this management, after having separated him from his wife and from his children, and after having shown him how painful are all his duties, you will then excite in him the desire of another existence. Man is a born rebel. Stir up the desire of rebellion until it

---

[1] EDITOR'S NOTE: See Monsignor Dillon's original footnote in appendix I provided at the end of this chapter.

becomes a conflagration, but in such a manner that the conflagration may not break out. This is a preparation for the grand work that you should commence. When you shall have insinuated into a few souls disgust for family and for religion (the one nearly always follows in the wake of the other), let fall some words which will provoke the desire of being affiliated to the nearest lodge. That vanity of the citizen or the burgess, to belong to Freemasonry, is something so common and so universal that it always makes me wonder at human stupidity.

I begin to be astonished at not seeing the entire world knock at the gates of all the Venerables, and demand from these gentlemen the honor to be one of the workmen chosen for the reconstruction of the Temple of Solomon. The prestige of the unknown exercises upon men a certain kind of power, that they prepare themselves with trembling for the phantasmagoric trials of the initiation and of the fraternal banquet.

To find oneself a member of a lodge, to feel oneself called upon to guard from wife and children a secret which is never confided to you, is for certain natures a pleasure and an ambition. The lodges, today, can well create gourmands, they will never bring forth citizens. There is too much dining amongst right worshipful and right reverend brethren of all the Ancients. But they form a place of depot, a kind of stud (breeding ground), a center through which it is necessary to pass before coming to us. The lodges form but a relative evil, an evil tempered by a false philanthropy, and by songs yet more false as in France. All that is too pastoral and too gastronomic; but it is an object which it is necessary to encourage without ceasing. In teaching a man to raise his glass to his lips you become possessed of his intelligence and of his liberty, you dispose of him, turn him round about, and study him. You divine his inclinations, his affections, and his tendencies; then, when he is ripe for us, we direct him to the secret society of which Freemasonry can be no more than the antechamber.

The Alta Vendita desires that under one pretense or another, as many princes and wealthy persons as possible should be introduced into the Masonic lodges. Princes of a sovereign house, and those who have not the legitimate hope of being kings by the grace of God, all wish to be kings by the grace of a Revolution.

The Duke of Orleans is a Freemason, the Prince of Carignan was one also. There are not wanting in Italy and elsewhere, those amongst them, who aspire to the modest-enough honors of the symbolic apron and trowel. Others of them are disinherited and proscribed.

Flatter all of their number who are ambitious of popularity; monopolize them for Freemasonry. The Alta Vendita will afterwards see what it can do to utilize them in the cause of progress. A prince who has not a kingdom to expect, is a good fortune for us. There are many of them in that plight. Make Freemasons of them. The lodge will conduct them to Carbonarism.

A day will come, perhaps, when the Alta Vendita will deign to affiliate them. While awaiting they will serve as birdlime for the imbeciles, the intriguing, the *bourgeoisie*, and the needy. These poor princes will serve our ends, while thinking to labor only for their own. They form a magnificent sign board, and there are always fools enough to be found who are ready to compromise themselves in the service of a conspiracy, of which some prince or other seems to be the ringleader.

Once that a man, that a prince, that a prince especially, shall have commenced to grow corrupt, be persuaded that he will hardly rest upon the declivity. There is little morality even amongst the most moral of the world, and one goes fast in the way of that progress. Do not then be dismayed to see the lodges flourish, while Carbonarism recruits itself with difficulty. It is upon the lodges that we count to double our ranks. They form, without knowing it, our preparatory novitiate. They discourse without end upon the dangers of fanaticism, upon the happiness of social equality, and upon the grand principles of religious liberty. They launch amidst their feastings thundering anathemas against intolerance and persecution. This is positively more than we require to make adepts. A man imbued with these fine things is not very far from us. There is nothing more required than to enlist him. The law of social progress is there, and all there. You need not take the trouble to seek it elsewhere.

In the present circumstances never lift the mask. Content yourselves to prowl about the Catholic sheepfold, but, as good wolves, seize in the passage the first lamb who offers himself in the desired conditions.

The burgess has much of that which is good for us, the prince still more. For all that, these lambs must not be permitted to turn themselves into foxes like the infamous Carignan. The betrayal of the oath is a sentence of death; and all those princes whether they are weak or cowardly, ambitious or repentant, betray us, or denounce us. As good fortune would have it, they know little, in fact not anything, and they cannot come upon the trace of our true mysteries.

Upon the occasion of my last journey to France, I saw with profound satisfaction that our young initiated exhibited an extreme ardor for the diffusion of Carbonarism; but I also found that they rather precipitated the movement a little. As I think, they converted their religious hatred too much into a political hatred.

The conspiracy against the Roman See should not confound itself with other projects. We are exposed to see germinate in the bosom of secret societies, ardent ambitions; and the ambitious, once masters of power, may abandon us. The route which we follow is not as yet sufficiently well traced so as to deliver us up to intriguers and tribunes.

It is of absolute necessity to de-Catholicize the world. And an ambitious man, having arrived at his end, will guard himself well from seconding us. The Revolution in the Church is the Revolution *en permanence*. It is the necessary overthrowing of thrones and dynasties.

Now an ambitious man cannot really wish these things. We see higher and farther. Endeavour, therefore, to act for us, and to strengthen us. Let us not conspire except against Rome. For that, let us serve ourselves with all kinds of incidents; let us put to profit every kind of eventuality. Let us be principally on our guard against the exaggerations of zeal. A good hatred, thoroughly cold, thoroughly calculated, thoroughly profound, is of more worth than all these artificial fires and all these declamations of the platform. At Paris they cannot comprehend this, but in London I have seen men who seized better upon our plan, and who associated themselves to us with more fruit. Considerable offers have been made to me. Presently we shall have a printing establishment at Malta placed at our disposal. We shall then be able with impunity, with a sure stroke, and under the British flag, to scatter from one end of Italy to the other, books, pamphlets, etc., which the Alta Vendita shall judge proper to put in circulation.

This document was issued in 1822. Since then, the instructions it gives have been constantly acted upon in the lodges of Carbonarism, not only in Italy but everywhere else. "Prowl about the Catholic sheepfold and seize the first lamb that presents himself in the required conditions." This, and the order to get into Catholic confraternities, were as well executed by the infamous Carey[2] under the influence of

---

[2] EDITOR'S NOTE: William Paulet Carey (1789–1839) was an Irish art critic and publicist who joined the Society of United Irishmen. He later faced charges of sedition, and testified in the case against them.

"No. 1," as they were by any Italian conspirator and assassin, under the personal inspiration of Piccolo Tigre. Carey, the loud-spoken Catholic—the Catholic who had Freemason or Orange friends able to assist him in the truly Masonic way of getting members of the craft as Town-Councilors, or Aldermen, or Members of Parliament—was, we now know, a true secret-society hypocrite of the genuine Italian type. He prowled with effect round the Catholic sheep-fold. He joined "with fruit" the confraternities of the Church. Well may we pray that God may guard from such satanic influences the noble, generous-hearted, faithful young men of Ireland at home and in all the lands of their vast colonization. The scoundrel that presents the "knife" or the "prayer-book" ready to swear them in, is a murderer in intention, and in effect whenever he dares to be, with a chance of impunity. He is ready to drag them in the toils of the Carbonari, for whether a secret society be Irish, English, or American; whether Fenian or Invincible, no matter by what name it may be called, it is still black Masonry—Carbonarism pure and simple. And the lost hypocrite and assassin who tempts incautious youth, under the pretense of patriotism, to join any such society, is ever, like Carey, as ready to betray as he is to "swear in" his victim.

Another curious instruction given by the Alta Vendita to the Carbonari of the lower lodges, is the way to catch a priest and make the good, simple man unconsciously aid the designs of the revolutionary sectaries. In the permanent instruction of the Alta Vendita, given to all the lodges, you will recollect the passage I read for you relative to the giving of bad names to faithful Prelates who may be too knowing

or too good to do the work of the Carbonari against conscience, God, and the souls of men. "Ably find out the words
and the ways to make them unpopular" is the sum of that
advice. Has it not been attempted amongst ourselves?

But the main advice of the permanent instruction is to
seduce the clergy. The ecclesiastic to be deceived is to be led
on by patriotic ardor. He is to be blinded by a constant,
though, of course, false, and fatal popularity. He is to be made
believe that his course, so very pleasant to flesh and blood, is
not only the most patriotic but the best for religion. "A free
Church in a free State," was the cry with which the sectaries
pulled down the altars, banished the religious, seized upon
Church property, robbed the Pope, and despoiled the Propaganda.[3] There were ecclesiastics so far deceived, at one time,
as to be led away by these cries in Italy, and ecclesiastics have
been deceived, if not by these, at least by cries as false and
fatal elsewhere to our knowledge. The seduction of foremost
ecclesiastics, prelates, and bishops was the general policy of
the sect at all times, and it remains so everywhere to this day.

The rank and file of the Carbonari had to do with local
priests and local men of influence. These were, if possible,
to be corrupted, unnerved, and seduced. Each Carbonaro
was ordered to try and corrupt a fellow Christian, a man of
family, by means that the devil himself incarnate could not
devise better for the purpose.

At the end of his letter, Piccolo Tigre glances at means of
corruption which he hoped then—and his hopes were soon

---

[3] EDITOR'S NOTE: Propoganda refers to the Vatican congregation established by Pope Gregory XV in 1622 for spreading the Gospel, which was
called the Propaganda Fide.

realized to the full—to have in operation for the scattering
of Masonic "light" throughout Italy. We have another document which will enable us to judge of the nature of this
"light." It is contained in a letter from Vindex to Nubius,
and was meant to cause the ideas of the Alta Vendita to pass
through the lodges. It is found in that convenient form of
questioning which the Sultan propounds to the Sheik-ul-
Islam when he wants to make war. He puts his reasons in a
set of questions, and the Sheik replies in as many answers.
Then the war is right in the sight of Allah, and so all Islam
goes to fight in a war so sanctified. The new Islam does the
same. A skillfully devised set of questions are posed for the
consideration of one member of the Alta Vendita by another,
and the answer which has been well concocted in secret conclave, is of course either given or implied to be given by
the nature of the case. The horrible quality of the diabolical
measures proposed by Vindex to Nubius in this form for the
desired destruction of the Church, cannot be surpassed. If
he discountenances assassination, it is not from fear or loath-
ing of that frightful crime, but simply because it is not the
best policy. He certainly did fall in upon the only blow that
could—if that were possible, which, thank God, it is not—
destroy the Church of God, and place, as he well says, Catholicity in the tomb. This is a translation of the document:

CASTELLAMARE, 9th August, 1838
The murders of which our people render themselves
culpable now in France, now in Switzerland, and
always in Italy, are for us a shame and a remorse. It is
the cradle of the world, illustrated by the epilogue of

Cain and Abel, and we are too far in progress to content ourselves with such means. To what purpose does it serve to kill a man? To strike fear into the timid and to keep audacious hearts far from us? Our predecessors in Carbonarism did not understand their power. It is not in the blood of an isolated man, or even of a traitor, that it is necessary to exercise it; it is upon the masses. Let us not individualize crime. In order to grow great, even to the proportions of patriotism and of hatred for the Church, it is necessary to generalize it. A stroke of the dagger signifies nothing, produces nothing. What does the world care for a few unknown corpses cast upon the highway by the vengeance of secret societies? What matters it to the world, if the blood of a workman, of an artist, of a gentleman, or even of a prince, has flown in virtue of a sentence of Mazzini,[4] or certain of his cut-throats playing seriously at the *Holy Vehme*?[5]

The world has not time to lend an ear to the last cries of the victim. It passes on and forgets; it is we, my Nubius, we alone, that can suspend its march. Catholicism has no more fear of a well-sharpened stiletto than monarchies have, but these two bases of social order can fall by corruption. Let us then never cease to corrupt. Tertullian was right in saying, that the blood of martyrs was the seed of Christians. Let us, then, not make martyrs, but let us popularize vice amongst the

---

[4] EDITOR'S NOTE: See footnote 2 of chapter 13.

[5] EDITOR'S NOTE: A form of secretive lay courts for fraternal organizations that were active in Germany in the Middle Ages.

multitudes. Let us cause them to draw it in by their five senses; to drink it in; to be saturated with it; and that land which Aretinus[6] has sown is always disposed to receive lewd teachings. Make vicious hearts, and you will have no more Catholics. Keep the priest away from labor, from the altar, from virtue. Seek adroitly to otherwise occupy his thoughts and his hours. Make him lazy, a gourmand, and a patriot. He will become ambitious, intriguing, and perverse. You will thus have a thousand times better accomplished your task, than if you had blunted the point of your stiletto upon the bones of some poor wretches. I do not wish, nor do you anymore, my friend Nubius, to devote my life to conspiracies, in order to be dragged along in the old ruts.

It is corruption *en masse* that we have undertaken: the corruption of the people by the clergy, and the corruption of the clergy by ourselves; the corruption which ought, one day to enable us to put the Church in her tomb. I have recently heard one of our friends, laughing in a philosophic manner at our projects, say to us: "in order to destroy Catholicism it is necessary to commence by suppressing woman." The words are true in a sense; but since we cannot suppress woman, let us corrupt her together with the Church, *corruptio optimi pessima* ["corruption of the best is the worst of all"]. The object we have in view is sufficiently good to tempt men such as we are; let us not separate

---

[6] EDITOR'S NOTE: Guido Aretinus, or Guido of Arezzo (c. 991/992–after 1033) was an Italian music theorist.

ourselves from it for some miserable personal satisfaction of vengeance. The best poniard with which to
strike the Church is corruption. To work, then, even
to the very end.

The horrible program of impurity here proposed was at once
adopted. It was after all but an attempt more determined
than ever, to spread the immorality of which Voltaire and
his school were the apostles. At the time the Alta Vendita
propounded this infernal plan they were resisting an inroad
upon their authority on the part of Joseph Mazzini, just then
coming into notoriety, who, however, overcame them.

Mazzini developed and taught, in his grandiloquent style,
as well as practiced the doctrine of assassination[7] which
formed, we know, a part of the system of all secret societies,
and which the Alta Vendita deprecated because they feared
that it was about to be employed, just then, against the
members of their own body. Mazzini speaks of having arisen
from his bed one morning fully satisfied as to the lawfulness
of removing whomsoever he might be pleased to consider an
enemy by the dagger, and fully determined to put that horrible principle into execution. He cherished it as the simplest
means given to an oppressed people to free themselves from
tyrants. But however much he labored to make his terrible
creed plausible, as being only permissible against tyrants
and traitors, it was readily foreseen how easily it could be
extended, until it became a capital danger for the sectaries
themselves. Human nature could never become so base

---

[7] EDITOR'S NOTE: See Monsignor Dillon's original footnote in appendix II provided at the end of this chapter.

and so blinded as not to revolt against a principle so pernicious. It may last for a season amidst the first pioneers of the
Alta Vendita, amongst the Black-Hand in Spain, amongst
the Nihilists in Russia, amongst the Invincibles in Ireland,
amongst the Trade-Unionists of the Bradlaugh[8] stamp in
England, or amongst the Communists of Paris. It may serve
as a means to hold in terror the unfortunate prince or leader
who may be seduced in youth or manhood to join secret
societies from motives of ambition; and when that ambition
was gratified, might refuse to go the lengths for Socialism
which the Alta Vendita required. But otherwise assassination
did not by experience prove such a sovereign power in the
hands of the Carbonari as Mazzini expected. His more astute
associates soon found out this; and not from any qualms of
conscience, but from a strong sense of its inexpediency for
their ends, they determined to reject it. They found out a
more effective, though a far more infamous, way for attaining the dark mastery of the world. It was by the assassination
not of bodies but of souls—by deliberate, systematic, and
persevering diffusion of immorality.[9]

The Alta Vendita, then, sat down calmly to consider the
best means to accomplish this design. Satan and his fallen
angels could devise no more efficacious methods than
they found out. They resolved to spread impurity by every
method used in the past by demons to tempt men to sin, to
make the practice of sin habitual, and to keep the unhappy

---

[8] EDITOR'S NOTE: Charles Bradlaugh (1833–91) was an English political activist and atheist, founder of the National Secular Society, and
member of Parliament for Northampton from 1880 to 1891.
[9] EDITOR'S NOTE: See Monsignor Dillon's original footnote in appendix III provided at the end of this chapter.

victim in the state of sin to the end. They had, being living men, means to accomplish this purpose, which devils could not use without the aid of men.

Christian civilization established upon the ruins of the licentiousness of Paganism had kept European society pure. Vice, when it did appear, had to hide its head for shame. Public decency, supported by public opinion, kept it down. So long as morality existed as a recognized virtue, the Revolution had no chance of permanent success; and so the men of the Alta Vendita resolved to bring back the world to a state of brutal licentiousness not only as bad as that of Paganism, but to a state at which even the morality of the Pagans would shudder.

To do this they proceeded with caution. Their first attempt was to cause vice to lose its conventional horror, and to make it free from civil punishment. The unfortunate class of human beings who make a sad trade in sin, were to be taken under the protection of the law, and to be kept free from disease at the expense of the State. Houses were to be licensed, inspected, protected, and given over to their purposes. The dishonor attached to their infamous condition was, so far as the law could effect it, to be taken away. That wholesome sense of danger and fear of disease which averted the criminally disposed from sin was to disappear. The agents of the Alta Vendita had instructions to increase the number and the seductiveness of those unfortunate beings, while the State, when revolutionized, was to close its eyes to their excesses, and to connive at their attempts upon the youth of the country. They were to be planted close to great schools and universities, and wherever else they could ruin the rising generation in every country in which the sect should obtain power.

Then literature was systematically rendered as immoral as possible, and diffused with a perseverance and labor worthy of a better cause. Railway stations, newspaper stands, book shops, and restaurants, were made to teem with infamous productions, while the same were scattered broadcast to the people over every land.

The teaching of the Universities and of all the middle schools of the State, was not only to be rendered Atheistic and hostile to religion, but was actually framed to demoralize the unfortunate alumni at a season of life always but too prone to vice.

Finally, besides the freest license for blasphemy and immorality, and the exhibition and diffusion of immoral pictures, paintings, and statuary, a last attempt was to be made upon the virtue of young females under the guise of educating them up to the standard of human progress.

Therefore, middle and high-class schools were, regardless of expense, to be provided for female children, who should be, at any cost, taken far away from the protecting care of nuns. They were to be taught in schools directed by lay masters, and always exposed to such influences as would sap, if not destroy, their purity, and, as a sure consequence, their faith. These schools have since been the order of the day with Masonry all over the world. "If we cannot suppress woman let us corrupt her togeher with the Church," said Vindex, and they have faithfully acted upon this advice.

The terrible society which planned these infernal means for destroying religion, social order, and the souls of men, continued its operations for many years. Its "permanent instruction" became the Gospel of all the secret societies of Europe. Its agents, like Piccolo Tigre, travelled unceasingly in every country. Its orders were received, according to the system of Masonry, by the heads and the rank and file of the lodges as so many inevitable decrees.

But unfortunately for the world, it permitted too much political action to the second lines of the great conspiracy. In the latter, ambitious spirits arose, who, while embracing to the full the doctrines of Voltaire and the principles of Weishaupt, began to think that the Alta Vendita halted actual revolution too much. This state of feeling became general when that high lodge refused admittance to Mazzini, who wished to become one of the invisible forty—the number beyond which the supreme governing body never permitted itself to pass.

The jealousy of Nubius—for jealousy is a quality of demons not wanting from the highest intelligence in Atheistic organization to the lowest—prevented his being admitted. But he was already far too powerful with the rank and file of the Carbonari to be refused a voice in the supreme management. He raised a cry against the old chiefs as being impotent and needing change. Nubius consequently passed mysteriously away. M. Cretineau-Joly[10] is clearly of opinion that it was by poison; and as it was a custom with the unfortunate chief to betray for his own protection, or for punishment, some lodges of Carbonari to the Pontifical Government, it is more than probable that it was by his provision or information that the same Government came into the possession of the

---

[10] ORIGINAL FOOTNOTE: Opus, cit. ii. 23.

whole archives of the Alta Vendita, and that the Church and society have the documents which I have quoted and others still more valuable to guide them in discovering and defeating the attempts of organized Atheism.

The Alta Vendita subsequently passed to Paris, and since, it is believed, to Berlin. It was the immediate successor of the Inner Circle of Weishaupt. It may change in the number of its adepts and in the places of its meetings, but it always subsists. There is over it, a recognized Chief like Nubius or Weishaupt. But in his lifetime this Chief is usually unknown, at least to the world outside "Illuminated" Masonry. He is unknown to the rank and file of the common lodges. But he wields a power which, however, is not, as in the case of Nubius and Mazzini, always undisputed.

Since that time, if not before it, there have been two parties under its Directory, each having its own duties, well defined. These are the Intellectual and the War Party in Masonry.

Appendix I (footnote 1)

Mazzini, after exhorting his followers to attract as many of the higher classes as possible to the secret plotting, which has resulted in united Italy, and is meant to result in republican Italy as a prelude to republican Europe, says:

> Associate, associate. All is contained in that word. The secret societies can give an irresistible force to the party who are able to invoke them. Do not fear to see them divided. The more they are divided the better it will be. All of them advance to the same end by different paths. The secret will be often unveiled. So much the

better. The secret is necessary to give security to members, but a certain transparency is necessary to strike fear into those wishing to remain stationary. When a great number of associates who receive the word of command to scatter an idea abroad and make it public opinion, can concert even for a moment, they will find the old edifice pierced in all its parts, and failing, as if by a miracle, at the least breath of progress. They will themselves be astonished to see kings, lords, men of capital, priests, and all of those who form the carcass of the old social edifice, fly before the sole power of public opinion. Courage, then, and perseverance.

Appendix II (footnote 7)

The following extracts from the rules of the Carbonari of Italy, "Young Italy," will give an idea of the spirit and intent of the order as improved by the warlike and organizing genius of Mazzini:

> Art. I—The society is formed for the indispensable destruction of all the Governments of the Peninsula and to form of Italy one sole State under a Republican Government.

> Art. II—Having experienced the horrible evils of absolute power and those yet greater of constitutional monarchies, we ought to work to found a Republic one and indivisible.

> Art. XXX—Those who do not obey the orders of the secret society, or who shall reveal its mysteries, shall be

poniarded without remission. The same chastisement for traitors.

Art. XXXI—The secret tribunal shall pronounce the sentence and shall design [sic] one or two affiliated members for its immediate execution.

Art. XXXII—Whoever shall refuse to execute the sentence shall be considered a perjurer, and as such shall be killed on the spot.

Art. XXXIII—If the culpable individual escape he shall be pursued without intermission in every place, and he ought be struck by an invisible hand, even should he take refuge in the bosom of his mother or in the tabernacles of Christ.

Art. XXXIV—Every secret tribunal shall be competent not only to judge the culpable adepts, but also to cause to be put to death every person whom it shall have stricken with anathema.

Art. XXXIX—The officers shall carry a dagger of antique form, the sub-officers and soldiers shall have guns and bayonets, together with a poniard a foot long attached to their cincture, and upon which they will take oath, etc.

A large number of inspectors of police, generals, and statesmen were assassinated by order of these tribunals. The lodges assisted in that work. Eckart says:[11]

---

[11] ORIGINAL CITATION: *La Franc-Maçonnerie*, t. ii., p. 218, 219.

Mazzini was the head of that Young Europe and of the warlike power of Freemasonry, and we find in the *Latomia* that the minister Nothorub, who had retired from it, say to M. Vesbugem, even in the national palace in presence of six deputies, that the actual Freemasonry in Belgium had become a powerful and dangerous arm in the hands of certain men, that the Swiss insurrection had its resting place in the machinations of the Belgian lodges, and that Brother Defacqz, Grand Master of these lodges, had undertaken, in 1844, a voyage to Switzerland, only in order to prepare that agitation.

Appendix III (footnote 9)

Nubius, who, in conjunction with the Templars of France, and the secret friends of the Revolution in England, had caused all the troubles endured by the Church and the Holy Father during the celebrated Congress of Rome and during the entire reign of Louis Philippe,[12] and had so ably planned the revolutions afterwards carried out by Palmerston and Napoleon III,[13] was written to before his death by one of his fellow-conspirators in the following strain:

> We have pushed most things to extremes. We have taken away from the people all the gods of heaven and earth that they had in homage. We have taken away their religious faith, their monarchical faith, their

[12] EDITOR'S NOTE: Louis Philippe I (1773–1850) was the last king of the French, reigning from 1830 to 1848.

[13] EDITOR'S NOTE: Napoleon III (1808–73) was the first president of France (1848–52), the last emperor of the French (1852–70), and the last French monarch.

virtue, their probity, their family virtue; and, meantime, what do we hear in the distance but low bellow-
ing; we tremble, for the monster may devour us. We
have little by little deprived the people of all honorable
sentiment. They will be without pity. The more I think
on it the more I am convinced that we must seek delay
of payment.

CHAPTER 16

The Intellectual and War Party in Masonry

"They secretly sustain what in public they strongly reprobate, and if necessary disown and denounce. This is a point worthy of deep consideration, and shows more than anything else, the ability and astuteness with which the whole organization has been planned. . . . It is the deeply hidden Chief and his Council that concoct and direct all. They wield a power with which, as is well known, the diplomacy of every nation in the world must count."

—Monsignor Dillon

ECKERT[1] SHOWS THAT at present all secret societies are divided into two parties—the party of direction, and the party of action or war party. The duty of the intellectual party is to plot and to contrive; that of the party of action is to combine, recruit, excite to insurrection, and fight. The members of the war party are always members of the intellectual party, but not *vice versa*. The war party thus know

---

[1] ORIGINAL FOOTNOTE: *La Franc-Maçonnerie dans sa véritable signification*, par Eckert, avocat à Dresde, trad. par Gyr (Liège 1854), t. I., p. 287, appendice. See also *Les Societes Revolutionnaires, Introduction de faction des Societes Secretes au xix. Siècle. Par M. Claudio Jannel, Deschamps, Opus cit.* xciii.

what is being plotted. But the other party, concealed as common Freemasons amongst the simpletons of the lodges, cover both sections from danger. If the war party succeed, the peace party go forward and seize upon the offices of state and the reins of power. Their men go to the hustings,[2] make speeches that suit, are written up in the press, which, all the world over, is under Masonic influence. They are cried up by the adroit managers of mobs. They become the deputies, the ministers, the Talleyrands,[3] the Fouchès,[4] the Gambettas,[5] the Ferrys;[6] and of course they make the war party generals, admirals, and officers of the army, the navy, and the police. If the war party fails, the intellectual party, who close their lodges during the combat, appear afterwards as partisans, if possible, of the conquering party, or if they cannot be that, they silently conspire. They manage to get some friends into power. They agitate. They, in either case, come to the assistance of the defeated war party. They extenuate the faults, while condemning the heedless rashness of ill-advised, good-natured, though too ardent, young men. They cry for mercy. They move the popular compassion. In time, they free the culprits, and thus prepare for new commotions.

All Freemasonry has been long thus adapted, to enable the intellectual party to assist the war party in distress. It must

---

[2]   EDITOR'S NOTE: A meeting where election candidates address voters.

[3]   EDITOR'S NOTE: See footnote 8 of chapter 9.

[4]   EDITOR'S NOTE: See footnote 7 of chapter 9.

[5]   EDITOR'S NOTE: Léon Gambetta (1838–82) was a French statesman who served in various capacities in the French government, proclaiming the French Third Republic in 1870, and serving as its prime minister from 1881 to 1882.

[6]   EDITOR'S NOTE: See footnote 7 of the preface.

be remembered that every Carbonaro is in reality a Freemason. He is taught the passes and can manipulate the members of the craft. Now, at the very threshold of the admission of a member to Freemasonry, the Master of the Lodge, the "Venerable," thus solemnly addresses him:

> Masons [says he] are obliged to assist each other by every means, when occasion offers. Freemasons ought not to mix themselves up in conspiracies; but if you come to know that a Freemason is engaged in any enterprise of the kind, and has fallen a victim to his imprudence, you ought to have compassion upon his misfortune, and the Masonic bond makes it a duty for you, to use all your influence and the influence of your friends, in order to diminish the rigor of punishment in his favor.

From this it will be seen, with what astute care Masonry prepares its dupes from the very beginning, to subserve the purposes of the universal Revolution. Under plea of compassion for a brother in distress, albeit through his supposed imprudence, the Mason's duty is to make use not only of all his own influence, but also "of the influence of his friends," to either deliver him altogether from the consequences of what is called "his misfortune," or "to diminish the rigor of his punishment."

Masonry, even in its most innocent form, is a criminal association. It is criminal in its oaths, which are at best rash; and it is criminal in promising obedience to unknown commands coming from hidden superiors. It always, therefore, sympathizes with crime. It hates punishment of any repressive kind, and does what it can to destroy the death penalty even for murder. In revolution, its common practice is to open jails, and let felons free upon society. When it cannot do this, it raises on their behalf a mock sympathy.

Hence, we have Victor Hugo pleading with every government in Europe in favor of revolutionists; we have the French Republic liberating the Communists; and there is a motion before the French Parliament to repeal the laws against the party of dynamite—the Internationalists, whose aim is the destruction of every species of religion, law, order and property, and the establishment of absolute Socialism.

With ourselves, there is not a revolutionary movement created that we do not find at the same time an intellectual party apparently disconnected with it, often found condemning it, but in reality supporting it indirectly but zealously. The Odgers[7] and others of the Trades Union, for instance, will murder and burn; but it is the Bradlaughs[8] and men theorizing in Parliament if they can, or on the platform if they cannot, who sustain that very party of action. They secretly sustain what in public they strongly reprobate, and if necessary disown and denounce. This is a point worthy of deep consideration, and shows more than anything else, the

---

[7]　EDITOR'S NOTE: George Odger (1813–77) was a British trade unionist and radical who served as the president of the First International, or International Workingmen's Association, which combined socialist, communist, anarchist, and trade union groups in supposed service of the working class.

[8]　EDITOR'S NOTE: See footnote 8 of chapter 15.

ability and astuteness with which the whole organization has been planned.

Again, we must remember, that while the heads of the party of action are well aware of the course being taken by the intellectual party, it does not follow that the intellectual party know the movements of the party of action, or even the individuals, at least so far as the rank and file are concerned. It therefore can happen in this country, that Freemasons or others who are in communication only with the Supreme Council on the Continent, get instructions to pursue one line of conduct, and that the war party for deep reasons get instructions to oppose them. This serves, while preventing the possibility of exposure, to enable the work of the Infidel Propaganda to be better done.

It is the deeply hidden Chief and his Council that concoct and direct all. They wield a power with which, as is well known, the diplomacy of every nation in the world must count. There are men either of this Council, or in the first line of its service, whom it will never permit to be molested. Weishaupt, Nubius, Mazzini,[9] Piccolo Tigre, De Witt, Misley,[10] Garibaldi,[11] Number One, Hartmann, may have been arrested, banished, etc., but they never found the prison that could contain them long, nor the country that would dare deliver them up for crime against law or even life. It is determined by the Supreme Directory that at any cost, the

---

[9] Editor's Note: See footnote 2 of chapter 13.

[10] Editor's Note: Enrico Misley (1801–63) was an Italian lawyer and revolutionary involved in the failed rebellions of 1831. However, it is possible Monsignor Dillon is referring to the same Henry Misely he mentions in the next chapter.

[11] Editor's Note: See footnote 4 of the preface.

men of their first lines shall not suffer; and from the beginning they have found means to enforce that determination against all the crowned heads of Europe.

Now you must be curious to know who succeeded to the Chieftaincy of this formidable conspiracy when Nubius passed away. It was one well known to you, at least by fame. It was no other than the late Lord Palmerston.[12]

---

[12] EDITOR'S NOTE: Lord Palmerston (1784–1865) was an English Whig-Liberal statesman whose political career included serving as British foreign secretary (1830–34, 1835–41, and 1846–51) and prime minister (1855–58 and 1859–65).

CHAPTER 17

Lord Palmerston

"He was a noble, without a hope of issue, or of a near heir to his title and estates. He therefore preferred the designs of the Atheistic conspiracy he governed to the interests of the country which employed him, and he sacrificed England to the projects of Masonry."

—Monsignor Dillon

THE BARE ANNOUNCEMENT of this fact will, no doubt, cause as much surprise to many here tonight as it certainly did to myself when it became first known to me. I could with difficulty believe that the late Lord Palmerston knew the veritable secret of Freemasonry, and that for the greater part of his career he was the real master, the successor of Nubius, the Grand Patriarch of the Illuminati, and as such, the Ruler of all the secret societies in the world. I knew, of course, that as a statesman, the distinguished nobleman had dealings of a very close character with Mazzini,[1] Cavour,[2] Napoleon III,[3] Garibaldi,[4] Kossuth,[5] and the other leading revolutionary

---

[1] EDITOR'S NOTE: See footnote 2 of chapter 13.
[2] EDITOR'S NOTE: See footnote 3 of the preface.
[3] EDITOR'S NOTE: See footnote 13 of chapter 15.
[4] EDITOR'S NOTE: See footnote 4 of the preface.
[5] EDITOR'S NOTE: Lajos Kossuth (1802–94) was a Hungarian political reformer who helped lead Hungary's struggle for independence from

spirits of Europe in his day, but it was never for a moment suspected that he went so far as to accept the supreme direction of the whole dark and complex machinery of organized Atheism, or sacrificed the welfare of the great country he was supposed to serve so ably and so well, to the designs of the terrible secret conclave whose acts and tendencies were so well known to him. But the mass of evidence collected by Father Deschamps and others[6] to prove Lord Palmerston's complicity with the worst designs of Atheism against Christianity and monarchy—not even excepting the monarchy of England—is so weighty, clear, and conclusive, that it is impossible to refuse it credence.

Father Deschamps brings forward in proof the testimony of Henry Misley, one of the foremost Revolutionists of the period, when Palmerston reigned over the secret Islam of the Sects, and other no less important testimonies. These I would wish, if time permitted, to give at length. But the whole history, unhappily, of Lord Palmerston proves them.

In 1809, when but twenty-five years of age,[7] we find him War Minister in the Cabinet of the Duke of Portland.[8] He

---

Austria. He played a role in the Revolutions of 1848 in Hungary, which were aborted by Russian armies. He died in exile.

[6] EDITOR'S NOTE: See Monsignor Dillon's original footnote in appendix I provided at the end of this chapter.

[7] EDITOR'S NOTE: Monsignor Dillon mistakenly said he was twenty-three years old at the time.

[8] EDITOR'S NOTE: Palmerston assumed the post of secretary at war under Spencer Perceval (1762–1812), who served as prime minister from 1809 to 1812. Perceval's immediate predecessor as prime minister was William Cavendish-Bentinck, Third Duke of Portland, to whom Monsignor Dillon refers.

remained in this office until 1828, during the successive administrations of Mr. Perceval, the Earl of Liverpool, Mr. Canning, Lord Goderick, and the Duke of Wellington.[9] He left his party—the Conservatives—when the last-named Premier insisted upon accepting the resignation of Mr. Huskisson.[10] In 1830, he accepted the position of Foreign Secretary in the Whig Ministry of Earl Grey.[11]

Up to this period he must have been well informed in the policy of England. He saw Napoleon in the fullness of youth, and he saw his fall. He knew and approved of the measures taken after that event by the advisers of George IV,[12] for the conservation of legitimate interests in Europe, and for the preservation for the Pope of the Papal States. The balance of power, as formed by the Congress of Vienna,[13] was considered by the wisest and most patriotic English statesmen the best safeguard for British interests and influence on the Continent. While it existed, the multitude of small States in Italy and Germany could be always so manipulated by British diplomacy as effectually to prevent that complete isolation which England feels today so keenly, and which

---

[9] EDITOR'S NOTE: Spencer Perceval; Robert Jenkinson, Second Earl of Liverpool; George Canning; F. J. Robinson, First Viscount Goderich; and Arthur Wellesley, First Duke of Wellington, were all British prime ministers from 1809 to 1834.

[10] EDITOR'S NOTE: William Huskisson (1770–1830) was a British statesman, financier, and member of Parliament who resigned from the government of the Duke of Wellington in 1828.

[11] EDITOR'S NOTE: Charles Grey, Second Earl Grey (1764–1845) was a British politician who served as prime minister from 1830 to 1834.

[12] EDITOR'S NOTE: George IV (1762–1830) was the king of the United Kingdom from 1820 to 1830. In 1811, he became prince regent for his father, King George III, who had gone insane.

[13] EDITOR'S NOTE: See footnote 2 of chapter 12.

may prove so disastrous within a short period to her best interests.

If this sound policy has been since changed, it is entirely owing to Palmerston, who appears, after leaving the ranks of the Tories, to have thrown himself absolutely into the hands of that Liberalistic Freemasonry which, at the period, began to show its power in France and in Europe generally. On his accession to the Foreign Office in 1830, he found the Cabinet freed from the influence of George IV, and from Conservative traditions, and he at once threw the whole weight of his energy, position, and influence to cause his government to side with the Masonic program for revolutionizing Europe.

With his aid, the sectaries were able to disturb Spain, Portugal, Naples, the States of the Church, and the minor States of Italy. The cry for a constitutional government received his support in every State of Europe, great and small. The Pope's temporal authority and every Catholic interest were assailed. England, indeed, remained quiet. Her people were fascinated by that fact. Trade interests being served by the distractions of other States, and religious bigotry gratified at seeing the Pope, and every Catholic country harassed, they all gave a willing, even a hearty support to the policy of Palmerston. They little knew that it was dictated, not by devotion to their interests, but in obedience to a hidden power of which Palmerston had become the dupe and the tool, and which permitted them to glory in their own quiet, only to gain their assistance and, on a future day, to compass with greater certainty their ruin.

Freemasonry, as we have already seen, creates many "figure-head" Grand Masters from the princes of reigning houses, and the foremost statesmen of nations, to whom, however, it only shows a small part of its real secrets. Palmerston was an exception to this rule. He was admitted into the very recesses of the Sect. He was made its Monarch, and as such ruled with a real sway over its realms of darkness. By this confidence he was flattered, cajoled, and finally entangled beyond the hope of extrication in the meshes of the sectaries. He was a noble, without a hope of issue, or of a near heir to his title and estates. He therefore preferred the designs of the Atheistic conspiracy he governed to the interests of the country which employed him, and he sacrificed England to the projects of Masonry.

As he advanced in years, he appears to have grown more infatuated with his work. In 1837, in or about the time when Nubius was carried off by poison, Mazzini, who most probably caused that Chief to disappear, and who became the leader of the party of action, fixed his permanent abode in London. With him came also several counsellors of the "Grand Patriarch," and from that day forward the liberty of Palmerston to move England in any direction, except in the interest of the secret conspiracy, passed away forever.

Immediately, plans were elaborated destined to move the program of Weishaupt another step towards its ultimate completion.[14] These were, by the aid of well-planned Revolutions, to create one immense Empire from the small German States in the center of Europe, under the house of

---

[14] EDITOR'S NOTE: See Monsignor Dillon's original footnote in appendix II provided at the end of this chapter.

Brandenburg; next to weaken Austrian dominion; then to annihilate the temporal sovereignty of the Pope by the formation of a United Kingdom of Italy under the provisional government of the house of Savoy; and lastly, to form of the discontented Polish, Hungarian, and Slavonian populations an independent kingdom between Austria and Russia.

After an interval during which these plans were hatched, Palmerston returned to office in 1846, and then the influence of England was seen at work in the many revolutions which broke out in Europe within eighteen months afterwards.[15] If these partly failed, they eventuated at least in giving a Masonic Ruler to France in the person of the Carbonaro, Louis Napoleon.[16] With him Palmerston instantly joined the fortunes of England, and with him he plotted for the realization of his Masonic ideas to the very end of his career.

Now here comes a most important event, proving beyond question the determination of Palmerston to sacrifice his country to the designs of the Sect he ruled. The Conservative feeling in England shrank from acknowledging Louis Napoleon or approving of his *coup d'état*. The country began to grow afraid of revolutionists, crowned or uncrowned. This feeling was shared by the Sovereign, by the Cabinet, and by the Parliament, so far that Lord Derby[17] was able to move

---

[15] EDITOR'S NOTE: The Revolutions of 1848 were a series of republican revolts against European monarchs in Sicily, France, Germany, Italy, and the Austrian Empire. All of them were repressed.

[16] EDITOR'S NOTE: This refers to Napoleon III, who became the first president of France in 1848. See footnote 13 of chapter 15.

[17] EDITOR'S NOTE: Edward Stanley, Fourteenth Earl of Derby (1799–1869), was a British statesman and leader of the Conservative Party

a vote of censure on the government because of the foreign policy of Lord Palmerston. For Palmerston, confiding in the secret strength he wielded, and which was not without its influence in England herself, threw every consideration of loyalty, duty, and honor overboard, and without consulting his Queen or his colleagues, he sent, as Foreign Secretary, the recognition of England to Louis Napoleon. He committed England to the Empire,[18] and the other nations of Europe had to follow suit.

On this point Chambers' Encyclopedia, Article "Palmerston," has the following notice:

> In December 1852, the public was startled at the news that Palmerston was no longer a member of the Russell Cabinet.[19] He had expressed his approbation of the *coup d'état* of Louis Napoleon (gave England's official acknowledgment of the perpetration) without consulting either the Premier or the Queen; and as explanations were refused, Her Majesty exercised her constitutional right of dismissing her minister.

Palmerston had also audaciously interpolated dispatches signed by the Queen. He acted, in fact, as he pleased. He had the agents of his dark realm, in almost every Masonic lodge in England. The Press at home and abroad, under

---

from 1846 to 1868, who served as prime minister three times, for several months in 1852, from 1858 to 1859, and finally from 1866 to 1868.

[18] EDITOR'S NOTE: The Second French Empire, which lasted from January 14, 1852 to October 27, 1870.

[19] EDITOR'S NOTE: John Russell, First Earl Russell (1792–1878), was a British Whig and Liberal statesman who served as prime minister from 1846 to 1852, and again from 1865 to 1866.

Masonic influences, applauded his policy. The Sect so acted that his measures were productive of immediate success. His manner, his *bonhomie* [geniality], his very vices fascinated the multitude. He won the confidence of the trading classes, and held the Conservatives at bay. Dismissed by the Sovereign, he soon returned into power her master, and from that day to the day of his death ruled England and the world in the interests of the Atheistic Revolution, of which he thought himself the master spirit.[20]

In a few moments we shall see the truth of this when considering the political action of the Sect he led, but first it will be necessary to glance at what the Church and Christianity generally had to suffer in his day by the war of the intellectual party.

Appendix I (footnote 6)

M. Eckert (*opus cit.*) was a Saxon lawyer of immense erudition, who devoted his life to unravel [sic] the mysteries of secret societies, and who published several documents of great value upon their action. He has been of opinion that "the interior order" not only now but always existed and governed the exterior mass of Masonry, and its cognate and subject secret societies. He says:

> Masonry being a universal association is governed by one only chief called a Patriarch. The title of Grand Master of the Order is not the exclusive privilege of a family or of a nation. Scotland, England, France, and

---

[20] EDITOR'S NOTE: See Monsignor Dillon's original footnote in appendix III provided at the end of this chapter.

Germany have in their time had the honor to give the order its supreme chief. It appears that Lord Palmerston is clothed today [Eckert wrote in Lord Palmerston's time] with the dignity of Patriarch.

At the side of the Patriarch are found two committees, the one legislative and the other executive. These committees, composed of delegates of the Grand Orients (mother national lodges) alone know the Patriarch, and are alone in relation with him.

All the revolutions of modem times prove that the order is divided into two distinct parties—the one pacific, the other warlike.

The first employs only intellectual means—that is to say, speech and writing.

It brings the authorities or the persons whose destruction it has resolved upon to succumb or to mutual destruction.

It seeks for the profit of the Order all the places in the State, in the Church (Protestant), and in the Universities; in one word, all the positions of influence.

It seduces the masses and dominates over public opinion by means of the press and of associations.

Its Directory bears the name of the Grand Orient, and it closes its lodges (I will say why presently) the moment the warlike division causes the masses which they have won over to secret societies to descend into the street.

At the moment when the pacific division has pushed its works sufficiently far that a violent attack has chances of success, then, at a time not far distant, when men's passions are inflamed; when authority is sufficiently weakened; or when the important posts are occupied by traitors, the warlike division will receive orders to employ all its activity.

The Directory of the belligerent division is called the Firmament.

From the moment they come to armed attacks, and that the belligerent division has taken the reins, the lodges of the pacific division are closed. These tactics again denote all the ruses of the order.

In effect, they thus prevent the order being accused of co-operating in the revolt.

Moreover, the members of the belligerent division, as high dignitaries, form part of the pacific division, but not reciprocally, as the existence of that division is unknown to the great part of the members of the other division—the first can fall back on the second in case of want of success. The brethren of the pacific division are eager to protect by all the means in their power the brethren of the belligerent division, representing them as patriots too ardent, who have permitted themselves to be carried away by the current in defiance of the prescriptions of order and prudence.

Appendix II (footnote 14)

In page 340 of his work on Jews, etc., already quoted, M. G. Demousseaux reproduces an article from the Political Blueter, of Munich, in 1862, in which is pointed out the existence in

Germany, in Italy, and in London, of directing-lodges unknown to the mass of Masons, and in which Jews are in the majority.

At London, where is found the home of the revolution under the Grand Master, Palmerston, there exists two Jewish lodges which never permit Christians to pass their threshold. It is there that all the threads and all the elements of the revolution are reunited which are hatched in the Christian lodges.

Further, M. Demousseaux cites the opinion (p. 368) of a Protestant statesman in the service of a great German Power, who wrote to him in December 1865:

> At the outbreak of the revolution of 1845[21] I found myself in relation with a Jew who by vanity betrayed the secret of the secret societies to which he was associated, and who informed me eight or ten days in advance of all the revolutions which were to break out upon every point of Europe. I owe to him the immovable conviction that all these grand movements of "oppressed people" etc., are managed by a half-a-dozen individuals who give their advice to the secret societies of the entire of Europe.

Henry Misley, a great authority also, wrote to Père Deschamps:

> I know the world a little, and I know that in all that "grand future" which is being prepared, there are not more than four or five persons who hold the cards. A

---

[21] EDITOR'S NOTE: This was likely intended to be 1848, the year multiple revolutions broke out across Europe.

great number think they hold them, but they deceive themselves.

Appendix III (footnote 20)

Mr. F. Hugh O'Donnell, the able MP [Member of Parliament] for Dungarvan, contributed to the pages of the Dublin *Freeman's Journal* a most useful and interesting paper which showed on his part a careful study of the works of Monsignor Segur and other continental authorities on Freemasonry. In this, he says, regarding his own recollections of contemporary events:

> It is now many years since I heard from my lamented master and friend, the Rev. Sir Christopher Bellew, of the Society of Jesus, these impressive words. Speaking of the tireless machinations and ubiquitous influence of Lord Palmerston against the temporal independence of the Popes, Sir Christopher Bellew said:
>
>> Lord Palmerston is much more than a hostile statesman. He would never have such influence on the Continent if he were only an English Cabinet Minister. But he is a Freemason and one of the highest and greatest of Freemasons. It is he who sends what is called the Patriarchal Voice through the lodges of Europe. And to obtain that rank he must have given the most extreme proofs of his insatiable hatred to the Catholic Church.
>
> Another illustration of the manner in which European events are moved by hidden currents was given

me by the late Major-General Burnaby, MP, a quiet
and amiable soldier, who, though to all appearance
one of the most unobtrusive of men, was employed in
some of the most delicate and important work of British policy in the East. General Burnaby was commis-
sioned to obtain and preserve the names and addresses
of all the Italian members of the foreign legion enlisted
for the British service in the Crimean War. This was
in 1855 and 1856. After the war these men, mostly
reckless and unscrupulous characters—"fearful scoundrels" General Burnaby called them—dispersed to
their native provinces, but the clue to find them again
was in General Burnaby's hands, and when a couple
of years later Cavour and Palmerston, in conjunction
with the Masonic lodges, considered the moment
opportune to let loose the Italian Revolution, the list
of the Italian foreign legion was communicated to the
Sardinian Government and was placed in the hands
of the Garibaldian Directory, who at once sought
out most of the men. In this way several hundreds of
"fearful scoundrels," who had learned military skill
and discipline under the British flag, were supplied
to Garibaldi[22] to form the corps of his celebrated
"Army of Emancipation" in the two Sicilies and the
Roman States. While the British diplomatists at Turin
and Naples carried on, under cover of their character
as envoys, the dangerous portion of the Carbonarist
conspiracy, the taxpayers of Great Britain contributed
in this manner to raise and train an army destined to

---

[22] EDITOR'S NOTE: See footnote 4 of the preface.

confiscate the possessions of the Religious Orders and the Church in Italy, and, in its remoter operation, to assail, and, if possible, destroy the world-wide mission of the Holy Propaganda itself.

CHAPTER 18

War of the Intellectual Party

*"Well the Infidels knew that in proportion as nations fell away
from the holy restraints of the Church, and as the sanctity
and inviolability of the marriage bond became weakened,
the more Atheism would enter into the human family. . . . A
hundred other able means were devised to efface the Christian
aspect of the nations until they presented an appearance
more devoid of religion than that of the very pagans."*

—Monsignor Dillon

DURING WHAT MAY be called the reign of Palmerston, the
war of the intellectual party against Christianity, intensified
in the dark counsels of the Alta Vendita, became accentuated
and general throughout Europe. It chiefly lay in the propagandism of immorality, luxury, and naturalism amongst all
classes of society, and then in the spread of Atheistic and
revolutionary ideas. During the time of Palmerston's influence not one iota of the advices [sic] of the Alta Vendita was
permitted to be wasted. Wherever, therefore, it was possible to advance the program mapped out in the "Permanent
Instruction," in the letter of Piccolo Tigre, and in the advices
of Vindex, that was done with effect. We see, therefore,
France, Italy, Germany, Spain, America, and the rest of the

world, deluged with immoral novels, immodest prints, pictures, and statues, and every legislature invited to legalize a system of prostitution, under pretense of expediency, which gave security to sinners, and a kind of recognized status to degraded women. We find, wherever Masonry could effect it, these bad influences brought to bear upon the universities, the army, the navy, the training schools, the civil service, and upon the whole population. "Make corrupt hearts and you will have no more Catholics," said Vindex, and faithfully, and with effect, the secret societies of Europe have followed that advice. Hence, in France under the Empire, Paris, bad enough before, became a very pandemonium of vice; and Italy just in proportion to the conquests of the Revolution, became systematically corrupted on the very lines laid down by the Alta Vendita.

Next, laws subversive of Christian morality were caused to be passed in every State, on, of course, the most plausible pretexts. These laws were first that of divorce, then, the abolition of impediments to marriage, such as consanguinity, order, and relationship, union with a deceased wife's sister, etc. Well the Infidels knew that in proportion as nations fell away from the holy restraints of the Church, and as the sanctity and inviolability of the marriage bond became weakened, the more Atheism would enter into the human family.

Moreover, the few institutions of a public, Christian nature yet remaining in Christian States were to be removed one after another on some skillfully devised, plausible plea. The Sabbath which in the Old as well as in the New Dispensation, proved so great an advantage to religion and to man—to nations as well as to individuals—was marked out for desecration. The leniency of the Church which permitted certain necessary works on Sunday, was taken advantage of, and the day adroitly turned into one of common trading in all the great towns of Catholic Continental Europe. The Infidels, owing to a previous determination arrived at in the lodges, clamored for permission to open museums and places of public amusement on the days sacred to the services of religion, in order to distract the population from hearing Mass and worshipping God. Not that they cared for the unfortunate working man. If the Sabbath ceased tomorrow, he would be the slave on Sunday that they leave him to be during the rest of the week. The one day of rest would be torn from the laboring population, and their lot drawn nearer than before to that absolute slavery which always did exist and would exist again, under every form of Idolatry and Infidelity.

Pending the reduction of men to Socialism, the secret conclave directing the whole mass of organized Atheism has therefore taken care that in order to withdraw the working man from attending divine worship and hearing the Word of God, theaters, cafes, pleasure gardens, drinking saloons, and other still worse means of popular enjoyment shall be made to exert the utmost influence on him upon that day. This sad influence is beginning to be felt amongst ourselves. Then, besides the suppression of State recognition to religion, chaplains to the army, the navy, the hospitals, the prisons, etc., were to be withdrawn on the plea of expense or of being unnecessary. Courts of justice, and public assemblies were to be deprived of every Christian symbol. This was to be done on the plea of religion being too sacred to be permitted to enter into such places. In courts, in society, at dinners, etc., Christian habits, like that of grace before meals, etc., or any social recognition of God's presence, were to be scouted as not in good taste. The company of ecclesiastics was to be shunned, and a hundred other able means were devised to efface the Christian aspect of the nations until they presented an appearance more devoid of religion than that of the very pagans.

But of all the attacks made by Infidels during the reign of Palmerston, that upon primary, middle-class, and superior education was the most marked, the most determined, and decidedly, when successful, the most disastrous.

We must remember that from the commencement of the war of Atheism on Christianity, under Voltaire and the Encyclopedists, this means of doing mischief was the one most advocated by the chief leaders. They then accumulated immense sums to diffuse their own bad literature amongst every class. Under the Empire, the most disastrous blow struck by the Arch-Mason Talleyrand[1] was the formation of a monopoly of education for Infidelity in the foundation of the Paris University. But it was left for the Atheistic plotters of this century to perfect the plan of wresting the education of every class and sex of the coming generations of men from out of the hands of the Church, and the influence of Christianity.

This plan was apparently elaborated as early as 1826, by intellectual Masonry. About that time appeared a dialogue between Quintet and Eugene Sue, in which after the

---

[1] EDITOR'S NOTE: See footnote 8 of chapter 9.

manner of the letter of Vindex to Nubius the whole program of the now progressing education war was sketched
out. In this the hopes which Masonry had from Protestantism in countries where the population was mixed,
were clearly expressed. The jealousy of rival Sects was to be
excited, and when they could not agree, then the State was
to be induced to do away with all kinds of religion "just for
peace sake," and establish schools on a purely secular basis,
entirely removed from "clerical control," and handed over
to lay teachers, whom in time Atheism could find means
to "control" most surely. But in purely Catholic countries,
where such an argument as the differences of Sects could
not be adduced, then the cry was to be against clerical ver-
sus lay teaching. Religious teachers were to be banished by
the strong hand, as at present in France, and afterwards it
could be said that lay teachers were not competent or willing to give religious instruction, and so that, too, in time,
could be made to disappear.[2]

We may here call to mind the fact that it was while Lord
Palmerston directed Masonry as Monarch, and English pol-
icy as Minister, that an insidious attempt was made to intro-
duce secularism into higher education in Ireland by Queen's
Colleges, and into primary education by certain acts of
the Board of National Education. The fidelity of the Irish
Episcopacy and the ever-vigilant watchfulness of the Holy
See, disconcerted both plans, or neutralized them to a great
extent. Attempts of a like kind are being made in England.
There, by degrees, board schools with almost unlimited

---

[2] EDITOR'S NOTE: See Monsignor Dillon's original footnote in Appendix I provided at the end of this chapter.

assistance from taxes have been first made legal, and then encouraged most adroitly. The Church schools have been systematically discouraged, and have now reached the point of danger. This has been effected, first, by the Masonry of Palmerston in high places, and secondly, by the Masonry of England generally, not in actual league and knowingly, with the dark direction I speak of, but unknowingly influenced by its well-devised cries for the spread of light, for the diffusion of education amongst the masses, for the banishment of religious discord, etc.

It was, of course, never mentioned, that all the advantages cried up could be obtained, together with the still greater advantage of a Christian education, producing a future Christian population. It was sedulously kept out of sight that the people who would be certain to use board schools, were those who never went themselves to any church, and who would never think of giving religious instruction of any kind to their children. Nothing can show the power of Freemasonry in a stronger light than the stupor it was able to cast over the men who make laws in both Houses of the English Parliament, and who were thus hoodwinked into training up men fitted to take position, wealth, and bread itself, from themselves and their children; to subject, in another generation, the moneyed classes of England to the lot that befell other blinded "moneyed people" in France during the last century. In England, the Freemasons had, unfortunately, the Dissenters as allies. Hatred for church schools caused the latter to make common cause with Atheists against God, but the destruction of the Church of England—they do not hope for the destruction of the vigorous Catholic Church of the country—will never compensate even Socinians for a spirit of instructed irreligion in England—a spirit which, in a generation, will be able and only too willing to attempt Atheistic levelling for its own advantage, and certainly not for the benefit of wealthy Dissenters, or Dissenters having anything at all to lose.

The same influences of Atheism were potent, and for the same reasons, in all Australian legislatures. There the influence of continental Freemasonry is stronger than at home, and conservative influences which neutralize Atheistic movements of too democratic a nature in England and Scotland, are weaker. Hence, in all Australian Parliaments, Acts are passed with but a feeble resistance from the Church Party, abolishing religious education of every kind, and making all the education of the country "secular, compulsory, and free." That is, without religion, enforced upon every class, and at the general expense of the State. Hence, after paying the taxation in full, the Catholic and the conscientious Christian of the Church of England, have to sustain in all those colonies their own system of education, and this, while paying for the other system, and while bearing the additional burden of the competition of State schools, richly and completely endowed with every possible requisite and luxury out of the general taxes.

A final feature in the education-war of Atheism against the Church especially, and against Christianity of every kind, is the attempted higher education without religion of young girls. The expense which they have induced every legislature to undertake for this purpose is amazing; and how the nations tolerate that expense is equally amazing. It is but carrying out to the letter the advice of Vindex: "If we cannot suppress woman, let us corrupt her together with the Church." For this purpose those infamous hot-beds of foul vice, "lodges of adoption," lodges for women, and "androgynes"—lodges for libertine Masons and women— were established by the Illuminati of France in the last century. For the same purpose schools for the higher education of young girls are now devised. This we know by the open avowal of leading Masons. They were introduced into France, Belgium, Italy, and Germany for the purpose of withdrawing young girls of the middle and upper classes from the blessed, safe control of nuns in convents, and of leading them to positive Atheism by Infidel masters and Infidel associates. This design of the lodges is succeeding in its mission of terrible mischief; but, thank God, not amongst the daughters of respectable Christians of any kind, who value the chastity, the honor, or the future happiness here and hereafter of that sex of their children, who need most care and delicacy in educating.

In the extract from the permanent instruction of the Alta Vendita, you have already seen how astutely the Atheists compassed the corruption of youth in Universities. It is since notorious that in all high schools over which they have been able to obtain influence, the students have been deprived of religion, taught to mock and hate it, allured to vicious courses, and have been placed under professors without religion or morality. How can we be surprised if the Universities of the Continent have become the hot-beds of vice, revolution, and Atheism? Moreover, when Masonry governs, as in France, Italy, and Germany, the only way for youth to obtain a livelihood on entering upon life is by being affiliated to Masonry; and the only way to secure advancement is to be devoted to the principles, the intrigues, and the interests of the Sect.

The continuous efforts of Masonry, aided by an immoral and Atheistic literature, by a corrupt public opinion, by a zealous Propagandism of contempt for the Church, for her ministers and her ministrations, and by a sleepless, able Directory devoted to the furtherance of every evil end, are enough in all reason to ruin Christianity if that were not Divine.

But, in addition to its intellectual efforts, Masonry has had from the beginning another powerful means of destroying the existing social and Christian order of the world in the interests of Atheism. We shall see what this is by a glance at the action of the war party under Palmerston.

Appendix I (footnote 2)

The late celebrated Monsignor Dupanloup published, in 1875, an invaluable little treatise, in which he gave, from the expressions of the most eminent Masons in France and elsewhere, from the resolutions taken in principal lodges, and from the opinions of their chief literary organs, proofs that what is here stated is correct. The following extracts regarding education will show what Masonry has been doing in regard to that most vital question. Monsignor Dupanloup says:

> In the great lodge called the "Rose of Perfect Silence,"
> it was proposed at one time for the consideration

of the brethren: "Ought religious education be suppressed?" This was answered as follows: "Without any doubt the principle of supernatural authority, that is faith in God, takes from a man his dignity; is useless for the discipline of children, and there is also in it, the danger of the abandonment of all morality. . . . The respect, specially due to the child, prohibits the teaching to him of doctrines, which disturb his reason."[3]

To show the reason of the activity of the Masons, all the world over, for the diffusion of irreligious education, it will be sufficient to quote the view of the *Monde Maçonnique* on the subject. It says, in its issue of May 1, 1865:

An immense field is open to our activity. Ignorance and superstition weigh upon the world. Let us seek to create schools, professorial chairs, libraries.

Impelled by the general movement thus infused into the body, the Masonic (French) Convention of 1870 came unanimously to the following decision:

The Masonry of France associates itself to the forces at work in the country to render education gratuitous, obligatory, and laic [non-clerical, lay].

We have all heard how far Belgium has gone in pursuit of these Masonic aims at Infidel education. At one of the principal festivals of the Belgian Freemasons a certain brother Boulard exclaimed, amidst universal applause:

---

[3]   EDITOR'S CITATION: Monsignor Dupanloup, Bishop of Orleans, *A Study of Freemasonry* (Newark, NJ: J.J. O'Connor & Co., 1876), 50. This has a slightly different, but essentially the same, translation.

> When ministers shall come to announce to the coun-
> try that they intend to regulate the education of the
> people I will cry aloud, "to me a Mason, to me alone
> the question of education must be left; to me the
> teaching; to me the examination; to me the solution."

Monsignor Dupanloup also attacked the Masonic project
of having professional schools for young girls, such as are
now advocated in the Australian colonies and elsewhere in
English-speaking countries. At the time, the movement was
but just being initiated in France, but it could not deceive
him. In a pamphlet, to which all the Bishops of France
adhered, and which was therefore called the Alarm of the
Episcopate, he showed clearly that these schools had two
faces, on one of which was written "Professional Instruction
for Girls," and on the other, "Away with Christianity in life
and death." "Without woman," said Brother Albert Leroy
at an International Congress of Masons, at Paris, in 1867,
"all the men united can do nothing"—nothing to effectually
de-Christianize the world.

The French "Education League" had the same object. At
the time it was introduced, the lodges were busy with getting
up a statue to Voltaire. And the *Monde Maçonnique*, speaking of both, said in April 1867:

> May the Education League and the statue of Brother
> Voltaire find in all the lodges the most lively sympa-
> thy. We could not have two subscriptions more in har-
> mony: Voltaire, that is the destruction of prejudices
> and superstitions: the Education League, that is the
> building up of a new society founded solely upon

science and upon instruction. All our brethren understand the matter in this manner.

It is needless to remark here that by "superstition" the *Monde
Maçonnique* means religion, and, by "science and instruction," these acquirements, not only without, but directly
hostile to religion. This newspaper constantly teaches that all
religions are so many darknesses, that Masonry is the light;
that God, the soul, the life to come, are nothing but supposi-
tions and fantasies, and that, as a consequence, a man ought
to be reared up independent of every kind of Christianity.
Therefore, it adds, "All masons ought to adhere in mass to
*the league of instruction, and the lodges ought to study in the
peace of their temples the best means to render it efficacious.*"
In fact the Education League and Masonry are declared to
be identical by Brother Mace, who, at a general banquet,
drank: "To the entrance of all Masons into the League. To
the entrance into Masonry of all those who form part of the
League." "To the triumph of the light, the watchword common to the League and to Masonry."

In fine, the author of a history of Freemasonry, and
one evidently well up in its aims, Brother Coffin, writes as
follows:

> Whenever Masonry accords the entrance into its
> temple to a Hebrew, to a Mahometan [Muslim], to a
> Catholic, or to a Protestant, that is done on the con-
> dition that he becomes a new man, that he abjures all
> his past errors, *that he rejects the superstitions in which
> he was cradled from his youth.* Without all this what has
> he to do in our Masonic assemblies?

But as we have seen, the great aim of the Alta Vendita was to corrupt woman. "As we cannot suppress her," said Vindex to Nubius, "let us corrupt her together with the Church." The method best adapted for this was to alienate her from religion by an infidel education. The Freemasons, no doubt, obtained from the higher grades the word of command, and, accordingly, proceeded to force, everywhere, the establishment of superior schools for young girls where they might be surely deprived of their religion and their morality. In the "Lodge of Beneficence and Progress," at Boulogne, on the July 19, 1867, "Massol" thus spoke:

> By means of instruction, women will become able to shake off the clerical yoke, and to liberate themselves from the superstitions which impede them from occupying themselves with an education in harmony with the spirit of the age.

To give one proof only of this, where is the English, German, or American woman, who to the two religious questions which her own children can propose to her: "Who made the world?" "Do we continue to live after death?" would dare to answer that she knew nothing and that no one knew anything about it. Well, then, this boldness the instructed French woman will possess.

CHAPTER 19

The War Party under Palmerston

"There are sure signs in all the countries where the
Atheistic Revolution has made decided progress that
this final catastrophe is planned already, and that
its instruments are in course of preparation."

—Monsignor Dillon

FATHER DESCHAMPS, ON the authority of Eckert and Misley, gives an interesting description of all that Freemasonry, under the direction of Lord Palmerston, attempted and effected after the failure of the revolutionary movements, conducted by the party of action, under Mazzini,[1] in 1848. These were fomented to a large extent by British diplomacy and secret service money manipulated by Lord Palmerston. Under his guidance and assistance, Mazzini had organized all his revolutionary Sects. Young Italy, Young Poland, Young Europe, and the rest sprang as much from the one as from the other.

But after years of close union, Mazzini, who was probably hated by Palmerston, and dreaded as the murderer of Nubius, began to wane in influence. He and his party felt,

---

[1] EDITOR'S NOTE: See footnote 2 of chapter 13.

of course, the inevitable effects of failure; and the leader subsided without, however, losing any of his utility for the Sect. Napoleon III[2] appears to have supplanted him in the esteem of Palmerston, and would, had he dared, have ceased to follow the Carbonari. Mazzini accordingly hated Napoleon III with a deadly hatred, which he lived to be able to gratify signally when Palmerston was no more. As he was the principal means of raising Palmerston to power in the Alta Vendita, so, after Palmerston had passed away, he introduced another great statesman, to the high conductors, if not into the high conduct itself, of the whole conspiracy; and caused a fatal blow to be given to France and to the dynasty of Napoleon.

Meanwhile, from 1849 to the end of the life of Palmerston, the designs formed by the high council of secret Atheism, were carried out with a perfection, a vigor, and a success never previously known in their history. Nothing was precipitated; yet everything marched rapidly to realization. The plan of Palmerston—or the plan of the deadly council which plotted under him—was to separate the two great conservative empires of Russia and Austria, while, at the same time, dealing a deadly blow at both. It was easy for Palmerston to make England see the utility of weakening Russia, which threatened her Indian possessions. France could be made to join in the fray by her ruler, and the powerful Masonic influence at his command: hence the Russian campaign of 1853.[3]

---

[2]   Editor's Note: See footnote 13 of chapter 15.
[3]   Editor's Note: Monsignor Dillon originally wrote 1852 but was likely referring to the onset of the Crimean War, which lasted from October 1853 to February 1856, in which Russia lost to an alliance of France, the United Kingdom, the Ottoman Empire, and Kingdom of Sardinia.

But it was necessary for this war to keep Prussia and Austria quiet. Prussia was bribed by a promise to get, in time, the Empire of United Germany. Austria was frightened by the resolution of England and France to bring war to the Danube, and so form a projected Kingdom in Poland and Hungary. The joint power of England, France, and Turkey could easily, then, with the aid of the populations interested, form the new kingdom, and so effectually curb Russia and Austria.

But it was of more importance for the designs of the sect upon the Temporal Power of the Pope, and upon Austria herself, to separate the Empires. Palmerston succeeded with Austria, who withdrew from her alliance with Russia. The forces therefore of England and France were ordered from the Danube to the barren Crimea, as payment for her neutrality. This bribe proved the ruin of Austrian influence. As soon as Russia was separated from her, and weakened beyond the power of assisting her, if she would, France, countenanced by England, dealt a deadly blow at Austrian rule in Italy, united Italy, and placed the Temporal Power of the Pope in the last stage of decay.

On the other hand, Prussia was permitted to deal a blow soon after at Austria. This finished the prestige of the latter as the leading power in Germany, and confined her to her original territory, with the loss of Venice, her remaining Italian province. After this war, Palmerston passed away, and Mazzini came, once more, into authority in the Sect. He remembered his grudge against Napoleon, and at once used his influence with the high direction of Masonry to abandon France and assist Germany; and, on the promise of Bismarck[4]—a promise fulfilled by the May Laws[5]—that Germany should persecute the Church as it was persecuted in Italy, Masonry went over to Germany, and Masons urged on Napoleon to that insane expedition which ended in placing Germany as the arbiter of Europe, and France and the dynasty of Napoleon in ruins.[6] In the authorities quoted, there is abundant proof that Masonry, just as it had assisted the French Revolution and Napoleon I, now assisted the Germans. It placed treason on the side of the French, and sold in fact the unfortunate country and her unscrupulous ruler. Mazzini forced Italy not to assist Napoleon, and was gratified to find before his death that the liar and traitor who, in the hope of getting assistance he did not get from Masonry, had dealt his last blow at the Vicar of Christ, and placed Rome and the remnant of the States of the Church in the hands of the King of Italy, had lost the throne and gained the unenviable character of a coward and a fool.[7]

---

[4] EDITOR'S NOTE: Otto von Bismarck (1815–98) was a German statesman and diplomat who served as the prime minister of Prussia, founded the first German Empire in 1871, and served as its first chancellor until 1890.

[5] EDITOR'S NOTE: A series of laws promulgated by the Prussian minister of culture, Adalbert Falk, from 1873 to 1875 during the *kulturkampf* ["culture struggle"] against the Catholic Church by Otto von Bismarck. The laws exercised strict control over religious training and ecclesiastical appointments, secularized education, expelled the Jesuits and other religious orders from the empire, and made civil marriage obligatory.

[6] EDITOR'S NOTE: A reference to France's loss in the Franco-Prussian War which lasted from 1870 to 1871 and ended with the establishment of the German Empire, formally proclaimed in the Hall of Mirrors at the Palace of Versailles outside of Paris on January 18, 1871.

[7] EDITOR'S NOTE: With the outbreak of the Franco-Prussian War in 1870, Napoleon III withdrew his garrison from Rome, which left it vulnerable to Italian nationalists who had managed to unify most of

This is necessarily but a brief glance at the program, which Atheism has both planned and carried out since the rule of Palmerston commenced. Wherever it prevailed, the worst form of persecution of the Church at once began to rage.

In Sardinia, as soon as it obtained hold of the King and Government, the designs of the French Revolution were at once carried out against religion. The State itself employed the horrible and impure contrivances of the Alta Vendita for the corruption and demoralization of every class of the people. The flood gates of hell were opened. Education was at once made completely secular. Religious teachers were banished. The goods of the religious orders were confiscated. Their convents, their land, their very churches were sold, and they themselves were forced to starve on a miserable pension, while a succession was rigorously prohibited. All recognition of the Spiritual Power of Bishops was put to an end. The priesthood was systematically despised and degraded. The whole ministry of the Church was harassed in a hundred vexatious ways. Taxes of a crushing character were levied on the administration of the sacraments, on masses, and on the slender incomes of the parish clergy. Matrimony was made secular, divorce legalized, the privileges of the

---

the Italian peninsula, of which the Papal States were the last remaining holdout. They took advantage of the situation, crossed the frontier of the Papal States on September 11, 1870, and captured the city on September 20. The captured territory was officially annexed to the Kingdom of Italy in October 1870, marking the end of the Papal States *de facto*. The popes refused any accommodation with the Kingdom of Italy for decades, and the dispute between the two parties was known as "the Roman Question." Pope Pius XI formally renounced the Papal States *de jure* and consented to the establishment of the State of the Vatican City in the Lateran Treaty which was signed on February 11, 1929.

clerical state abrogated. Worse than all, the *leva* or conscription was rigorously enforced. Candidates for the priesthood at the most trying season of their career were compelled to join the army for a number of years, and exposed to all the snares which the Alta Vendita had astutely prepared to destroy their purity, and with it, of course, their vocations. "Make vicious hearts, and you will have no more Catholics." Besides these measures made and provided by public authority, every favor of the State, its power of giving honors, patronage and place, was constantly denied to Catholics. To get any situation of value in the army, navy, civil service, police, revenue, on the railways, in the telegraph offices, to be a physician to the smallest municipality, to be employed almost anywhere, it was necessary to be a Freemason, or to have powerful Masonic influence. The press, the larger mercantile firms, important manufactories, depending as such institutions mostly do on State patronage and interest, were also in the hands of the Sectaries. To Catholics was left the lot of slaves. If permitted to exist at all, it was as the hewers of wood and the drawers of water.[8] The lands which those amongst them held who did not forsake religion were taxed to an unbearable extent. The condition of the faithful Catholic peasants became wretched from the load of fiscal burdens placed upon them. The triumph of Atheism could not be more complete, so far as having all that the world could give on its side, and leaving to the Church scarcely more than covered her Divine Founder upon the Cross.

---

[8] EDITOR'S NOTE: An idiom for menial laborers drawn from Joshua 9:21.

Bismarck, though assisted in his wars against France by the brave Catholic soldiers of the Rhine, and of the Fatherland generally, no sooner had his rival crushed, and his victory secured, than he hastened to pay to Freemasonry his promised persecution of the Church. The Freemasons in the German Parliament, and the Ministers of the Sect, aided him to prepare measures against the Catholic religion as drastic as those in operation in Italy, even worse in many respects. The religious orders of men and women were rigorously suppressed or banished, as a first installment. Then fell Catholic education to make way for an Infidel propagandism. Next came harassing decrees against the clergy by which Bishops were banished or imprisoned and parishes were deprived in hundreds of their priests. All the bad, immoral influences, invented and propagated by the Sectaries, were permitted to run riot in the land. A schism was attempted in the Church. Ecclesiastical education was corrupted in the very bud, and all but the existence of Catholics was proscribed.

Wherever we find the dark sect triumphant we find the same results. In the Republics of South America, where Freemasonry holds the highest places, the condition of the Church is that of normal persecution and vexation of every kind. It has been so for many years in Spain and Portugal, in Switzerland, and to whatever extent Freemasons can accomplish it in Belgium and in Austria.

The dark Directory succeeding Weishaupt, the Alta Vendita, and Palmerston, sits in Paris and in Berlin almost openly, and prepares at leisure its measures, which are nothing short of first, the speedy weakening of the Church, and then a bloody attempt at her extermination. If it goes on slower than it did during the French Revolution, it is in order to go on surer. Past experience, too, and the determinations of the sect already arrived at, show but too clearly that a single final consummation is kept steadily in view. The impure assassins who conduct the conspiracy have had no scruple to imbue their hands in the blood of Christians in the past, and they never will have a scruple to do so, whenever there is hope of success. In fact, from what I have seen and studied on the Continent, an attempt at this ultimate means of getting rid at least of the clergy and principal lay leaders amongst Catholics, might take place in France and even in Italy at any moment. In France, some new measure of persecution is introduced every day. The Concordat is broken openly. The honor of the country is despised. Subventions belonging by contract to the clergy are withdrawn. The insolence of the Atheistical Government, relying on the strength of the army and on the unaccountable apathy or cowardice of the French Catholic laity, progresses so fast, that no act of the Revolution of 1789 or of the Commune[9] can be thought improbable within the present decade; and Italy would be sure to follow any example set by France in this or in any other method of exterminating the Church.

There are sure signs in all the countries where the Atheistic Revolution has made decided progress that this final catastrophe is planned already, and that its instruments are in course of preparation. These instruments are something the same as were devised by the illuminated lodges, when the power of the French Revolution began to pass from the National Assembly to the clubs. The clubs were the open

---

[9]   EDITOR'S NOTE: See footnote 6 of the preface.

and ultimate expression of the destructive anti-Christianity of Atheism; and when the lodges reached so far, there was no further need for secrecy. That which in the jargon of the Sect is called "the object of the labor of ages" was attained. Man was without God or Faith, King or Law. He had reached the level aimed at by the Commune, which is itself the ultimate end of all Masonry, and all that secret Atheistic plotting which, since the rise of Atheism, has filled the world.

In our day, if Masonry does not found Jacobite or other clubs, it originates and cherishes movements fully as Satanic and as dangerous. Communism, just like Carbonarism, is but a form of the illuminated Masonry of Weishaupt. "Our end," said the Alta Vendita, "is that of Voltaire and the French Revolution." Names and methods are varied, but that end is ever the same. The clubs at the period of the French Revolution were, after all, local.

Masonry now endeavors to generalize their principles and their powers of destructive activity on a vastly more extended scale. We therefore no longer hear of Jacobins or Girondins, but we hear of movements destined to be for all countries what the Jacobins and the Girondins were for Paris and for France. As surely, and for the same purpose, as the clubs proceeded from the lodges in 1789, so, in the latter half of the nineteenth century, the lodges sent out upon the whole civilized world, for the very same intent, the terrible Socialist organizations, all founded upon the lines of Communism, and called according to the exigencies of time, place, and condition, the association of the brethren of the International, the Nihilists, the Black Hand, etc.

CHAPTER 20

The International, the Nihilists, the Black Hand, etc.

"Our only chance lies in a return to God, of which, alas, there are as yet but little signs amongst those who hold power amongst us. I mean of course a return to the public Christianity of the past."

—Monsignor Dillon

THERE ARE MULTITUDES in Freemasonry—even in the most "advanced" Freemasonry of Italy and France—who have no real wish to see the principles of these anarchists predominate. Those, for instance, who in advocating the theories of Voltaire, and embracing for their realization the organization of Weishaupt, saw only a means to get for themselves honors, power, and riches, which they could never otherwise obtain but by Freemasonry, would be well pleased enough to advance no further, once the good things they loved had been gained. *"Nous voulons, Messieurs,"* said Thiers,[1] *"la republique, mais la republique conservatrice"* ["We want, gentlemen, the republic, but the conservative republic"]. He and his desired, of course, to have the Republic which gave them all this world had to bestow, at the expense of former

---

[1] EDITOR'S NOTE: See footnote 5 of the preface.

possessors. They desired also the destruction of a religion which crossed their corrupt inclinations, and which was suspected of sympathy for the state of things which Masonry had supplanted.

But they had no intention, if they could help it, to descend again to the level of the masses from which they had sprung.

In Italy, for instance, this class of Freemasons have had supreme power in their hands for over a quarter of a century. They obtained it by professing the strongest sympathy for the down-trodden millions whom they called slaves. They stated that these slaves—the bulk of the Italian people in the country and in the cities—were no better than tax-paying machines, the dupes and drudges of their political tyrants. Victor Emmanuel,[2] when he wanted, as he said, "to liberate them from political tyrants," declared that a cry came to him from the "enslaved Italy" composed of these down-trodden, unregenerated millions. He and his Freemasons and Carbonari—the party of direction and the party of action—therefore drove the native princes of the people from their thrones, and seized supreme sway throughout the Italian peninsula. Were the millions of "slaves" served by the change? The whole property of the Church was seized upon. Were the burdens of taxation lightened? Very far from it. The change simply put hungry Freemasons, and chiefly those of Piedmont, in possession of the Church lands and revenues. It dispossessed many ancient Catholic proprietors, in order to put Freemasons in their stead.

---

[2] EDITOR'S NOTE: Victor Emmanuel II (1820–78) was king of Sardinia-Piedmont from 1849 to 1861, and then became the first king of a united Italy from 1861 to 1878.

But with what consequence to the vast mass of the people, to the peasantry and the working population—some twenty four out of the twenty-six millions of the Italian people? The consequence is this, that after a quarter of a century of vaunted "regenerated Masonic rule," during which "the liberators" were at perfect liberty to confer any blessings they pleased upon the people as such, the same people are at this moment more miserable than at any past period of their history, at least since Catholicity became predominant as the religion of the country. If their natural princes ever "whipped them with whips" for the good of the state, Freemasonry, under the House of Savoy, slashes them with scorpions, for the good of the fraternity.[3] To keep power in the hands of the Atheists, an army ten times greater and ten times more costly than before had to be supported by the "liberated" people. A worthless but ruinously expensive navy has been created and must be kept by the same unfortunate "regenerated" people. These poor people, "regenerated and liberated," must man the fleets and supply the rank and file of army and navy; they must give their sons, at the most useful period of their lives, to the "service" of Masonic "United Italy." But the officials in both army and navy—and their number is legion—supported by the taxes of the people, are Freemasons or the sons of Freemasons. They vegetate in absolute uselessness, so far as the development of the country is concerned, living in comparative luxury upon its scanty resources. The civil service, like the army and navy, is swelled with "government

---

[3] EDITOR's NOTE: An allusion to 1 Kings 12:11, in which King Rehoboam, the son of King Solomon, promises further oppression of the northern tribes of Israel.

billets," out of all proportion to the wants of the people. It is filled with Freemasons. It is a paradise of Freemasons, where Piedmontese patriots, who have intrigued with Cavour[4] or fought under Garibaldi,[5] enjoy *otium cum dignitate* ["leisure with dignity"] at the expense of the hard earnings of a people very poor at any time, but by the present "regenerated" regime made more wretched and miserable than any Christian peasantry—not even excepting the peasantry of Ireland—on the face of the earth.

The consequence of the "liberation" wrought by the Freemasons in Italy is this: they clamored for representative institutions. All their revolutions were made under the pretext that these were not granted—and the mass of Italian people, seven-eighths of them—are as yet unenfranchised, after a quarter of a century of Masonic supremacy in the land. The Masons represented the lot of the poor man as insupportable under the native princes. But under themselves the poor man's condition, instead of being ameliorated, has been made unspeakably worse. He is positively, at present, ground down, in every little town of Italy, by insupportable exactions. His former burdens are increased four-fold—in many cases, ten-fold. To find money for all the extravagances of Masonic rule—to make fortunes for the men at the top, and comfortable places for the rank and file of the sect—a system of taxation, the most elaborate, severe, and searching ever yet invented to crush a nation, has been devised. The peasant's rent is raised by Masonic greed whenever a Mason becomes a proprietor, as is often

4   EDITOR'S NOTE: See footnote 3 of the preface.
5   EDITOR'S NOTE: See footnote 4 of the preface.

the case with regard to confiscated church lands. Land taxes cause the rents to rise everywhere. The tenant must bear them. Then every article of the produce of his little rented holding is taxed as he approaches the city gates to sell it. At home his pig is taxed, his dog, if he can keep one, his fowl, his house, his fireplace, his window light, his scanty earnings, *titulo servizio* ["service title"], all are specially, and for the poor, heavily taxed.

The consequence of this is, that few Italian peasants can, since Italy became "United," drink the wine they produce, or eat the wheat they grow. Flesh meat, once in common use, is now as rare with them as it used to be with the peasantry in Ireland. Milk or butter they hardly ever taste. Their food, often sadly insufficient, is reduced to *pizzi*, a kind of cake made of Maize or Indian meal and vegetables or fruit when in season. Their drink is plain water. They are happy when they can mingle with it a little *vinaccio*, a liquid made after the grapes are pressed and the wine drawn off by pouring water on the refuse. Their homes are cheerless and miserable, their children left to live in ignorance, without schooling, employed in coarse labor, and clothed in rags. The Grand Duke of Tuscany had by wise and generous regulations placed hundreds, yea, even thousands of these peasants, happy as independent farmers on their own land. The crushing load of taxation has caused these to disappear, and their little holdings have been sold by auction to pay taxes, and have passed, of course, into the hands of speculators, generally Freemasons, who, when they become landlords, vie with the worst of their class, in Ireland, in greed.

In the States of the Church, where the careful, most Christian, and compassionate spirit and legislation of the Vicar of Christ prevailed, the peasantry ate their own bread, drank their own wine, and were decently, nay even picturesquely clad, as all travelers know, before the "liberation" of the Masonic Piedmontese. Not a family was without a little hoard of savings for the age of the old, and for the provision and placing in life of the young. Now, gaunt misery, even starvation, is the characteristic of these populations, after only some fifteen years of Masonic rule. The vast revenues of the Church are gone, none know whither. The nation is none the better for them, and the populace, in their dire poverty, can no longer go to the convent-gate, where before the poor never asked for bread in vain. The religious, deprived of their possessions, and severely repressed, have no longer food to give. They are fast disappearing, and the people already experience that the promises of Freemasonry, like the promises of its real author [Satan], are but apples of ashes, given but to lure, to deceive, and to destroy.

But to return. The Freemasonry of France and other Continental nations, which has done so much to give effect to the principles of Voltaire and Weishaupt, wishes decidedly not to go beyond the *role* played by the Freemasonry of Italy. But in France, as in Italy, an inexorable power is behind them, pushing them on, and also fanatically determined to push them off the scene when the time is ripe for doing so. This the Freemasons of Italy well know; this the men now in power in France feel. But if they move against the current coming upon them from the depths of Freemasonry, woe to them. The knife of the assassin is ready. The sentence of death is there, which they are too often told to remember, and which has before now reached the very foremost men of the sect who refused, or feared, for motives good or bad, to advance as quickly as the hidden chiefs of the Revolution desired and decreed. It "removed" Nubius in the days of Mazzini.[6] It "removed" Gambetta[7] before our eyes. It aimed frequently at Napoleon III,[8] and would most assuredly have struck home, but its aim was only to terrify him so that he as a Carbonaro would be made to do its work soon and effectively. Masonry obtained its end, and Napoleon marched to the Italian war, and to his doom.

It is this invisible power, this secret, sleepless, fanatical Directory, which causes the solidarity most evidently subsisting between Freemasonry in its many degrees and aspects, and the various parties of anarchists which now arise everywhere in Europe. In the last century kings, princes, and nobles, took up Masonry. It swept them all away before that century closed. In the beginning and progress of this century, the *bourgeoisie* took it up with still greater zest, and made it all their own. For a long time they would not tolerate such a thing as a poor Mason. Poverty was their enemy. What has come to pass? The *bourgeoisie* at this moment are the peculiar enemy of the class of workmen who have invaded "Black" or "Illuminated" Masonry, and made it at last completely theirs. The *bourgeoisie* are now called upon by the Socialists to be true to the real levelling principles of the brotherhood—to practice as well as preach "liberty,

---

6 Editor's Note: See footnote 2 of chapter 13.
7 Editor's Note: See footnote 5 of chapter 16.
8 Editor's Note: See footnote 13 of chapter 15.

equality, and fraternity"; to divide their possessions with the working men—to descend to that Elysium of Masonry, the level of the Commune[9]—or die.

It is passing strange how Masonry, being what it is, has always managed to get a princely or noble leader for every one of its distinct onward movements against princes, property, and society. It had Égalité[10] to lead the movement against the throne of France in the last century. It had the Duke of Brunswick,[11] Frederick II[12], and Joseph II[13] to assist. In this century we see it ornamented by Louis Philippe,[14] Napoleon III, Victor Emmanuel, and others as figure-heads; Nubius and Palmerston, both won from the leaders of the Conservative nobility, were its real chiefs. Now, when it appears in its worst possible form, it is championed by no less a personage than a Russian Prince, of high lineage, a representative of the wealthiest, most exclusive, and perhaps richest aristocracy in the world. We find that in all cases of seduction like this, the promise of mighty leadership has been the bait by which the valuable dupe has been caught by the sectaries. The advice of Piccolo Tigre for the seduction of princes has thus never been without its effect.

These new anarchical societies are not mere haphazard associations. They are most ably organized. There is, for instance, in the International, three degrees, or rather distinct societies, the one, however, led by the other. First come

---

[9] EDITOR's NOTE: See footnote 6 of the preface.
[10] EDITOR's NOTE: See footnote 1 of chapter 5.
[11] EDITOR's NOTE: See footnote 2 of chapter 7.
[12] EDITOR's NOTE: See footnote 2 of chapter 3.
[13] EDITOR's NOTE: See footnote 10 of chapter 5.
[14] EDITOR's NOTE: See footnote 12 of chapter 15.

the International Brethren. These know no country but the Revolution; no other enemy but "reaction." They refuse all conciliation or compromise, and they regard every movement as "reactionary" the moment it ceases to have for its object, directly or indirectly, the triumph of the principles of the French Revolution. They cannot go to any tribunal other than a jury of themselves, and must assist each other, lawfully or otherwise, to the "very limits of the possible." No one is admitted who has not the firmness, fidelity, intelligence, and energy considered sufficient by the chiefs, to carry out as well as to accept the program of the Revolution. They may leave the body, but if they do, they are put under the strictest surveillance, and any violation of the secret or indiscretion, damaging to the cause, is punished inexorably by death. They are not permitted to join any other society, secret or otherwise, or to take any public appointment without permission from their local committee; and then they must make known all secrets which could directly or indirectly serve the International cause.

The second class of Internationalists are the National Brethren. These are local socialists, and are not permitted even to suspect the existence of the International Brethren, who move among them and guide them in virtue of higher degree. They figure in the meetings of the society, and constitute the grand army of insurrection. They are, without knowing it, completely directed by the others. Both classes are formed strictly upon the lines laid down by Weishaupt.

The third class comprises all manner of workmen's societies. With these the two first mingle, and direct to the profit of the Revolution. The death penalty for indiscretion or trea-son is common in every degree.

The Black Hand and the Nihilists are directed by the same secret agency, to violence and intrigue. Amongst them, but unknown to most of them, are the men of the higher degrees, who in dark concert easily guide the others as they please. They administer oaths, plan assassinations, urge on to action, and terrorize a whole country, leaving the rank and file who execute these things to their fate. It is unneces-sary to dwell longer upon these sectaries, well known by the outrages they perpetrate.

These terrible societies are unquestionably connected with, and governed by, the dark directory, which now, as at all times since the days of Weishaupt, rules the secret societ-ies of the world. Mahometanism [Islam] permitted the assas-sins gathered under the "old man of the mountain," to assist in spreading the faith of Islam by terrorizing its Christian enemies. For a like purpose, whenever it judges it oppor-tune, the dark Alta Vendita employs the assassins wholesale and retail of the secret societies. It believes it can control when it pleases these ruthless enemies of the human race. In this, as Nubius found out, it is far mistaken.

But the encouragement of murderers as a "skirmishing" party of the Cosmopolitan Revolution remains since the day of Weishaupt—a policy kept steadily in view. Today, that party is used against some power such as that of the Popes, or the petty princes of Italy. Great powers like England, in the belief that the mischief will stop in Italy, rejoice in the results attained by assassination. Tomorrow, it suits the policy of the Alta Vendita to make a blow at aristocracy in England, at despotism in Russia, at monarchy in Spain; and at once we find Invincibles formed from the advanced amongst the Fenians; Nihilists and the Black Hand from the ultras of the Carbonari; and Young Russia, ready to use dynamite and the knife and the revolver, reckless of every consequence, for the ends of the secret Directory with which the diplomacy of the world has now to count. The professional lectures on the use and manufacture of dynamite given to Nihilists in Paris, the numbers of them gathered together in that capital, the retreat afforded them there to the known murderers of the Emperor Alexander,[15] excited little comment in England. If referred to at all in the press, it was not with that vigorous abhorrence which such proceedings should create. Often a chuckle of satisfaction has been indulged in by some at the fact. The utterances of the "advanced" members of the Masonic Intellectual party in the French Senate excusing Nihilists were quoted with a kind of "faint damnation" equivalent to praise.

I have no doubt but in Russia a similar kind of tender treatment is given to the Fenian dynamitards employed by O'Donovan Rossa.[16] So long as the leading nations in Europe do not see in these anarchists and desperate miscreants the irreconcilable enemies of the human race, Paris, completely Masonic as it is, will afford them a shelter; and when French tribunals fine or imprison them, it will be as in Italy with a tenderness still further exhibited in jails.

---

[15] EDITOR'S NOTE: Alexander II (1818–81) was emperor of Russia from 1855 to 1881. His reign came to an end by an assassin's bomb which mortally wounded him as he was traveling through St. Petersburg on his regular route.

[16] EDITOR'S NOTE: Jeremiah O'Donovan Rossa (1831–1915) was an Irish Fenian leader and member of the Irish Republican Brotherhood.

The salvation of Europe depends upon a manly abhorrence of secret societies of every description, and the pulling up root and branch from human society of the sect of the Freemasons whose "illuminated" plottings have caused the mischief so far, and which if not vigorously repressed by a decided union of Christian nations will yet occasion far more. *Deus fecit nationes sanabiles* ["God made nations to be healed"]. The nations can be saved. But if they are to be saved, it must be by a return to Christianity and to public Christian usages; by eradicating Atheism and its socialistic doctrines as crimes against the majesty of God and the well-being of individual men and nations; by rigorously prohibiting every form of secret society for any purpose whatever; by shutting the mouth of the blasphemer; by controlling the voice of the scoffer and the impure in the press and in every other public expression; by insisting on the vigorous Christian education of children; and, if they can have the wisdom of doing it, by opening their ears to the warning voice of the Vicar of Jesus Christ. It is not an expression of Irish discontent finding a vent in dynamite which England has most to fear from anarchy. Its value to the Revolution is the knowledge it gives to those millions whom English education methods are depriving of faith in God, of the use of a terrible engine against order, property, and the very existence of the country as such.

The dark directory of Socialism is powerful, wise, and determined. It laughs at Ireland and her wrongs. It hates, and ever will hate, the Irish people for their fidelity to the Catholic faith. But it seizes upon those subjects which Irish discontent in America affords, to make them teach the millions everywhere the power of dynamite, and the knife, and the revolver, against the comparatively few who hold property. This is the real secret of dynamite outrages in England, in Russia, and all the world over; and I fear we are but upon the threshold of a social convulsion which will try every nation where the wiles of the secret societies have obtained, through the hate of senseless Christian sectaries, the power for Atheism to dominate over the rising generation, and deprive it of Christian faith, and the fear and the love of God. I hope these my forebodings may not be realized, but I fear that even before another decade passes, Socialism will attempt a convulsion of the whole world equal to that of France in 1789; and that convulsion I fear this country shall not escape. Our only chance lies in a return to God, of which, alas, there are as yet but little signs amongst those who hold power amongst us. I mean of course a return to the public Christianity of the past.

To this pass Freemasonry has brought the world and itself. Its hidden Directory no outsider can know. Events may afterwards reveal who they were. Few can tell who is or is not within that dark conclave of lost but able men. There is no staying the onward progress of the tide which bears on the millions in their meshes to ruin. The only thing we can hope to do is to save ourselves from being deceived by their wiles. This, thank God, we may and will do. We can, at least, in compliance with the advice of our Holy Father, open the eyes of our own people, of our young men especially, to the nature and atrocity of the evil, that seeing, they may avoid the snare laid for them by Atheism.

To do this with greater effect we shall now, for a while, consider the danger as it appears amongst ourselves. We shall also see what relation it has with its kind in other countries, and so we shall take a brief survey of Freemasonry with ourselves.

CHAPTER 21

Freemasonry with Ourselves

*"The Alta Vendita and the intellectual party in Masonry have
for a long time endeavored to revive practices which Christianity
did away with, and which were distinctly pagan. Amongst others
they have made every exertion to destroy the Christian respect
for the dead, and every respect for the dead which kept alive in
the living the belief in the immortality of the soul. . . . [Satan's]
followers in the secret societies established by him, and which he
keeps in such unity of aim and action, second his desire to the
utmost by doing away with whatever may keep alive in man
the thoughts of his last end and of a future resurrection, and, of
course, of judgment. . . . In opposition to these, Christian people
should carefully study to keep the joy of Christmas, the penitential
fasts, the sanctity of Holy Week, the splendor of Easter, the feasts
of God's holy Mother and of the saints—to fill themselves, in
one word, with the Christian spirit of the Ages of Faith."*

—Monsignor Dillon

WE HEAR FROM every side a great deal regarding the difference said to exist between Freemasonry as it has remained
in the United Kingdom, and as it has developed itself on
the Continent of Europe since its introduction there chiefly,
we must remember, by British Jacobites, in the last century.
It is argued, that the Illuminism of Weishaupt, or that of

213

Saint-Martin,[1] did not cross the Channel to any great extent; and that on the whole the lodges of England, Ireland, and Scotland remained loyal to Monarchy and to religion.

There is much truth in all this. The Conservative character of the mass of English Freemasons, and the fact, that amongst them were found the real governors and possessors of the country, made it impossible that such men could conspire against their own selves. But, as I have already shown, the fact that British lodges have always had intercourse with the lodges of the Continent,[2] makes it equally impossible that some, at least, of the theories of the latter should not have got into the lodges on this side of the water. I believe it is owing mainly to this influence over British Freemasons, that so many revolutionary movements have found favor with our legislators, who are, when they are not Catholics, generally of the craft. It was through it, that the fatal foreign policy of Lord Palmerston obtained such support, even against the conviction and instincts of the best and most farseeing statesmen of the country, as, for instance, the late Lord Derby.[3] It was through it, certainly, that the cry for secular education was welcomed amongst us, that divorce and "liberal" marriage laws came into force, and that attacks were permitted upon the sanctity of the Sabbath and other Christian institutions.

Speaking of this latter subject, I must say, that one change in the habits of the people of England, and Scotland, too, struck me very forcibly on my return to the United Kingdom

---

[1] EDITOR'S NOTE: See footnote 5 of chapter 5.
[2] EDITOR'S NOTE: See Monsignor Dillon's original footnote in appendix I provided at the end of this chapter.
[3] EDITOR'S NOTE: See footnote 17 of chapter 17.

after a long absence. When, some twenty-three years ago I last visited these Islands, it was a pleasure—and when one thought of the desecration of the Sabbath on the Continent, it was a pride—to witness the state of the streets of our great cities on Sundays. The shops were as shut up as at midnight. Every thoroughfare manifested a religious quiet, which reverentially and most emphatically proclaimed the reign of God in the country.

On my return, I found that a new departure from good, old, holy customs had commenced, which to me looked anything but an improvement. I found in London and elsewhere, a multitude of shops with shutters removed, and goods displayed in the most tempting profusion, marked for sale, and distracting the passers-by even more than they could do on a weekday. A contrivance to keep within the law was introduced in many cases. It was a kind of iron-rail door-way, which left the full inside of the shop or store visible, so that, to all intents and purposes, the interior was within the turn of a key of being as much in the way of business as shops of the same kind in Paris. What prevented business being done, and clerks and assistants being forced to labor as vigorously on the Sabbath as on any other day? The law alone. This, a breath might destroy; and public opinion, already accustomed to the sight of shop windows open on Sundays, would easily become reconciled to the turn of the key in the iron door. At first this would be only for a few hours, of course, but afterwards, just as in Paris, forever. No doubt, a large percentage of good, religious shopkeepers avoid this scandal, and I hope the public of our cities will make out these, and patronize them in preference to others, who put the thin end of the wedge of destruction into our observance of the Christian sanctity of the Sabbath—an observance which, in the midst of a world falling fast from God, sustains that great, divine institution; and, besides giving time to worship God, protects the liberties of the poor, and prevents them from again becoming slaves. The doing away by degrees of the "Lord's Day" is a favorite aim of Atheism; and it is by resisting this aim—by resisting all its aims on morality and religion—that we can hope to sustain the Christianity and the religious character of this country and its people.[4]

But granting that British lodges remain unaffected by Atheism and Anti-Christianity which, as we have seen, influence the whole mass of Continental Freemasonry, would they on that account be innocent? Could a conscientious man of any Christian denomination join them?

The question is, of course, decided for Catholics. The Church forbids her children to be members of British or any Freemasonry under penalty of excommunication. The reasons which have led the Church to make a law so stringent and so serious must have been very grave. We have seen some at least of these reasons, and it is certainly with a full knowledge of facts that she has decreed the same penalties against such of her children as join the English lodges as she has against those who join the lodges of the Continent.

Then, though parsons have become "chaplains" to lodges, Anglicans generally have shown no sympathy with the Freemasonry of England. I am not aware that

---

[4] EDITOR'S NOTE: See Monsignor Dillon's original footnote in appendix II provided at the end of this chapter.

Protestant denominations assume, or that their members grant them, the power of making laws which could bind in conscience. If they did possess such power, many of them, I have no doubt, would forbid Freemasonry, as dangerous and evil in itself. But it needs not a law from man to guide one in determining what is clearly prohibited by reason and revelation.

Now that which is called harmless Freemasonry with us, is, besides the evident danger to which it is exposed, of being made what it has become in the rest of the world, both sacrilegious and dangerous. If it be only a society for brotherly intercourse and mutual help, where can be the necessity of taking for such purposes a number of oaths of the most frightful character? I shall now quote some of these oaths— the most ordinary ones taken by every English Freemason who advances to the first three degrees of the Craft. Oaths far more blasphemous and terrible are taken in the higher degrees both in England and on the Continent. I shall also give you the passwords, grips, and signs for these three main degrees. One can then judge of the nature of the travesty that is made of the name of God for purposes utterly puerile, if not meant to cover such real and deadly secrecy as that of Continental Masonry.

The first of these oaths is administered to the candidate who wishes to become an apprentice. He is divested of all money and metal. His right arm, left breast, and left knee are bare. His right heel is slipshod. He is blindfolded, and a rope called a "cable tow," adapted for hanging, is placed round his neck. A sword is pointed to his breast, and in this manner he is placed kneeling before the Master of the

Lodge, in whose presence he takes the following oath, his hand placed on a Bible:

> I, [First and Last name], in the presence of the great Architect of the Universe, and of this warranted, worthy, and worshipful Lodge of free and accepted Masons, regularly assembled and properly dedicated, of my own free will and accord, do hereby and hereon, most solemnly and sincerely swear, that I will always hail, conceal, and never reveal, any part or parts, point or points, of the secrets and mysteries of, or belonging to, free and accepted Masons in masonry, which have been, shall now, or hereafter may be, communicated to me, unless it be to a true and lawful brother or brothers, and not even to him or them, till after due trial, strict examination, or sure information from a well-known brother, that he or they are worthy of that confidence, or in the body of a just, perfect, and regular lodge of accepted Freemasons. I further solemnly promise, that I will not write those secrets, print, carve, engrave, or otherwise them delineate, or cause or suffer them to be done so by others, if in my power to prevent it, on anything movable or immovable under the canopy of heaven, whereby or whereon any letter, character or figure, or the least trace of a letter, character or figure may become legible or intelligible to myself, or to any-one in the world, so that our secrets, arts, and hidden mysteries, may improperly become known through my unworthiness. These several points I solemnly swear to observe, without evasion, equivocation, or

mental reservation of any kind, under no less a penalty, on the violation of any of them, than to have *my throat cut across, my tongue torn out by the root, and my body buried in the sand of the sea at low water mark,* or a cable's length from the shore, where the tide regularly ebbs and flows twice in the twenty-four hours, or the more efficient punishment of being branded as a willfully perjured individual, void of all moral worth, and unfit to be received in this warranted lodge, or in any other warranted lodge, or society of Masons, who prize honor and virtue above all the external advantages of rank and fortune: So help me, God, and keep me steadfast in this my great and solemn obligation of an Entered Apprentice Freemason.

Worshipful Master:

What you have repeated may be considered a sacred promise as a pledge of your fidelity, and to render it a solemn obligation, I will thank you to seal it with your lips on the volume of the sacred law. (*Kisses the Bible*)

When the above oath is duly taken, the sign is given. This, for an Apprentice, consists of a gesture made by drawing the hand smartly across the throat and dropping it to the side. This gesture has reference to the penalty attached to breaking the oath. The grip is also a penal sign. It consists of a distinct pressure of the top of the right-hand thumb to the first joint from the wrist of the right-hand forefinger, grasping the finger with the hand. The password is BOAZ, and is given letter by letter.

There are a number of quaint ceremonial charges and lectures which may be seen by consulting any of the Manuals

of Freemasonry, and which are perfectly given in a treatise
by one Carlyle, an Atheist, who undertook for the benefit
of Infidelity to divulge the whole of the mere ceremonial
secrecy of English Freemasons in order to advance the real
secret of it all, namely, Pantheism or Atheism, and hatred for
every form of Christianity. The English Freemasons made
too much of the ceremonies and too little of Atheism, and
hence the design of real Infidelity to get the "real secret" into
English lodges by expelling the pretended one.

The oath of the second degree, that of Fellow-Craft, is as
follows:

> I, [First and Last name], in the presence of the Grand
> Geometrician of the Universe, and in this worshipful
> and warranted Lodge of Fellow-Craft Masons, duly
> constituted, regularly assembled, and properly dedi-
> cated, of my own free will and accord, do hereby and
> hereon most solemnly promise and swear that I will
> always hail, conceal, and never reveal any or either
> of the secrets or mysteries of, or belonging to, the
> second degree of Freemasonry, known by the name
> of the Fellow-Craft; to him who is but an Entered
> Apprentice, no more than I would either of them
> to the uninitiated or the popular world who are not
> Masons. I further solemnly pledge myself to act as a
> true and faithful craftsman, obey signs, and maintain
> the principles inculcated in the first degree. All these
> points I most solemnly swear to obey, without evasion,
> equivocation, or mental reservation of any kind, under
> no less a penalty, on the violation of any of them, in

addition to my former obligation, than to have my left breast cut open, my heart torn therefrom, and given to the ravenous birds of the air, or the devouring beasts of the field, as a prey: So help me Almighty God, and keep me steadfast in this my great and solemn obligation of a Fellow-Craft Mason.

After taking this oath with all formality, the Fellow-Craft is entrusted with the sign, grip, and password by the Master, who thus addresses him:

You, having taken the solemn obligation of a Fellow-Craft Freemason, I shall proceed to entrust you with the secrets of the degree. You will advance towards me as at your initiation. Now take another pace with your left foot, bringing the right heel into its hollow, as before. That is the second regular step in Freemasonry, and it is in this position that the secrets of the degree are communicated. They consist, as in the former instance, of a *sign, token,* and *word*; with this difference that the sign is of a three-fold nature. The first part of a threefold sign is called the sign of fidelity, emblematically to shield the repository of your secrets from the attacks of the cowan. (*The sign is made by pressing the right hand on the left breast, extending the thumb perpendicularly to form a square*) The second part is called the hailing sign, and is given by throwing the left hand up in this manner. (*Horizontal from the shoulder to the elbow, and perpendicular from the elbow to the ends of the fingers, with the thumb and forefinger forming a square*) The third part is called the penal sign, and is given by drawing the hand across the breasts and dropping it to the side. This is an allusion to the penalty of your obligation, implying that as a man of honor, and a Fellow-Craft, you would rather have your heart torn from your breast, than to improperly divulge the secrets of this degree. The grip, or token, is given by a distinct pressure of the thumb on the second joint of the hand or that of the middle finger. This demands a word; a word to be given and received with the same strict caution as the one in the former degree, either by letters or syllables. The word is JACHIN. As in the course of the evening you will be called on for this word, the Senior Deacon will now dictate the answers you will have to give.

The next oath is that of the highest substantial degree in old Freemasonry, namely, that of Master. Attention is specially to be paid to the words "or at my own option."

I, [First and Last name], in the presence of the Most High, and of this worthy and worshipful lodge, duly constituted, regularly assembled, and properly dedicated, of my own free will and accord, do hereby and hereon, most solemnly promise and swear, that I will always hail, conceal, and never reveal, any or either of the secrets or mysteries of, or belonging to, the degree of a Master Mason, to anyone in the world, unless it be to him or them to whom the same may justly and lawfully belong; and not even to him or them, until after due trials, strict examination, or full conviction, that he or they are worthy of that confidence,

or in the bosom of a Master Mason's Lodge. I further
most solemnly engage that I will keep the secrets of
the Third Degree from him who is but a Fellow-Craft
Mason, with the same strict caution as I will those of
the Second Degree from him who is but an Entered
Apprentice Freemason; the same or either of them,
from anyone in the known world, unless to true and
lawful Brother Masons. I further solemnly engage
myself to advance to the pedestal of the square and
compasses, to answer and obey all lawful signs and
summonses sent to me from a Master Mason's Lodge,
if within the length of my cable-tow, and to plead no
excuse except sickness, or the pressing emergency of
my own private or public avocations. I furthermore
solemnly pledge myself to maintain and support the
five points of fellowship, in act as well as in word; that
my hand given to a Mason shall be the sure pledge
of brotherhood; that my foot shall traverse through
danger and difficulties, to unite with his in forming
a column of mutual defense and safety; that the pos-
ture of my daily supplications shall remind me of his
wants, and dispose my heart to succor his distresses
and relieve his necessities, as far as may fairly be done
without detriment to myself or connections; that my
breast shall be the sacred repository of his secrets,
when delivered to me as such; murder, treason, felony,
and all other offences contrary to the law of God, or
the ordinances of the realm, being at all times most
especially excepted *or at my own option*: and finally,
that I will support a Master Mason's character in his

absence as well as I would if he were present. I will not revile him myself, nor knowingly suffer others to do so; but will boldly repel the slander of his good name, and strictly respect the chastity of those that are most dear to him, in the persons of his wife, sister, or his child: and that I will not knowingly have unlawful carnal connection with either of them. I furthermore solemnly vow and declare, that I will not defraud a Brother Master Mason, or see him defrauded of the most trifling amount, without giving him due and timely notice thereof; that I will also prefer a Brother Master Mason in all my dealings, and recommend him to others as much as lies in my power, so long as he shall continue to act honorably, honestly, and faithfully towards me and others. All these several points I promise to observe, without equivocation or mental reservation of any kind, under no less a penalty, on the violation of any of them, than to have my body severed in two, my bowels torn thereout, and burned to ashes in the center, and those ashes scattered before the four cardinal points of heaven, so that no trace or remembrance of me shall be left among men, particularly among Master Masons: So help me God, and keep me steadfast in this grand and solemn obligation, being that of a Master Mason.

A long ceremony follows, in which the newly-made Master is made to sham a dead man and to be raised to life by the Master, grasping, or rather clawing his hand or wrist, by putting his right foot to his foot, his knee to his knee, bringing up the right breast to his breast, and with his hand over the back. This is practiced in Masonry as the five points of Fellowship.

Then the Master gives the signs, grip, and password, saying:

> Of the signs, the first and second are casual, the third is penal. The first casual sign is called the sign of horror, and is given from the Fellow-Craft's hailing sign, by dropping the left hand and elevating the right, as if to screen the eyes from a painful sight, at the same time throwing the head over the right shoulder, as a remove or turning away from that sight. It alludes to the finding of our murdered Master Hiram by the twelve Fellow-Crafts. The second casual sign is called the sign of sympathy or sorrow, and is given by bending the head a little forward, and by striking the right hand gently on the forehead. The third is called the penal sign, because it alludes to the penalty of your obligation, and is given by drawing the hand across the center of the body, dropping it to the side, and then raising it again to place the point of the thumb on the navel. It implies that, as a man of honor and a Master Mason, you would rather be severed in two than improperly divulge the secrets of this Degree. The grip or token is the first of the five points of fellowship. The five points of fellowship are: first, a grip with the right hand of each other's wrist, with the points of the fingers; second, right foot parallel with right foot on the inside; third, right knee to right knee; fourth, right breast to right breast; fifth, hand over shoulder, supporting the back. It is in this position, and this only,

except in open lodge, and then but in a whisper, that
the word is given. It is MAHABONE or MACBENACH.
The former is the ancient, the latter the modern word.

I have here given an idea of the principal ceremonies used
in making English Freemasons. I could not in the space I
have allotted to myself, enter, as I would wish to do, upon
other features of its ridiculous rites and observances, many
of which in still higher degrees, get a gradually opening,
Atheistic, and most anti-Christian interpretation. But it will
suffice for my purpose to bring one fact under your observation. In the ceremonies accompanying initiations, many
charges are made to the candidates, and lectures and cate-
chizings are given. In these, in the highest degrees, the real
secret is gradually divulged in a manner apparently the most
simple. For instance in the degree of the Knights Adepts of
the Eagle or the Sun, the Master in his charge describing the
Bible, Compass, and Square, says:

> By the *Bible*, you are to understand that it is the
> only law you ought to follow. It is that which Adam
> received at his creation, and which the Almighty
> engraved in his heart. *This law is called natural law*,
> and shows positively that there is but *one God*, and to
> adore only him without any sub-division or interpo-
> lation. The *Compass* gives you the faculty of judging
> for yourself, that whatever God has created is well,
> and he is the sovereign author of everything. Existing
> in himself, nothing is either good or evil, because we
> understand by this expression an action done which
> is excellent in itself, is relative, and submits to the

human understanding, judging to know the value and price of such action, and that God, with whom everything is possible, communicates nothing of his will but such as his great goodness pleases; and everything in the universe is governed as he has decreed it with justice, being able to compare it with the attributes of the Divinity. I equally say, that in himself there is no evil, because he has made everything with exactness, and that *everything exists according to his will; consequently, as it ought to be.* The distance between good and evil, with the Divinity, cannot be more justly and clearly compared than by a circle formed with a compass: from the points being reunited there is formed an entire circumference; and when any point in particular equally approaches or equally separates from its point, it is only a faint resemblance of the distance between good and evil, which we compare by the points of a compass, forming a circle, *which circle, when completed, is God!*

From this it will be clear, to what the so-called veneration for the Bible and for religion comes to, at last, in all Freemasonry. From apparent agreement with Christianity it ends in Atheism. In the essentially Jewish symbolism of Masonry, the Trinity is ignored from the commencement, and God reduced to a Grand Architect. The mention of Christ is carefully avoided. By degrees the Bible is not revelation at all—only the laws written on the heart of every man by the one God—the one God, yet, however, somewhat respected. But in a little while, we find the "one God" reduced to very small dimensions indeed. You may judge for yourself by the Compass that God exists in himself, "*therefore*"—though it is hard here to see the *therefore*—"nothing is either good or evil." Here is a blow at the moral law. Finally, "God" spoken of with such respect in all the preceding degrees, is reduced to a nonentity—"*which circle when completed is God.*" This is a perfect introduction on Weishaupt's lines to Weishaupt's Pantheism.

But the theories of Masonry, however developed, do less practical mischief than the conduct it fosters. The English, happily for themselves, are, in many useful respects, an eminently inconsistent people. The gentry amongst them can join Freemasonry and yet keep, in the most illogical manner possible, their very diluted form of Christianity. It has been otherwise with the more reasoning Continental Masons. They either abandon the Craft or abandon their Christianity. But the morality inculcated by Freemasonry has done immense damage in English-speaking countries, nevertheless. The very oath binding a Master Mason to respect the chastity of certain near relations of another Master Mason, insinuates a wide field for license; and Masons, even in England, have never been the most moral of men. It leads them, we too well know, to the neglect of home duties, and it leads them to an unjust persecution of outsiders, for the benefit of Craftsmen—a matter more than once complained of as injurious in trade, politics, and social life. I need not call to your mind what mischief—what foul murder—it has led to in America. I prefer to let Carlyle, the Infidel apologist of dark Masonry, speak on this point. He says:[5]

---

[5]   EDITOR'S CITATION: Alfred Carlile, *An Introduction to the Science of the Modern Mysteries of Masonry, Christianity, and Judaism* (London: Alfred Carlile, 1836), xi–xii.

My exposure of Freemasonry in 1825 led to its exposure in the United States of America; and a Mason there
of the name of William Morgan, having announced
his intention to assist in the work of exposure, was kid-
napped under pretended forms and warrants of law, by
his brother Masons, removed from the State of New
York to the borders of Canada, near the falls of Niag-
ara, and there most barbarously murdered. This happened in 1826.[6] The States have been for many years
much excited upon the subject; a regular warfare has
arisen between Masons and anti-Masons; societies of
anti-Masons have been formed; newspapers and magazines started; and many pamphlets and volumes, with
much correspondence, published; so that, before the
Slavery Question was pressed among them, all parties
had merged into Masons and anti-Masons. Several persons were punished for the abduction of Morgan; but
the murderers were sheltered by Masonic Lodges, and
rescued from justice. This was quite enough to show
that Masonry, as consisting of a secret association, or

---

[6] EDITOR'S NOTE: After the Morgan incident, John Quincy Adams—son
of second president John Adams, and the sixth president of the United
States—wrote a series of anti-Masonic letters and addresses. In a letter
addressed to Edward Ingersoll, Esq. on September 22, 1831, he wrote as
follows: "It has therefore been in my opinion, ever since the disclosure of
the Morgan-murder crimes, and of the Masonic Oaths and Penalties by
which they were instigated, the indispensable duty of the Masonic Order
in the United States, either to dissolve itself, or to discard forever from its
constitution and laws all *oaths*, all *penalties*, all *secrets*, and as ridiculous ap-
pendages to them, all *mysteries* and *pageants*." John Quincy Adams, *Letters
on the Masonic Institution* (Boston: Press of T.R. Marvin, 1847), 23.

an association with secret oaths and ceremonies, is a political and social evil.

While writing this, I have been informed that individual members of Orange Lodges have smiled at the dissolution of their lodges, with the observation, that precisely the same association can be carried on under the name of Masonry. This is an evil that secret associations admit. No form of anything of the kind, when secret, can protect itself from abuses; and this is a strong reason why Masonic associations should get rid of their unnecessary oaths, revise their constitutions, and throw themselves open to public inspection and report. There is enough that may be made respectable in Masonry, in the present state of mind and customs, to admit of scrutinizing publicity.

The question of the death of Morgan, and other unhappy incidents in the history of Freemasonry in the United States, are very fully treated by Father Muller, C.SS.R. Yet, strange to say, notwithstanding anti-Masonic societies being formed extensively in the Great Republic, and the horror created by the murder of Morgan, there is no part of the world where Masonry flourishes more than in America. I believe it will yet become the greatest enemy of the free institutions of that country.

I am willing to admit, however, that Freemasonry has, thank God, made little progress amongst Catholics in Ireland, or Catholics of Irish birth or blood anywhere. This is true, and the same may be said of millions of Protestants who have not joined Masonry. But the evil is amongst us for all that, and it is necessary that we should know what it is and how it manifests itself.

We know too, that besides the movements which Masonry has been called upon to serve by means of Masonic organs, and resolutions inspired by Atheism, and advocated by its hidden friends scattered through British lodges, there have been at all times, at least in London, some lodges affiliated to Continental lodges, and doing the work of Weishaupt. Of this class were several lodges of foreigners and Jews, which existed in London contemporaneously with Lord Palmerston, and which aided him in the government and direction of the secret societies of the world, and in the Infidel Revolution which was carried on during his reign with such ability and success. In the works of Deschamps, a detailed account will be found of several of these high temples of iniquity and deadly, anti-Christian intrigue.

But besides Masonry of any description—and every description, for reasons already stated, even the most apparently harmless, is positively bad—bad, because of its oaths, because of its associations, and because of its un-Christian character, there were other societies formed on the lines of Illuminated Masonry under various names in Great Britain, and especially in Ireland, of which I deem it my duty while treating of the subject to speak as plainly as I possibly can. The most notable amongst these is Fenianism.

Appendix I (footnote 2)

A curious proof of this fact is preserved in the records of Dublin Castle, where, upon a return of the members and officers of Freemasonry, as it is with us, having been asked for by the government, the names of the delegates from the Irish Lodges to various continental national Grand Lodges were given. I do not place much value upon the fact as a means to connect British Freemasonry with its kind on the Continent, because the Real Secret was, as a rule, kept from British and Irish Masons. But the intercourse had an immense effect in causing the vanguard cries of the continental lodges to find a fatal support from British Masons in and out of Parliament. These delegates brought back high-sounding theories about "education" without "denominationalism," etc., but they were never trusted with the ultimate designs of the Continental directory to destroy the Throne, the Constitution, and lastly, the very property of British Masons. These designs are communicated only to reliable individuals, who know full well the Real Secret of the sect—and keep it.

Appendix II (footnote 4)

The Alta Vendita and the intellectual party in Masonry have for a long time endeavored to revive practices which Christianity did away with, and which were distinctly pagan. Amongst others they have made every exertion to destroy the Christian respect for the dead, and every respect for the dead which kept alive in the living the belief in the immortality of the soul. Death is with man a powerful means to keep alive in him a wholesome fear of his Creator and respect for religion. Spiritual writers—following the advice of the Holy Ghost in the Scriptures, "Remember thy last end and thou shalt never sin" [Sir. 7:40], always place before Christians the thought of death as the most wholesome lesson in the spiritual life. The demon from the beginning tried to do away with this salutary thought as the most opposed to his designs. When Eve feared to eat the forbidden fruit, it was because of the terror with which death inspired her. The devil lied in telling her, "No, ye shall not die the death" [Gen. 3:4]. She believed the liar and the murderer. His followers in the secret societies established by him, and which he keeps in such unity of aim and action, second his desire to the utmost by doing away with whatever may keep alive in man the thoughts of his last end and of a future resurrection, and, of course, of judgment. Weishaupt taught his disciples to look upon suicide as a praiseworthy means of flying the horrors of death and present inconvenience. Cremation, instantly destroying the terrors of corruption—the death's head and cross-bones—the worst features in mortality, as exhibited in a corpse, is therefore largely advocated by the secret societies on plausibly devised sanitary, aesthetic, and economical grounds. But it is a pagan practice, opposed to that followed ever since the creation of the world by all that had the knowledge of the true God in the Primeval, Jewish, and Christian dispensations. The Revolution in Italy has established at Rome, Milan and Naples means of cremating bodies, and advanced Freemasons, like Garibaldi,[7] have in their wills, directed that their bodies should be cremated.

A little reflection, however, will show that neither for rich nor poor, for sanitary, for economical or any other reasons can cremation be advocated in preference to burial. For besides the fact that the earth which is always the best, safest, and readiest solvent for corruption, may be had everywhere in abundance, and at a safe enough distance from cities if so

---

[7] EDITOR'S NOTE: See footnote 4 of the preface.

desired, there is the fact before us that the Roman poor and slaves were thrown into pits to save expense; while cremation, where practiced by the rich, led to most extravagant expenses and excesses. Christians, when they find plausibly given, interesting notices of cremation in journals of any kind, may be quite sure that the writer who writes them is influenced by the secret sect, and these scribes are found everywhere and find means to ventilate their ideas—unsuspected by the proprietors—sometimes into journals professedly Catholic. They are advocating, it is thought, a harmless sanitary arrangement not condemned by the Church; but they are doing all the while, consciously or unconsciously, the work of the secret Atheistic sect. As it is with cremation, so it is with the eating of horse flesh and other apparently harmless practices advocated by the sectaries solely because in practice or in theory, discountenanced by, or not practiced by, Christians.

When in these days, a distinctive anti-Christian custom is seen advocated without any urgent reason in the press, now almost entirely in the hands of members of the Sect, and generally Jewish members, Christians may fear that the cloven foot is in the matter. The cold water, the ridicule, the contempt thrown upon religious observances, the attempt to rob them of their purely Christian character are other methods employed by the sects to loosen the influence of Christianity. In opposition to these, Christian people should carefully study to keep the joy of Christmas, the penitential fasts, the sanctity of Holy Week, the splendor of Easter, the feasts of God's holy Mother and of the saints—to fill themselves, in one word, with the Christian spirit of the Ages of Faith.

CHAPTER 22

Fenianism

*"The Fenian movement after being nursed in America, appeared in
Ireland, as a society founded upon lines not very unlike those of the
Carbonari of Italy. It was Illuminated Freemasonry with, of course,
another name, in order not to avert the pious Catholic men it meant
to seduce and destroy from its ranks. But being what it was, it could
not long conceal its innate, determined hostility to the Catholic
religion; and it proved itself in Ireland, and wherever it took a hold
of the people in the three kingdoms, one of the most formidable
enemies to the souls of the Irish people that had ever appeared."*

—Monsignor Dillon

FROM THE ESTABLISHMENT of Illuminated Masonry, its
Supreme Council never lost sight of a discontented population in any part of the earth. Aspiring to universal rule, it carefully took cognizance of every national or social movement
among the masses, which gave promise of advancing its aims.

It was thus it succeeded with the operative [working] and
peasant population of France, so as to accomplish the first
and every subsequent revolution in that country. The letters of the Alta Vendita and of Piccolo Tigre especially, have
carefully had in view the corruption of the masses of working men, so as to de-Christianize them adroitly, and fit and
fashion them into revolutionists.

235

Now amongst all the peoples of the earth, those who most impeded Atheistic designs, were the Catholics of Ireland. Forced to leave their country in millions, they brought to Scotland, to England, to the United States, to Canada, to the West Indies, to our growing Colonies—all empires in germ—of Australia, and as soldiers of England, to India, Africa, and China, the strongest existing faith in that very religion which Atheistic Freemasonry so much desires to destroy. It would be impossible to imagine, that the dark Directories of the Illuminati did not take careful account of this population. And they did.

In the years preceding 1798, they had emissaries, like those sent subsequently amongst the Catholic Carbonari of Naples, active amongst the ranks of the United Irishmen. France, then completely under the control of the Illuminati, sent aid which she sorely wanted at home, at the instigation of these very emissaries, to found an Irish Republic, of course on the Atheistic lines, upon which all the Republics then founded by her arms were established. That expedition ended in failure; but organizations on the lines of Freemasonry continued for many years afterwards to distract Ireland.

As in Italy, the Illuminati had taught the peasantry of Ireland how to conspire in secret, oath bound, and, of course, often murderous, but always hopeless, league against their oppressors. These societies never accomplished one atom of good for Ireland. They did much mischief. But what cared the hidden enemies of religion for the real happiness of the Irish? Their gain consisted in placing antagonism between the faithful pastors of the people and the members of those secret societies of Ribbonmen, Molly Maguires, and other such associations, organized by designing and, generally, traitorous scoundrels.

In 1848, there was something like a tendency in Ireland to imitate the secret revolutionary movements established on the Continent by Mazzini.[1] We had a Young Ireland Organization. That was not initiated as a secret society. Neither was the Society of United Irishmen at first. But the open United Irishmen led to the secret society; and so very easily might the Young Ireland movement of 1848, if it had not been prematurely brought to a conclusion. As it was, it led, without its leaders desiring it—indeed against the will of many of them—to the deepest, most cunningly devised, widespread, and mischievous, secret organization into which heedless young Irishmen have been ever yet entrapped. This was the Fenian Secret Society.

We can speak of the action of the originators of this movement as connected with the worst form of Atheistic, Continental, secret-society organization; for they boasted of having gone over to France "to study" the plans elaborated by the most abandoned revolutionists in that country. For my own part, I believe that these hot-headed young men, as they were at the time, never took the initiative themselves, but were entrapped into this course of action by agents of the designing Directory of the Atheistic movement, at that moment presided over by Lord Palmerston himself. That the association of the Fenians should be created and afterwards sacrificed to England, would be but in keeping with the tradition of the Alta Vendita, in whose place Lord Palmerston and his council stood.

---

[1] EDITOR'S NOTE: See footnote 2 of chapter 13.

We read in the life of the celebrated Nubius, the monarch who preceded Palmerston, that he often betrayed into the hands of the Pontifical Government some lodges of the Carbonari under his own rule, for the purpose of screening himself and of punishing those very lodges. If he found a lodge indiscreet, or possessing amongst its members too much religion to be tractable enough to follow the Infidel movement, he betrayed it. He told the government how to find it out; where it had its arms concealed; who were its members; and what were their misdeeds. They were accordingly taken red-handed, tried, and executed. Nubius got rid of a difficult body, for whom he felt nothing but contempt; and his position at Rome was rendered secure to gnaw, as he himself expressed it, at the foundations of that Pontifical power, which thought that any connection such a respectable nobleman as he was might have with assassins could be only in reality for the good of religion and the government, to which by station, education, and even class-interest he was allied.

Palmerston, too, if he wanted a blind to lead his colleagues astray, could, in the knowledge to be obtained of Fenian plots in Ireland and America, have a ready excuse for his well-known, constant intercourse with the heads of the Revolution of the world. What scruple would he have, any more than his predecessor Nubius, in urging on a few men whom he despised to revolution, and then using means to strangle their efforts and themselves if necessary? It was good policy in the sight of some at least of his colleagues, to manifest Ireland as revolutionary, especially when such a man as Palmerston had all the threads of the conspiracy which aimed at the revolution in his hand. They knew that he knew where to send his spies, and thwart at the opportune moment the whole movement. He could cause insurrections to be made in the most insane manner, as to time and place, just as they were made, and cover the conspirators with easy defeat and ridicule.

However this may be, the Fenian movement after being nursed in America, appeared in Ireland, as a society founded upon lines not very unlike those of the Carbonari of Italy. It was Illuminated Freemasonry with, of course, another name, in order not to avert the pious Catholic men it meant to seduce and destroy from its ranks. But being what it was, it could not long conceal its innate, determined hostility to the Catholic religion; and it proved itself in Ireland, and wherever it took a hold of the people in the three kingdoms, one of the most formidable enemies to the souls of the Irish people that had ever appeared.

When I say this, do not imagine that I mean for a single moment to infer that many of those who joined it held or knew its views. If all I have hitherto stated proves anything, it is this: the nature of the infernal conspiracy which we are considering is essentially hypocritical. It comes as Freemasonry comes, with a lie in its mouth. It comes under false pretenses always. So it came to Italy under the name of Carbonarism. It came, not only professing the purest Catholic religion, but absolutely made the saying of prayers, the frequentation of the sacraments, the open confession of the Faith, and devotion to the Vicar of Christ, a matter of obligation.

I do not believe that Fenianism came to Ireland with so many pious professions. But it came in the guise of patriotism, which in Ireland, for many centuries, was so bound up with religion that in the minds of the peasantry the one became inseparably connected with the other. The friend of the one was looked upon as the friend of the other; and the enemy of the one was regarded as the enemy of the other. Hence, in the minds of the Irish, in my own boyhood, the French who came over under Hoche,[2] were regarded as Catholic. The Irish held that France was then, as she was when the "wild geese" went over to fight for the Bourbons, a Catholic nation. The truth was, of course, quite the opposite; but so long had the Irish people been accustomed to regard the French as Catholic that they still cherished the delusion, and would hear or believe nothing to the contrary. It was enough, therefore, for Fenianism to appear in the guise of a national movement meant to free the country from Protestant England, that it should without question be looked upon as—at least in the first instance—essentially Catholic.

Nevertheless, after its leaders had gone to Paris to study the methods of the French and Italian Carbonari, and returned to create circles and centers on the plan of the *Vendite* of the Italians, they showed a large amount of the Infidel spirit of the men they found in France, and determined to spread it in Ireland. They well knew that the Catholic clergy would be sure to oppose and denounce them as would every wise and

---

[2]   EDITOR'S NOTE: Lazar Hoche (1768–97) was a French soldier who became a general of the Revolutionary Army, and was appointed to lead the troops who in 1796 were to help the United Irishmen in their rebellion against British rule.

really patriotic man in the country. The utter impossibility of any military movement which could be made by any available number of destitute Irish peasantry succeeding at the time, was in itself reason enough why men of any humanity, not to speak at all of the clergy, should endeavor to dissuade the people from the mad enterprise of the Fenians.

Every good and experienced Irishman, Smith O'Brien, the editors of the *Nation*, and others, did so; yet strange to say, the leaders of the disastrous movement, the Irish and the American organizers, were permitted by the English government, at least so long as Lord Palmerston lived, to act almost as they pleased in Ireland. The government knew that while impotent to injure England, these agitators and conspirators were doing the work which English anti-Catholic hate desired to do, more effectively than any delusion, or bribe, or persecution which heresy had been able to invent. They were undermining the Faith of the people and destroying secretly but surely that love and respect for the clergy which had distinguished the country ever since the days of St. Patrick.

A paper edited by one of these men was circulated for at least two years in the homes of nearly all the population. It contained, to be sure, much incitement to revolution; but it contained also that which in Lord Palmerston's eyes compensated for the kind of revolution Fenians could make a thousand-fold—it contained the most able, virulent, and subtle attacks upon the clergy. This paper remained undisturbed until Palmerston passed away and affairs in America made Fenianism a real danger for his successors in office. Its issues contained letters written in its own office, but purporting to come from various country parishes, calumniating many of the most venerable of the priests of the people. Men who so loved their flocks as to sacrifice all for them during the famine years[3]—men who had lived with them from youth to old age, were now so artfully assailed as foes of their country's liberation, that the people, maddened and deluded by such attacks, passed them on the road without the usual loving salutation Catholics in Ireland give to and receive from their priests. The Sect backed up the action of the newspaper. Its leaders got the "word of command" for that purpose, and had to be obeyed. Matters proceeded daily from bad to worse, until at last Divine Providence manifested clearly the deadly designs against religion underlying the Fenian movement, and the people of Ireland recoiled from it and were saved.

And then it was hard to keep even the leaders themselves bad to the end. At death, few of them like to face the God they have outraged without reconciliation. But in life these men, like the informers with whom they are so often in alliance, do desperate things to deceive first, and then, for a passing interest, to ruin their unfortunate dupes afterwards. For my own part, I am of [the] opinion that the man who deludes a number of brave young hearts to rush into a murderous enterprise, hopeless from the outset, is as dangerous as the man who seduces men to become assassins and then sacrifices their lives to save his own neck from the halter. At most there is but the difference of degree in the guilt and malignity of the leaders who urged on impetuous youth to

---

[3] EDITOR'S NOTE: Refers to the Great Famine, a period of mass starvation and disease that swept Ireland from 1845–49. Upwards of a million died, and more than two million left Ireland for opportunities elsewhere.

such risings as those of the snowstorms in 1867,[4] and of the scoundrel who planned assassination, entrapped and excited the same kind of youth to execute it, and then swore their lives away to save himself from his justly deserved doom.

I am led to this conclusion inevitably from the account given of the Fenian rising by one of the purest Irish patriots of this century, one just gone amidst the tears of his fellow-countrymen, with stainless name after a career of glorious labor, to his eternal reward. Mr. Alexander M. Sullivan[5] in his interesting "Story of Ireland," says:

> There was up to the last a fatuous amount of delusion maintained by the "Head Center" on this side of the Atlantic, James Stephens, a man of marvelous subtlety and wondrous powers of plausible imposition; crafty, cunning, and quite unscrupulous as to the employment of means to an end. However, the army ready to hand in America, if not utilized at once, would soon be melted away and gone, like the snows of past winters. So in the middle of 1865 it was resolved to take the field in the approaching autumn.
>
> It is hard to contemplate this decision or declaration without deeming it either insincere or wicked on the part of the leader or leaders, who at the moment knew the real condition of affairs in Ireland. That the enrolled members, howsoever few, would respond when called upon, was certain at any time; for the Irish are not cowards; the men who joined this desperate

---

[4] EDITOR'S NOTE: Refers to the Fenian Rising, an 1867 rebellion against British rule in Ireland organized by the Irish Republican Brotherhood.

[5] EDITOR'S NOTE: See footnote 9 of the preface.

enterprise were sure to prove themselves courageous, if not either prudent or wise. But the pretense of the revolutionary chief, that there was a force able to afford the merest chance of success, was too utterly false not to be plainly criminal.

Towards the close of 1865 came almost contemporaneously the Government swoop on the Irish Revolutionary executive, and the deposition—after solemn judicial trial, as prescribed by the laws of the society— of O'Mahony, the American "Head Center" for crimes and offenses alleged to be worse than mere imbecility, and the election in his stead of Colonel William R. Roberts, an Irish American merchant of high standing and honorable character, whose fortune had always generously aided Irish patriotic, charitable, or religious purposes. The deposed official, however, did not submit to the application of the society rules. He set up a rival association, a course in which he was supported by the Irish Head Center; and a painful scene of factious and acrimonious contention between the two parties thus antagonized, caused the English Government to hope—nay, for a moment—fully to believe— that the disappearance of both must soon follow.[6]

Mr. A. M. Sullivan, after speaking of the history of the Fenian movement in America, continues:

This brief episode at Ridgeway was for the confederated Irish the one gleam to lighten the page of their

---

[6] EDITOR'S CITATION: A. M. Sullivan, *Story of Ireland* (Dublin: M.H. Gill & Son, Ltd., 1909), 571–72.

history for 1866. That page was otherwise darkened and blotted by a record of humiliating and disgraceful exposures in connection with the Irish Head Center. In autumn of that year he proceeded to America, and finding his authority repudiated and his integrity doubted, he resorted to a course which it would be difficult to characterize too strongly. By way of attracting a following to his own standard, and obtaining a flush of money, he publicly announced that in the winter months close at hand, and before the new year dawned, he would (sealing his undertaking with an awful invocation of the Most High) be in Ireland, leading the long-promised insurrection. Had this been a mere "intention" which might be "disappointed," it was still manifestly criminal thus to announce it to the British Government, unless, indeed, his resources in hand were so enormous as to render England's preparations a matter of indifference. But it was not as an "intention" he announced it and swore to it. He threatened with the most serious personal consequences any and every man soever, who might dare to express a doubt that the event would come off as he swore. The few months remaining of the year flew by; his intimate adherents spread the rumor that he had sailed for the scene of action, and in Ireland the news occasioned almost a panic. One day, towards the close of December, however, all New York rang with the exposure that Stephens had never quitted for Ireland, but was hiding from his own enraged followers in Brooklyn. The scenes that ensued were such as may well be omitted from these pages. In that bitter hour thousands of honest, impulsive, and self-sacrificing Irishmen endured the anguish of discovering that they had been deceived as never had men been before; that an idol worshipped with frenzied devotion was, after all, a thing of clay.[7]

The plottings of the "Head Center," however, were not at an end. Mr. A. M. Sullivan continues:

In Ireland, where Stephens had been most implicitly believed in, the news of this collapse—which reached her early in 1867—filled the circles with keen humiliation. The more dispassionate wisely rejoiced that he had not attempted to keep a promise, the making of which was in itself a crime; but the desire to wipe out the reproach supposed to be cast on the whole enrollment by his public defection became so over-powering, that a rising was arranged to come off simultaneously all over Ireland on the 5th March, 1867.

Of all the insensate attempts at revolution recorded in history, this one assuredly was preeminent. The most extravagant of the ancient Fenian tales supplies nothing more absurd. The inmates of a lunatic asylum could scarcely have produced a more impossible scheme. The one redeeming feature in the whole proceeding was the conduct of the hapless men who engaged in it. Firstly, their courage in responding to such a summons at all, unarmed and unaided as they were. Secondly, their intense religious feeling. On the

---

[7] EDITOR'S CITATION: Sullivan, *Story of Ireland*, 576–77.

days immediately preceding the 5th March, the Catholic churches were crowded by the youth of the country, making spiritual preparations for what they believed would be a struggle in which many would fall and few survive. Thirdly, their noble humanity to the prisoners whom they captured, their scrupulous regard for private property, and their earnest anxiety to carry on their struggle without infraction in aught of the laws and rules of honorable warfare.

In the vicinity of Dublin, and in the Tipperary, Cork, and Limerick counties, attacks were made on the police stations, several of which were captured by or surrendered to the insurgents. But a circumstance as singular as any recorded in history intervened to suppress the movement more effectually than the armies and fleets of England ten times told could do. On the next night following the rising—the 6th of March—there commenced a snowstorm which will long be remembered in Ireland, as it was probably without precedent in our annals. For twelve days and nights without intermission, a tempest of snow and sleet raged over the land, piling snow to the depth of yards on all the mountains, streets, and highways. The plan of the insurrection evidently had for its chief feature desultory warfare in the mountain districts, but this intervention of the elements utterly frustrated the project, and saved Ireland from the horrors of a protracted struggle.[8]

---

[8]   Editor's Citation: Sullivan, *Story of Ireland*, 577–78.

Who that reads over this brief history of the contest between the Fenian leaders and the priesthood of Ireland, may not see the wisdom and goodness of the religious guides of the people, and the reckless cruelty and callousness of the secret society seducers? It was a life-and-death struggle. The true friends of the people could not look on and see them led to ruin of soul and body. They knew by a Light from on high, more certain than any that guides ships from danger, the real nature of the secret conspiracy that laid its meshes to deceive, to ruin, and to betray. They raised the warning voice, and for this were secretly assailed, maligned, circumvented, and even threatened in body, in life, in means, and in character. But the minister of God is not to be deterred by any such menaces. He that in the penal days braved the dungeon and the halter of them, and who everyday braves pestilence, want, and death if necessary for their sakes, who is of them and with them from the cradle to the grave, whose only interest is their interest, has surely more claims upon their love and allegiance than any conspirator. We learn wisdom from the end of all the secret society seducers—men first seduced themselves, and who then try to seduce others. But surely the Irish people and the young men of Ireland especially, have had experience enough of the whole lot of them. All seduce them into fatal courses under pretense of benefitting Ireland. Nearly all sell and betray them. All profit—if profit their wretched gain can be called—by the folly of our too fervid, too generous, too confiding youth.

Some of these same seducers are found, I am informed, plying their deadly trade amongst Irish working men in the large manufacturing districts of England and Scotland.

For aught I know they may be found in this very city or its neighborhood. They certainly are no friends of the Irish working man or of his family. Hopeless and criminal as were the Fenian conspiracies, the attempts of these openly lecturing, or worse still, secretly agitating, secret society seducers, are much worse. At best they are idlers who, instead of devoting themselves to honest toil, find it more congenial and easy to live upon the "subscriptions" of poor working men, who give to these oily tongued vagabonds a portion of their hard earnings "to liberate Ireland." God help us! To liberate Ireland by means of such heartless schemers, who would be only too happy to sell Ireland and their dupes into the bargain, for a wonderfully small consideration. It is well if these dangerous prowlers do not do worse and "swear in" some incautious, hot-headed, simple boys into societies which are seen to eventually bring the prison plank-bed if not the halter.

The Irish working man in England, in Scotland, or in America, has no worse enemy than these itinerant agitators who perambulate the country, creating excitement at one time, and encouraging secret-society practices at another. They render the condition of the Irish working man often intolerable. They lead him from home and to the public house. They encourage him in the worst possible habits for himself and his little family. They drag him from his God, from his religion, and often to his ruin.

The best way, believe me, for the Irish working man to serve Ireland in this country is to keep strictly sober, to mind his employment, to attend well to the Catholic education of his children, to live frugally, to practice economy, to become a respectable member of society. He will then have a voice and a voice that will be heard in the land, and when he comes to use the franchise [vote] he will benefit his fellows, and do something real and tangible in the Parliament of England, to serve Ireland. The victim of the secret society agitators is kept in his vices and drunkenness. He is never religious. He lives in rags and wretchedness, and dies in the workhouse or in the jail.

CHAPTER 23

Sad Ending of the Conspirators

*"How different is the case of the few apostates amongst them
who sold their faith! Who may not tell of the agony of mind, the
desolation, the suicides of these? But next to them in melancholiness
is the fate of the Irishman who first begins to listen to the seducer
of the secret society, and afterwards becomes himself a seducer, a
leader, perhaps a traitor, in the deadly, secret conspiracy to ruin
religion, to destroy God. . . . A life wasted, hopes blasted, happiness
departed, a cheerless, neglected, old age, are little recompense for the
free-thought and free-act which a system of Atheism and irreligion,
never really believed in, conferred upon any Catholic Irishman."*

—Monsignor Dillon

NOR CAN THERE be a spectacle presented by history more
sad than the fate of the unfortunate Fenian leaders. The Irish
who have died directly for their faith in the dungeon, on the
rack, or upon the gibbet, have had the crowning consolation
of martyrdom and the bright light of heaven when their sufferings were over. Those who fell victims of extermination, of
hunger, want, and exile, might, at least indirectly, trace their
sorrows to the same cause—grand, unalterable fidelity to the
Church of God. The martyrs' hope lit up their lives. The joy
they had even in famine, even in death, no man could take

251

from them. From their perishing bodies came forth the radiance of immortality. Their souls, naturally, the noblest souls, the most gifted, the very purest, given by God to this earth, conquered the very world that scorned and crucified them, with Him they loved and feared not to follow.

They endured the pangs of starvation, cold, and rags just as they did the jail, the fevership, and the gallows, with a sublime, godlike fortitude. Godlike, for it came from God indeed. Who ever heard of one of these millions of slowly-tormented victims seeking death by suicide—the remedy of the disbeliever? Who ever knew of one of them to seek to lengthen life by means which a section now condones, indeed half praises, in the case of the no more than equally tried man-slayers and cannibals in a shipwreck? Who that remembers the dread years of the great famine of 1847 and 1848 does not know of thousands and of tens of thousands of Irishmen and Irishwomen, aye, of Irish little children, that then laid down their lives in horrible agonies, sooner than receive from a hellish so-called "charity" the food, clothing, and patronage that would enable them to live in comfort—a "charity" which callous proselytizers offered everywhere at the price of one single act of apostasy—at the price of even eating meat on a Friday in contempt of God's Church? I myself have known of such cases. And I have seen this. I have seen downright honest pity manifested by these same starving but noble people of God for the rich man who lived in wealthy splendor, and then died in a great house near them, when they knew that by want of the Faith he ought to have, his life was without hope and his eternity without God.

Never since the days of Christ did a whole people realize more vividly or act more truly upon the teaching conveyed in the parable of the rich man lost and Lazarus saved [Luke 16:19-31]. The long eternity of hell, the want of the drop of water, never to be obtained, the eternal contempt and the eternal pain awaiting the sumptuously-living sinner, was no myth. It came from the mouth of Him who had the knowledge of the fact, because he was the Creator and the Judge. As vividly came the vision of their own bright, peaceful, wealthy rest, figured by the lot of Lazarus reposing in a bosom far brighter, far sweeter than that of Abraham—in the Heart of Jesus Christ, in the beautiful vision of God, in the embrace of Mary, the loved Mother of Ireland—and so these millions passed peacefully through the dark valley of famine, until, worn and weary, their bodies sank like the rain drops, forgotten, beneath the green sward[1] of Erin, and their souls passed forever to the joy of the blest.

How different is the case of the few apostates amongst them who sold their faith! Who may not tell of the agony of mind, the desolation, the suicides of these? But next to them in melancholiness is the fate of the Irishman who first begins to listen to the seducer of the secret society, and afterwards becomes himself a seducer, a leader, perhaps a traitor, in the deadly, secret conspiracy to ruin religion, to destroy God. His career is often this: At first a hopeful, young, ambitious student of his country's history, he begins to feel indignation at her wrongs, and wishes to right them. In a fatal hour he meets the tempter. He is sworn into the terrible sect. He gets a command, an importance in the organization. He is

---

[1] EDITOR'S NOTE: An expanse of short grass.

youthful, but the season of life wherein to make an honest livelihood passes rapidly in intrigue. He knows that the course into which he has fallen is bad, is injurious to religion, but he hopes to repent. Alas! little by little his conscience, his Faith passes from him. The day comes surely when he realizes his sad position, and knows the advice of the Church to be right. But having lived his best days to conspire, he now must "conspire to live," and inured to bad habits, he is at last ready for anything. Like the wretch who preys upon the little left to the Irish emigrant, now as a guide, now as a broker in New York or Liverpool, he, too, will wrench by every means fraud can devise the hard earnings of the poor, under pretense of injuring England, if not of liberating Ireland.

He will stop at nothing, and so the existing conspirator is made. He has no further scruple to join if he can the worst class of the Atheistic and Socialist plotters of Paris. He herds with them. And this is strange, for while the Irish conspirator may be as able to plot mischief as the worst of the miscreants with whom he associates in France, he differs from them in this, that in the secret of his soul he never loses his Faith. They know this well, and they watch him, use him, but never fully trust him. Many a broken Irish heart the children of the Revolution in Paris have made already. Many a one of those Irish victims wish again for the days of his boyish innocence and blessed faith. A life wasted, hopes blasted, happiness departed, a cheerless, neglected, old age, are little recompense for the free-thought and free-act which a system of Atheism and irreligion, never really believed in, conferred upon any Catholic Irishman.

CHAPTER 24

The Triumph of Irish Faith

"All secret societies and societies aiming at bad and irreligious
ends are no other than deadly Illuminated Freemasonry. Let
them be called by whatever name, they are a part of the system
of secret revolutionary fraud, invented and cast upon the earth
by Satan to compass the ruin of souls, and the destruction of
the reign of Jesus Christ. . . . All that secret organization of
which we have been speaking so much, is being framed by
Satan and his emissaries for one end long foreseen—that is,
to form, and that before very many years, the vast kingdom
of Antichrist, which already spreads its ramifications over the
whole earth. It is, you see, determined to leave no people, or
nation, or tribe, or tongue, unsubjected to its influence."

—Monsignor Dillon

THE SECRET SOCIETY onslaught on the attachment of the
people of Ireland to their spiritual guides and to their
ancient faith was treacherous, deadly, and long-continued.
But, thank heaven! the Church in Ireland, has survived the
shock, terrible though it was. My own Archbishop—at present, happily for Australia, placed by the Holy Father over
that extensive portion of the vineyard—a Prelate who knows
the Ireland of history better, I would say, than any living
man, and the Ireland of the present day, as well, certainly,

assured me that never since the days of Saint Patrick was the Faith stronger in the country than at the present moment. The frequentation of the sacraments was at no past period more general—if ever as general. Pious Confraternities spread their blessed influence everywhere. Temperance is progressing. The clergy, numerous and well supported by the people, enlighten all by the purity, self-denial, and laboriousness of their lives. They visit their people in every home, no matter how poor, in every cabin, in every garret. They are, as ever, of and with the people. Their little means are freely given to every want of education and religion, and, as far as these means can go, to the poor. This is a condition of things that must continue to bind the priests to the people, and the whole Church of Ireland to God. These holy pastors, whom every tie of nature, affection, and duty, bind to the Irish people, are the guides who have been with them for ages. Numerous, intelligent, learned, patriotic in the highest degree, sons of the saints, they alone can lead God's people aright. They have done so, and sad must be the hour when miserable adventurers, seeking their own gains, can so delude a nation as to seduce them from the side of God's anointed, to what did prove, and must ever prove, if pursued by the Irish people against the loving and intelligent advice of the Irish priests, "a mockery, a delusion, and a snare."

The time is come, however, when using their own intelligence Irishmen will everywhere be able to resist the wiles and temptations of the secret society seducer, and think for themselves. The leaders, the fathers who have never deceived them, whose advices [sic] are always given for their best advantage, who suffered and died for them in the past, and are ready to do so in the present and in the future, are the clergy of Ireland, led by the Bishops of Ireland, and all following the infallible teachings of the Vicar of Jesus Christ. God grant that this guidance may never fail; that the day may never dawn when it will not be heeded; and that the race of wretched men who have so often in the past ensnared generous-hearted, Catholic Irishmen in Ireland, in Great Britain, in America, and elsewhere, may end forever. From such false agents and from the machinations of all enemies to Irish Faith, we well may pray, GOD SAVE IRELAND!

I have no doubt whatever, but this our prayer will be heard. We only want a knowledge of the evil to avoid it. Even from what I have said this evening—and I have only stated plain, unvarnished facts—it must be evident that all secret societies and societies aiming at bad and irreligious ends are no other than deadly Illuminated Freemasonry. Let them be called by whatever name, they are a part of the system of secret revolutionary fraud, invented and cast upon the earth by Satan to compass the ruin of souls, and the destruction of the reign of Jesus Christ.

They are of the same kind as the Black Hand in Spain, as the Commune of Paris,[1] as the Nihilism that now dominates in Russia. With such associations the children of God have only one duty to discharge. It is: so far from giving them any countenance or support, to oppose them by every means possible.

I believe their strength has spent its force in Ireland. It only remains that the Irish abroad, who have crossed the seas to find a home, an honest living, and an honorable fortune

---

[1] EDITOR'S NOTE: See footnote 6 of the preface.

if they can in this and in other lands, should, as I have just advised, stand on their guard against emissaries who, under pretexts as seductive as those used by the Fenian leaders to lead our countrymen to ruin, or by that degraded seducer of brave, but heedless and passionate young men, Carey,[2] to drag his victims to murder and the gallows, may come to whisper words of conspiracy and lead far astray. The Catholic who hears the invitation from any quarter, were it from an angel from heaven, were it from a priest of God—fallen as that angel or priest should be to be able to give it—let him beware. It is a devil that speaks to him as sure as it was a devil that spoke to his mother Eve in the Garden of Eden. Let him renounce that devil and his tools and his works. Let him ask aid from on High—Good Counsel from God through the prayers of God's Virgin Mother, and he will triumph. He will stand firm on the side of God, and one day be rewarded at His Right Hand with the most glorious triumph that can be given to man to witness—the triumph of Christ coming in His Majesty to judge the living and the dead.

All that secret organization of which we have been speaking so much, is being framed by Satan and his emissaries for one end long foreseen—that is, to form, and that before very many years, the vast kingdom of Antichrist, which already spreads its ramifications over the whole earth. It is, you see, determined to leave no people, or nation, or tribe, or tongue, unsubjected to its influence. It seeks now the semi-civilized empires of Asia by means of Masonic France, and other European Masonic influences. It plants in Africa the germs of a European domination, which must speedily subject to

---

[2] EDITOR'S NOTE: See footnote 2 of chapter 15.

its authority the dark sons of Ham. I believe, so far as I can judge, it will soon send its telegraphs and its railways careering through that ancient Continent. Placing itself "above all that is worshipped or called God" [2 Thess. 2:4], it will in its pride and hate obliterate the polytheism of these countries to make room for its own Atheism; and that which Christianity has been hitherto unable to effect in destroying the false gods of the heathen, it will effect, in order to plant its own dark *non credo* instead.

It will thus one day be able to call to the standard of whoever is to be its last, long foretold leader [Antichrist], countless millions to battle with the elect of God. It may be—I believe it will be—checked, if but for a few years, to afford time for the Church of Christ to manifest her glory once more, and to gather in her strength for the final combat. But that it will advance to that combat is revealed to us.

Children of Ireland what a glorious place is reserved for you when that struggle does come! From the beginning you have been its opponents. When it cried—away with Christ—away with Christ's Vicar—let him be crucified—let his temporal and Spiritual Power be obliterated—and when, in the nations of Catholic Europe, and of the world, it raised its cries of secularism, of infidel education, of ruin to the Christian family and every Catholic institution, who of all the people of God most withstood it? Who best, from slender resources, in all the lands where English is spoken, supported the Vicar of Christ and every Catholic principle? In their island home, during these very saddest days, from the period of the great famine till this hour, the Irish people, scattered in their millions over this country and England;

over all the rising nations of great America; and the infant empires growing daily to maturity in Australia and New Zealand, and other islands of the Southern, the Indian, and the Pacific Oceans; by the coasts of Malabar and Coromandel; in the Colonies of Southern Africa; in the islands of the Caribbean Sea; amidst the decaying Christianity of Buenos Aires; in Canada; and all the other lands of the earth which give the best promise to Atheistic machinations, the Irish people lifted up the Cross of Christ, and sustained, by the sweat of their brow, the strong, vigorous reality of the Catholic religion. They gave their daughters to the cloister, their sons to the sanctuary, their all to the cause of God.

Freemasons thundered and intrigued in the legislatures round about them. Emissaries from the secret sects assailed them in the press, on the platform, everywhere. Fidelity to their religious principles was often visited with political, commercial, and even social ostracism. Ridicule and abuse rained in turn for their fidelity upon them. But the Faith of Saint Patrick and the hope of God's bright kingdom, the smile and the prayer of Mary in Heaven, were able to defeat and baffle all. In serried ranks with the pastors they had themselves brought forth, and nourished, and educated, and kept, they stood amidst the deluge of deception, allurement, and intrigue about them, firm as their own loved, distant land amidst the billows of the ocean, and went on advancing the mighty work of building up the Church which other nations were pulling down, until their very enemies paused, and wondered, and admired.

And often too when these enemies saw in the lands which the Irish had evangelized the Cross of the Catholic Church arise and pierce the heavens where it had never been seen before, or had been proscribed for generations, they cried out that Catholicity was immortal—was divine! It comes, for instance, by the Irish into this land, just as it was before the storm banished it, the same as their fathers once saw it. And they say rightly, "so that Church is now and so will it be forever."

Masonic Anti-Christianity will advance and do more damage than ever heresy effected. It will one day sweep the sects of heresy and the temples of idols utterly away; but it too will have its defeat, and in time must yield to Christ and to His cause the greatest triumph. Its union of all men in one vast republic; its bringing together of every people and nation; its destruction of every form of religion to make way for its sect; its advance in science, in education, in national progress, all will serve one day to place the Son of Mary supreme—to realize the prophecy made to His Mother: "And he shall be great, and be called the Son of the Most High, and the Lord God shall give him the throne of David His father, and He shall reign in the house of Jacob forever, and of His kingdom there shall never be an end" [Luke 1:32-33].

I say that when this consummation comes, as come it surely must, few nations shall have a more glorious record than the people of what is called "poor Ireland." Few nations shall have done more to prepare for the final combat, or shall have manifested to a greater extent in Christian heroism the last and most terrible trial. No nation whatever shall show a grander roll call of martyrs, confessors, virgins, and souls saved, than the land and the race evangelized by Saint Patrick, whose sacred name already adorns the most glorious and promising churches now existing in the world.

CHAPTER 25

Catholic Organization

"No hope, humanly speaking, appears on the horizon to warrant
us at this moment to look for a change for the better. But God
has promised never to desert His Church. That promise never
can be broken. When the darkest hour comes, it is not for
Catholics to look for dissolution, but for life and hope. The
crisis in the conflicts of Christianity is the hour of victory. . . .
In our day, the Atheistic Conspiracy is as determined as ever to
destroy, but it is wiser. Slowly it has surrounded God's Vicar."

—Monsignor Dillon

In conclusion, it is proper that I should say a word to you upon the attitude of the Church at the present moment, in the face of the forces of the Organized Atheism of the world. That organization has now arrived at the perfection of its dark wisdom, and is making rapid strides to the most complete and universal exercise of its power. It has succeeded. Through it the Church is despoiled. The Vicar of Christ is a prisoner, and has been so for over fourteen years. The religious orders are virtually suppressed in nearly every country of Europe. Freemasonry is supreme in the governments of France, Spain, Portugal, Italy, Switzerland, and works its will in nearly all the republics of Southern America. It rules

Germany, distracts Belgium, and secretly gnaws at the heart of Austria. Everywhere it advances with rapid strides both in its secret movements against Catholicity and the Christian religion generally, and in open persecution according to the measure of its opportunity and power.

No hope, humanly speaking, appears on the horizon to warrant us at this moment to look for a change for the better. But God has promised never to desert His Church. That promise never can be broken. When the darkest hour comes, it is not for Catholics to look for dissolution, but for life and hope. The crisis in the conflicts of Christianity is the hour of victory.

This has been realized more than once since the combat began between Atheistic Masonry and the Church. What hour could be darker than that which saw Pius VI taken prisoner to France in the white heat of its Revolution, and dying abandoned and forsaken in the dungeons by the Rhone? The Temporal Power [of the Pope] after an uninterrupted peace of nearly four centuries, during which the disturbances common to it in the middle ages had absolutely ceased, passed at a blow and apparently forever. Rome's treasures of art and religion were carried in triumph to grace the capital of Infidelity, or scattered throughout the earth. The Cross and Keys were without a defender, and the tricolor floated in triumph over the palace of the Popes.

The crisis had arrived when God's promise should be realized. In the twinkling of an eye, a strange force, under a strange commander, Suwarrow [sic],[1] descends like light-

---

[1] EDITOR'S NOTE: Aleksandr Vasilyevich Suvorov, Count Rimniksky (1729–1800), was a Russian military commander who won nota-

ning upon Italy. The power of the Revolution passes like an uneasy morning's dream. Rome belongs to the Pope, and Pius VII[2] sits calmly, as if nothing happened, upon the throne of his banished, I may add, martyred predecessor.

Another event more strange occurs. The Temporal Power falls again, and the legions of the strongest potentate Europe had seen since the days of the Caesars holds it as the heritage of his only son. The Pope is once more a prisoner—for years a persecuted circumvented prisoner. Napoleon mocks at his feebleness, and laughs at his predictions. The Temporal Power of the Popes was, he says, but never will be. The condition of the world is changed—the Empire returned. Is it so? The crisis has come for the hundredth time. The very cardinals are taken from the side of the Pontiff. He is alone in the power of his base tormentor as much as Saint Peter on Montorio[3] was in the power of Nero. Things cannot be darker. The light must dawn; and it does. In a month, God's elements blast the power of the

---

ble victories in the Russo-Turkish War of 1787–91 and in the French Revolutionary Wars. He conducted a series of quick campaigns in Italy from April to August 1799 that resulted in almost completely expelling French armies from Italy.

[2] EDITOR'S NOTE: Pius VII (1742–1823) was pope from 1800 to 1823. His conflicts with Napoleon helped restore the Church in France after its devastation during the pontificate of his predecessor, Pius VI. Rome was occupied by French troops in 1808, and Napoleon declared that the Papal States were annexed to France the following year. Pius VII excommunicated the invaders, after which he was taken prisoner in July 1809, and remained in exile until France was invaded in 1814.

[3] EDITOR'S NOTE: The San Pietro in Montorio is a church located at this site in Rome, just south of the Vatican, at a spot considered by some to be the site of Saint Peter's crucifixion. However, the ancient evidence points to Vatican hill being the site of Saint Peter's crucifixion during the reign of Nero.

tyrant, and while millions applaud the return of the Pontiff to the Chair of Saint Peter and to his power at Rome, Napoleon passes to his solitary dungeon in the midst of the waters, to ruminate on the verification which in his case, as in the case of every persecutor of the Church, attends the predictions of Peter.

In our day, the Atheistic Conspiracy is as determined as ever to destroy, but it is wiser. Slowly it has surrounded God's Vicar. It has taken care so to master the councils of every European country that help to him, when it assails, may be impossible. Under pretense of guaranteeing his independence, it has stolen from him everything. His trustiest servants are torn from his side, stripped, despoiled, degraded, scattered. His resources have been astutely lessened to the lowest possible point. A prisoner of the Infidels, as much as Pius VI or Pius VII in the strongholds of France, under the appearance of being free, he is really bound hand and foot and rendered completely impotent. His power is cancelled under pretext that his city is necessary to the unification of Italy. No other city will suit Italian jealousies as the capital of the new nation. And who will sacrifice the welfare of the new nation to the wants of the Pope?

Astuteness is now the characteristic of the Revolution, determined and callous as ever. But hope again appears. To the persecutions of Pius IX,[4] many and grievous as they were, God opposed a Pontiff simple as a dove in the snares of

---

[4] EDITOR'S NOTE: Pius IX (1792–1878) was pope from 1846 to 1878—the longest papacy in history. He solemnly defined both the Immaculate Conception of Our Lady (1854) and, during Vatican I, papal infallibility (1870). He steadfastly condemned the errors of liberalism, perhaps most famously in his *Syllabus of Errors* (1864). During his reign, the Papal States were destroyed, resulting in he and his successors, until Pius XI, essentially being imprisoned in the Vatican.

the spoiler. He took away from the ruffian hands of Masonry its only real argument.

But now when all is gone, help appears in the person of another Pontiff [Pope Leo XIII], whose greatest characteristic is wisdom, and whose wisdom, slowly but surely, is telling upon the nations. No Pontiff has been more firm in maintaining the rights of the Holy See, violently wrested as he found them, by the force and upon the pretexts used by Freemasonry. Despoiled of everything, he has nevertheless drawn together the scattered strength of the Church. Commencing with the foundation of all Christianity, its teaching, he has caused philosophy to be so purified, and so based on sound principles, as to be in reality a true handmaid to theology and a deadly foe to rationalistic, Atheistic, and infidel theories of whatever kind.[5] He has caused the teachings of Saint Thomas to assume more than at any past period, their supremacy in Christian schools. He has mastered the difficult, tangled web of European diplomacy. He has found out the true wants of Christian peoples. He has satisfied them: and then, finally, by his immortal Bull, *Humanum Genus*,[6] he has dealt a death blow to the progress of Freemasonry, and elevated into a system the means by which the guides of God's people are for the future to save these people from the evils of our days.

According to my humble ability, I have endeavored as best I could, this evening, to carry out the first part of the instruction of Our Sovereign Lord, Leo XIII, who is for me

---

[5] EDITOR'S CITATION: Pope Leo XIII, *Aeterni Patris: On the Restoration of Christian Philosophy* (1879).

[6] EDITOR'S NOTE: Monsignor Dillon meant "Encyclical." He refers to Pope Leo XIII's encyclical *Humanum Genus: On Freemasonry* (1884).

and for over two hundred millions like me, as much a Monarch, as if he reigned in the Quirinal instead of Humbert II.[7] That is, I have endeavored to show you what Secret Association was, and is, and ever will be, till the end.

I am persuaded that if the evils of secret society plotting have succeeded so far, it is mainly because from one reason or another, the mask was permitted to be worn by Freemasonry. Voices were raised, I know here and there, now and again, against it, and against Secret Societies of every kind; but they were either not heard at all, or, if heard, were very soon forgotten. The utmost efforts of Freemasonry of every kind were exerted to keep itself hidden, and that it had power to remain hidden is looked upon by Monsignor Segur, and Monsignor Ketteler, and others, as one of the most remarkable evidences of its real power. It had and still has means to silence all who may proceed against it. It murdered, as we have seen, in this very century, a free citizen of America, who attempted to write a book in which only the least part of its secrets—its absurd ceremonial, its grips, passwords, and oaths, were revealed to "the profane." It threatened and used the dagger, or calumny, or bribery, or whatever suited against those who attempted to expose it. Exposure is its death—the death at least of its influence over its intended dupes amongst Catholics.

Therefore, comes the word of command to us all, from the great Vicar of Christ—"Tear the mask from off Freemasonry"[8]—and consequently, it becomes a plain duty, a duty

[7] EDITOR'S NOTE: Monsignor Dillon perhaps anticipating the progeny of King Umberto ("Humbert") I of Italy, who reigned from 1878 to 1900.
[8] EDITOR'S CITATION: Pope Leo XIII, *Humanum Genus: On Freemasonry* (1884), no. 31.

not to be performed in any desultory manner, but in season and out of season [2 Tim. 4:2], to expose Freemasonry. The Supreme Pontiff, despoiled though he be, will find in the generous devotion of the children of the Church who fear no power of man or demon in the discharge of duty, not one but ten hundred thousand voices ready for the task. Thank God! the labors of devoted, Christian men—bishops, priests, and learned laymen—have resulted in enabling us to know the real character of Masonry, and enabling us to "tear the mask" off the horrible thing with ease.

Nor is this confined to the Continent or to ecclesiastics. The work has been nobly inaugurated already in our midst by Mr. O'Donnell, MP, and I trust will be continued by him and by many more. The religious orders will, in the solitude of their cells, make a special study of the machinations of the terrible sects, the secular clergy in their Colleges and home retreats, and above all, the Catholic press will not cease to expose the malignant hydra in constantly recurring references and discoveries.

The whole host of God is needed to march and to act against the foe in the manner indicated by our Holy Father; for the question is one of the salvation of the world, of the spread of the Gospel, of the happiness of families and individuals, of civil society, and of man. Surely upon such a movement the benediction of Heaven will descend.

The means to obtain that divine blessing are also pointed out by the Holy Father. He says to those whom it concerns, "unite the Catholic people in good societies and pious confraternities." He indicates, specially, the Third Order of Saint Francis and the confraternity which practices the recital of the

Holy Rosary. Father Anderledy, the newly appointed General of the Society of Jesus, who plainly says he speaks as he does with the knowledge and desire of the Holy Father, asks the Fathers of his Society to renew the holy habit of uniting those committed to their care in societies formed to honor Our Lady.

Behold, then, the true remedy for the ills that fall upon the world. That world is rushing wildly, madly, away from religion and true happiness. Who, under God, can be conceived more powerful to restore it to reason than Mary the Virgin Mother of God, who amongst many other holy titles, is honored by the Church as the special dispenser of the invaluable gift of Good Counsel, a gift She so wonderfully displayed in Her holy life, and which She obtains for God's people by Her powerful intercession. She too is called upon in the liturgy of the Church, to be glad and to rejoice, for She alone has destroyed all heresies throughout the whole world. Her power destroyed them singly in the past, and doubtless will also destroy their united force and malignity, as exhibited in Freemasonry and its kindred secret societies, in the future. Societies in honor of God's Mother cannot be too widely established. All should be under Her benign protection, as is the Catholic Young Men's Society of Edinburgh.

But there is one branch society of this Catholic Institute which I cannot help singling out for special praise. It is the Catholic Total Abstinence Society.

CHAPTER 26

Catholic Total Abstinence Societies

"The days of secret societies would for the Irish end forever, and for a certainty they would carry out to its fullness the glorious destiny given them of planting the Faith all the world over, and resisting to the bitter end the wiles, the deceits, and finally the last and most terrible onset of Antichrist against God, His Church, and Christian civilization throughout the world."

—Monsignor Dillon

No society can be conceived better adapted to keep working men from those bad associations which we have been considering, or more calculated to bring every blessing to individuals, and above all to homes. The public house, the drinking saloon, the music hall, the obscure "shebeen,"[1] wherever, in one word, drink is sold, is the ante-chamber of the secret society for men, and ruin both of men and women.

On this point permit me to be plain with you, my Catholic fellow-countrymen, as I may call you—for I find that the

---

[1] EDITOR'S NOTE: An unlicensed seller of alcohol; considered disreputable.

majority, indeed the mass of the Catholic congregations in Edinburgh, as well as in Glasgow, in Manchester, in Leeds, in Birmingham, and in all the large towns of England and Scotland, are, men and women, mainly, if not entirely, of Irish birth or Irish blood, the children of Irish parents. It is, the world knows, from you that the faith has come to Great Britain, by the providence of God in this nineteenth century.

In the Highlands, I am told, there are some twelve thousand genuine Scotch Catholics. In the Lowlands it is doubtful whether so many genuine Scotch Catholics can be found; but the number of Catholics in Scotland is a quarter of a million, and the excess comes from the Irish, whose migration has made the Church.

I believe the proportion in England, notwithstanding the conversion of so many by reason and grace, and the holding out of several old families, is still greater in favor of the Irish element. From the converts and the good old Catholic families come many blessed with vocations for the Priesthood, who devote their lives with great zeal to the service of the race which forms the majority—the mass of the Church.

Now I praise that mass, to which I myself belong, when it deserves to be praised; but you will allow me the liberty of a friend to blame a portion of it when it deserves blame. God, Who knows all hearts, knows that I desire to do the blaming as a friend. I praise you for what I see you do. The Churches, the Cathedrals—magnificent in many cases as both are—the Schools, the Houses of the Teaching Orders, are mainly the work of your hands. The Priesthood that has been brought to minister everywhere, and the active Orders of men and women who teach, are kept in the very largest measure, by you. Notwithstanding all your burdens, your poverty, and your local wants—great everywhere—you give with a willingness unequalled by any other race, to every good work. Of you, at home and abroad, generous, faithful people, it may be said, that you realize to the very letter the truth that it is better to give than to receive [Acts 20:35].

And what a blessing do you not in return receive in this laud, when you remain faithful to the teachings of that religion for which God has enabled you to do so much! There is not a city I have visited that I do not find some amongst you, who came to this country as poor as the rest, already risen to affluence and ease, sometimes to public and honorable position amongst their fellow-citizens differing from them more widely in religion than in race. There is no place where I have not been consoled with the signs of substantial prosperity amongst you. Pleasant it is for me, when visiting the many educational establishments now, thank God, so plentifully diffused over the face of the country, to find your sons in the Colleges, your daughters in the Convents, and to know that not a few of them dedicate themselves to the highest service of God. These prove the happy, holy homes which blessed them with true parental love and care, and cast round their childhood the influences of religion.

I have at this moment before my mind's eye the death of an Irish mother who passed to eternity, since I commenced my present journey, consoled by having her deathbed surrounded by children, every one of whom were holy, and several of whom had the happiness of being either Religious or Priests. This valiant Catholic mother came to one of the great cities of England the wife of an Irish working man. She had her reward surely in this life as well as in the next. In your own midst, there are instances of the honest prosperity which blesses the sober, well-conducted, though poor man, who comes to this country to make an honest livelihood. If he be but faithful to his religion, his life is always happy. His end is always holy. His children "rise up and call him blessed" [Prov. 31:28]. He is a blessing to the Church and to this country.

I could easily prolong this picture; but I must speak plainly upon another. I have seen even in this city hundreds of little children, as I passed yesterday, Sunday, through your streets; many of them were Catholics, certainly. Poor children! they saluted me reverently. They were, I found, sent—for the law happily forces that—to the Catholic School. That was the reason why the light of Faith was in their little eyes, which brightened at the sight of a Priest; but alas! the sign of hunger was upon the cheeks and upon the almost naked limbs of many of them, without shoes, without stockings, and in rags. I have seen children too, many of whom I know to be Catholic and Irish, selling newspapers in the streets on weekdays, and preparing, boys and girls, for careers I shudder to contemplate, after a very few years. On yesterday I had evidence of the cause of their sad state. I saw men and women, the fathers and mothers of these children, crowding round public-houses, openly intoxicated, and in consequent wretchedness upon the streets. I know of course that a large proportion of these were not Irish, but I know also from inquiries I made, that a large proportion was. These were the degraded, abominable parents who reduced their own little ones to the sad condition in which the whole

world could see them. I do not suppose that in a respectable
gathering like this such drunkards are found, but I allude
to the matter in the hope that my words and opinions may,
through you who are here, come to them; that they may
know, that while I praise my beloved fellow country people
for what they have done so nobly and so well for the works
of religion, I have no words strong enough to reprobate the
conduct of those who give themselves to drink in this country, at all. I say, at all. For to commence with—where, I ask,
is the working man to be found, or the working man's wife,
who, having undertaken the care and responsibility of the
present and the future of the numerous family it is generally their lot to have, can afford to spend earnings which
belong to their children, on the pernicious and expensive
luxury of drink? A working man needs every fraction he can
earn by his labor for the education and maintenance of his
children, for the rainy day, for the season of sickness, for an
honest independence in his old age. He cannot be honest
to his children, or to himself; he cannot advance religion,
education, or the cause of God, if he drinks. When a working man loses his employment, when he sickens, when he
gets into trouble, we invariably find drink at the bottom
of it. There is nothing that one can praise in the man who
practices this vice. He is mean, and he is cruelly dishon-
est always. He drinks the shoes off his children's feet, the
clothes off their backs, the bit from out their mouths, the
bed from under them, the home from over them, and sends
them upon society, boys degraded, and girls so lost that I
cannot contemplate the picture.

It is therefore that good pastors like Cardinal Manning, who (because of his numerous Irish flock, regards himself in London as an Irish Bishop) have undertaken a life and death crusade against this devil that preys upon the vitals of their most choice and devoted people. It is therefore that Cardinal MacCabe and others have made so many personal efforts to uproot this vice. My own Archbishop, for many years, while Bishop of Ossory, in Ireland, practiced total abstinence, in order to give his people an example. He is determined to make the same sacrifice in the new and vastly more extended field of labor which the Vicar of Christ has committed to his care at the Antipodes. I have great faith in such acts of self-denial coming from such quarters.

When those of the flock who need restraint see the pastors placed over them by God make such sacrifices for their salvation, there cannot, it seems to me, be much doubt about the issue. What they can do, what such men as the late Mr. A. M. Sullivan[2] and others have done, without any constraining necessity, others, who owe such restraint to themselves and their families, can do. For the mere temporal well-being of every working man, and every working man's family, I would be glad to see every such man a total abstainer. But when I consider the evils to which the eternal salvation of the Irish working man, in these countries especially, is exposed by the habit of drinking, I can find no words strong enough to express my anxiety to see him give up intoxicating drinks absolutely and forever. The sacrifice is small, the gain enormous.

---

[2]　Editor's Note: See footnote 9 of the preface.

God grant that all whom my words may reach—all Irish Catholics—may think with me on this point. Should that be so, the consequences would be indeed consoling. The Church of God might well rejoice. The days of secret societies would for the Irish end forever, and for a certainty they would carry out to its fullness the glorious destiny given them of planting the Faith all the world over, and resisting to the bitter end the wiles, the deceits, and finally the last and most terrible onset of Antichrist against God, His Church, and Christian civilization throughout the world.